This book lifts the curtain to explore the backgrounds and personal lives of some influential psychologists in the fields of personality, intelligence and their measurement. This brief book helps us understand how and why their backgrounds and private lives may have influenced their theories – and the controversies which frequently erupted. The book is engagingly written with a wry, light touch, such as describing Eysenck's 'physics envy'. It provides fascinating background to some influential theories and will appeal to both specialists and non-specialists.

Colin Cooper, School of Psychology, Queen's University, Belfast

Dear Steve

I thought chapter 23 might be of some interests. She's got one or two details wrong

Best Wishes
Peter Saville

Key Thinkers in Individual Differences

Key Thinkers in Individual Differences introduces the life, work and thought of 25 of the most influential figures who have shaped and developed the measurement of intelligence and personality. Expanding on from a résumé of academic events, this book makes sense of these psychologists by bringing together not only their ideas but the social experiences, loves and losses that moulded them.

By adapting a chronological approach, Forsythe presents the history and context behind these thinkers, ranging from the buffoonery and sheer genius of Charles Galton, the theatre of Hans Eysenck and John Phillipe Rushton, to the much-maligned and overlooked work of women such as Isabel Myers, Katherine Briggs and Karen Horney. Exploring all through a phenomenological lens, the background, interconnections, controversies and conversations of these thinkers are uncovered.

This informative guide is essential reading to anyone who studies, works in or is simply captivated by the field of individual differences, personality and intelligence. An invaluable resource for all students of individual differences and the history of psychology.

Alex Forsythe is Head of Certification for the Association for Business Psychology, Honorary Senior Lecturer at the University of Liverpool and Head of Psychology at the University of Wolverhampton. Among her various accomplishments, she is a Chartered Occupational Psychologist, BPS Specialist in test use, and in 2018 was awarded both Principal Fellowship of the Higher Education Academy and the prestigious National Teaching Fellowship. With extensive organisational experience working at senior levels in the private, public and voluntary sectors, Alex's specialisms include improving work performance through goal setting and by helping individuals develop healthy self-regulatory behaviours and relationships with feedback.

Key Thinkers in Psychology and Neuroscience

Key Thinkers in Psychology and Neuroscience is a collection of books focusing on the lives, work, and thought of the most influential figures in a given field. The books examine how these disciplines have been shaped and developed throughout history to the present day, and the impact of theory, research and practice from some of the most significant minds in psychology and neuroscience. These are insightful and indispensable companions for students in psychology.

Key Thinkers in Individual Differences
Alex Forsythe

Key Thinkers in Neuroscience
Andrew P. Wickens

Key Thinkers in Individual Differences

Ideas on Personality and Intelligence

Alex Forsythe

Routledge
Taylor & Francis Group

LONDON AND NEW YORK

First published 2019
by Routledge
2 Park Square, Milton Park, Abingdon, Oxon OX14 4RN

and by Routledge
52 Vanderbilt Avenue, New York, NY 10017

Routledge is an imprint of the Taylor & Francis Group, an informa business

© 2019 Alex Forsythe

The right of Alex Forsythe to be identified as author of this
work has been asserted by her in accordance with sections 77
and 78 of the Copyright, Designs and Patents Act 1988.

All rights reserved. No part of this book may be reprinted
or reproduced or utilised in any form or by any electronic,
mechanical, or other means, now known or hereafter
invented, including photocopying and recording, or in any
information storage or retrieval system, without permission
in writing from the publishers.

Trademark notice: Product or corporate names may be
trademarks or registered trademarks, and are used only for
identification and explanation without intent to infringe.

British Library Cataloguing-in-Publication Data
A catalogue record for this book is available from the
British Library

Library of Congress Cataloging-in-Publication Data
Names: Forsythe, Alex, author.
Title: Key thinkers in individual differences : ideas on
personality and intelligence / Alex Forsythe.
Description: Abingdon, Oxon ; New York, NY : Routledge,
2020. | Series: Key thinkers in psychology and neuroscience
| Includes bibliographical references and index.
Identifiers: LCCN 2019004651 (print) | LCCN 2019006839
(ebook) | ISBN 9781351026505 (Ebook) | ISBN
9781138494152 (hardback) | ISBN 9781138494213 (pbk.)
Subjects: LCSH: Personality and intelligence. | Individual
differences. | Psychology–History.
Classification: LCC BF698.9.I6 (ebook) | LCC BF698.9.I6
F67 2020 (print) | DDC 158.1–dc23
LC record available at https://lccn.loc.gov/2019004651

ISBN: 978-1-138-49415-2 (hbk)
ISBN: 978-1-138-49421-3 (pbk)
ISBN: 978-1-351-02650-5 (ebk)

Typeset in Sabon
by Swales & Willis, Exeter, Devon, UK

Printed in the United Kingdom
by Henry Ling Limited

For Brittany, Francesca and Henry
Failure is a beautiful thing, own it and you will be richly rewarded.

To Craig Ayre, I am indebted to your incorrigible optimism, your unyielding support, attention to detail and terrible jokes.

Contents

Preface

For the past 20 years, I have worked as a psychologist, trying to solve problems through careful observation and measurement. Psychology, unlike other sciences, taps straight into what it is to be human. Unlike chemistry or physics which are distant from human experience and emotions, psychology attempts to quantify, analyse and identify what it is to be human, to think like a human and to feel as a human. Because of this raw link, psychology can come in for much more criticism because everyone has an opinion on what it is to be a human. Plus, the fact that when you try to quantify, enumerate or analyse you run the risk of stereotyping and creating offence.

When it comes to creating offence, the field of individual differences has the capacity to outclass all others. Science should be secular, it should not be influenced, by politics, religion or public opinion. It is, after all, the pursuit of the truth and facts. Yet, from my earliest experiences as an undergraduate, I was told to stay away from the writings of people like J. P. Rushton and Richard Lynn. Of course, as a teenager growing up in the era of Frankie Goes to Hollywood, anything banned just becomes even more interesting.

Three experiences formulated my decision to study individual differences. My parents always believed I was bright. I was taught to read and write before attending school and leapt through primary school with few setbacks, but I failed my 11-plus and performed poorly at secondary school. I married early and had my first children in my 20s. I remember as an undergraduate, working through Herrnstein and Murray's book, with its 'checklist' of indicators of stupidity. By Herrnstein and Murray's deductions, my life choices meant that I was almost certainly of below average intelligence. Clearly, this was non-sense, I ended up with a first-class honours degree, but at the time, I felt some real shame and became convinced that my abilities were lacking.

Years later I grew to understand that academic talent is wasted if a child doesn't receive the right messages from their family and from society. As a girl growing up during 'the troubles', in a fundamentally Christian family, I had the deep-seated conviction that the only thing my parents truly wanted was for me to marry well. My mother often said she would 'put her head in the oven' if we came home pregnant. We had an electric oven, so I can only imagine she was planning to slow roast herself to death. So deep was God in our lives that my parents prevented my superiorly intelligent sister from going to university to study English; something I wonder if she ever really got over. At some point or another, we have all been trapped into believing we are somehow prisoners of our history, we act foolishly and feel unable to move forward. My personal chip on my shoulder eventually drove me to do the direct opposite of anything my father believed, and to the end of his life we had a truly abysmal relationship with one other.

In 1999, still shaken from my Herrnstein and Murray diagnosis, I was fortunate to see the great Arthur Jensen speak at Queens University Belfast. The auditorium was packed and hot but the then 76-year-old, 'Art', still gave an illuminating talk with complex factor matrices and other complexities. Thanks to the remarkable teaching of my tutor Colin Cooper I could smugly understand more than my less interested peers. I began to think that perhaps I was not as thick as a whale omelette. My most lasting memory, however, was the toe-curling mortification I felt as my measurement sceptic peers, having taken directly to heart the recently published Goleman book, began to mither Art with questions about emotional intelligence. Asking Arthur Jensen about emotional intelligence was akin to telling Hans Eysenck that Howard Gardner's multiple intelligences was a great idea. I remember sinking in my seat and hoping that Art would not think I was with the EI fool beside me.

Art wryly smiled and said, 'well that's probably just something to do with journalistic personality' and swatted the question away like it was a gnat. I then mustered my own, evidently 'high' levels of EI and resolved never to study emotional intelligence. That perspective quickly changed, however, when I spent a period of study at the Massachusetts Institute of Technology. An elderly Oliver Selfridge, often thought of as the Father of Machine Perception, took me for lunch. To say I was excited was an understatement. Before lunch, Oliver had shared with me his ideas for children's books on mathematics. This great man shone a spotlight on what was clearly my 'titanic' intellectual ability. Freud would probably have something to say about my deteriorating relationship with my father and my newly found obsession with 76-year-old men, but regardless off we went to lunch. Selfridge took me to one of the fanciest seafood restaurants in Boston, where to my horror, he proceeded to ask me to solve puzzle, after puzzle, after puzzle. Most of these brain teasers would make Pythagoras weep, but some were just based on the 9-dot problem which having studied them as an undergraduate, and I fully knew the answer. I was paralysed with fear. I could not think, and Selfridge must have seen my distress but showed no signs of stopping. When lunch was served, he merely shifted our food to one side, asked the waiter for more paper and continued testing me. Lunch was quite literally an IQ test which I was magnificently failing in the very public eye of the best of Boston society. I can still conjure up the exact feelings of shame and humiliation, feelings that I think most children share today when they are measured and found wanting. Perhaps there was something in emotional intelligence after all.

Academics often explain their lives as a series of scholastic events but their parents, their social experiences, loves and losses, moulded them in the same way that my parents shaped me. This book tries to get past the résumé of academic events by making sense of psychologists, often without very little direct evidence of what they were like. Fay Fransella in her book about George Kelly describes this process as *psychotherapy without the patient*. In trying to get close to these key thinkers, we attempt to understand their culture and their world at their point in time. The substance of this process is the substance of this book.

Here, one-dimensional psychologists, who are often reduced to their politically incorrect theories, emerge as complex, misunderstood individuals, battling against restrictions in free speech. Their complex, politically sensitive measurement ideologies and methods promised much; that those processes will be transparent and faithful. Their work is now proved either mostly right or mostly wrong, but even the blind alleys led to new ways of thinking and doing.

Deciding who should be included in a text such as this is always a challenge. The inclusion of Karen Horney, Isabel Myers and Katherine Briggs represents a breakthrough from other mainstream texts on this subject. Today, women represent the most substantial proportion of the undergraduate curriculum, but as in many areas of psychology, they do not feature heavily in the key-thinker literature. Horney provided feminist leadership to psychology, challenging the ways in which sexist values had internalised. Myers and Briggs are so effortlessly criticised within academic psychology, that it is almost impossible to understand how they could have developed the world's most popular psychometric test. I hope that by raising the profile of their work and lives, future students of psychology will be inspired to work in an area that has such an exceptional capacity to improve the lives of others.

For me, what was most impactful were the numbers of psychologists who were part of the waves of Jewish emigration to the United States. They or their parents were escaping persecution, restrictive laws and economic hardship. Once deemed a lesser people, these individuals and their children would go on and study how people differed from one another, in many cases making significant advances in educational and societal reform. The sheer impact that the Jewish community has had on the field of individual differences is remarkable; their psychology has helped us all to talk, to be understood and to change.

Alexandra Forsythe
January 7th, 2019

Acknowledgement

I wish to acknowledge Lewis Goldberg, John Ravens, Howard Gardner and Peter Saville, thank you for letting me into your lives to unpick your stories.

Chapter 1

Francis Galton

Hereditary Genius

February 16th, 1822 to January 17th, 1911

Erasmus Darwin (physician, philosopher poet and evolutionary theorist) was the grandfather of both Charles Darwin and Francis Galton. Erasmus' first wife Mary had four sons and two daughters, two of whom died in infancy. A third child, named Charles, died at the age of 30, so when their fourth child, Robert Waring Darwin became a father he named him Charles after his late brother. He is the Charles who is now immortalised in science and the half-cousin of Francis Galton.

Mary Darwin had long suffered from ill-health (probably gallstones). To manage the pain, she a self-medicated with copious amounts of alcohol and opium and died from cirrhosis of the liver at the age of 30. Erasmus, having five children to care for, hurriedly employed a young nanny, Mary Parker. Parker soon became his mistress and bore him two children. They never married because, by 1775, Erasmus' interests were set elsewhere. At the very much married Elizabeth Pole (nee Collier); a twentysomething, adventurous, humorous dark-haired beauty, and the pursuit for her attentions began.

Elizabeth was not exactly enthusiastic, Erasmus was much older than her and a rotund man. Neither Elizabeth's reluctance nor her marital state deterred Erasmus. Unrelenting in his pursuits he penned her love poems until in 1780, her much older husband conveniently died. Galton finally persuaded the indifferent but pragmatic Elizabeth to become his wife. Ultimately, Elizabeth made a matter-of-fact decision. Her previous husband had been 30 years her senior, so she was used to romantic hardship, and Galton was a wealthy man.

Erasmus had 15 children in total (and possibly one further illegitimate daughter), eight of whom were born to Elizabeth. Her daughter, Frances Ann Violetta shared Elizabeth's beauty and personality and would go on to marry the very conservative Samuel Tertius Galton, and the couple would eventually become the mother of Francis Galton.

Samuel Galton's family were wealthy Birmingham Quakers whose fortunes were founded on gun manufacturing. Frances Ann met her husband Samuel when his family began to move its business interests away from gun manufacturing, towards banking. Samuel and Erasmus shared both business and scientific interests, they were both members of the Birmingham Lunar Society, a dinner club and learned society for industrialists, philosophers and intellectuals, so the marriage was a good fit.

Their first four children, all daughters, were poorly. Agnes and Violetta lived only a few months, and Lucy and Adele were plagued with illness. Their children's deaths and illnesses prompted a crisis in faith, and the family moved away from the Quakers towards the Church of England. More children followed; four daughters and three sons, the youngest of which was Francis. The family was a happy and a very wealthy one, something that would later give Galton the freedom to roam and to study wherever and whatever he chose.

The young Francis was the object of devotion, most especially from his sister Adele. Isolated for large parts of her childhood because of curvature of the spine, Adele had spent long periods in bed rest strapped to a wooden board. Little Francis gave Adele the opportunity to expand the scope of her world, and she put all her time and energy into the needs of this adorable child. She proceeded to fill his world with as much information as his newly developing mind could master. By the time he was two and a half, Francis could read and write; by four he could multiply, begin to read French and Latin; by five he was reading Homer (in its original text). Despite these early achievements, Galton often complained of struggling with turning his thoughts into language throughout his life, leading some to suggest that he may have been struggling with dyslexia.

Francis was learning fast, but Adele was his primary source of education. The Galton family were becoming worried about Francis' lack of friends, so he was taken to the local school. While the school offered new social opportunities, the family were stunned by what was regarded as the complete ignorance of his fellow pupils, and thus, Francis was dispatched to board at the French coastal town of Boulogne-sur-Mer. Galton hated boarding school; he endured a harsh regime, corporal punishment and loneliness. His parents were rarely inclined to present themselves in France during school holidays, so for any kind of family news, Francis had to rely on letters.

Finally, in 1832 his time in Boulogne-sur-Mer came to an end. His father brought Francis home to England, to attend a new boarding school in a more enlightened environment where he could study not only the classics but science, carpentry and sports. He studied at Reverend Atwood's School until his thirteenth birthday, followed by King Edward's Grammar School where he experienced the 'best' that the Victorian educational regime could offer in the way of rote learning, humiliation and punishment.

Francis stayed at boarding school until 1838 when his parents took him on a tour of Europe. On his return, he followed his mother's long-held desire that he would follow in the footsteps of Erasmus Darwin and he commenced the study of medicine at Birmingham General Hospital. Francis never qualified in medicine. In an era of no proper anaesthesia, Galton was finding that the stress of applied medicine was taking a toll on his health. He was suffering sleep deprivation, digestive problems and headaches, but like most students still managed to find time to enjoy the sophistication of London; attending nights out at the opera, evening balls and the fencing club. His training had also managed to raise suspicions about the behaviour of his devoted sister, Adele. Francis began to suspect that her spinal problems were now more of an attention seeking device than an actual medical affliction and he began to create distance from her.

University education was not a resounding success. Francis went to the University of Cambridge (1840–1843) where he read mathematics, but he performed poorly and did not obtain a degree. He was distracted by the desire to travel and his family's wealth meant that Francis could pursue whatever interested him. His cousin Charles had just returned from his round-the-world trip on HMS Beagle and Galton wanted some action. Francis's heart was set on a Scandinavian venture, but his father negotiated this down to a working holiday in Germany to study with Justus von Liebig; the man now widely accepted as the father of organic chemistry. Francis, however, did not care much for von Liebig's teaching methods and decided to 'make a bolt' down the Danube for Constantinople and Athens. When Francis finally returned to England in September 1840, his father took Francis' flight from Germany in good humour, congratulating him on the great deal of experience he would have gained.

Four years later, Francis' beloved father died aged 61. He had suffered from asthma throughout his life and when it finally brought death the family were devastated. For Francis, there was an added complexity. It was his father's last wish that Francis should complete his medical career, but on his father's death, there was no real need to work at all. In the end, the decision was an easy one. A year after his father's death, Francis travelled to Egypt with the intention of following the Victorian tradition of murdering and stuffing exotic animals.

He travelled to Egypt, Sudan and across the Middle East, sailing, swimming and shooting as he went. Returning home only in 1856 following the death of his closest aide, Ali, from dysentery. Galton was not in good spirits or health. He had a recurrent fever, probably from venereal disease, and a significant ego-deficit caused by his inability to kill even one single hippopotamus. In what would be a recurring theme of buffoonery, Galton then made the calamitous decision to bring with him two monkey companions. On arrival home, the two monkeys were promptly locked in a freezing scullery by a housekeeper, and the poor animals were found dead in the morning, clinging to each other for warmth.

Undeterred, Galton was resolute in improving his hunting skills and began living primitively in a shelter on Culrain moor in the Highlands of Scotland. He shot seals (one can presume that on land they were easier to hit than a hippo) and took some basic instruction in rock-climbing which enabled him to raid the nests of seabirds. He intended to bring young birds and eggs back to add to his brother's Lakeland estate, but most of these sorry animals went the same way as the monkeys. Galton had the crates containing the birds strapped to the top of a transportation railway truck, and they died of hypothermia on the way back from Scotland. Only one oystercatcher survived. The bird was released into his brother's estate, and then during some particularly heavy frost, the little bird got stuck in ice. A fox quickly dispatched the animal, and all that remained in the morning was a little pair of orange legs stuck to the ice.

Galton was well placed within an affluent social circle and could have enjoyed a sedentary Victorian existence, but for the advice of a phrenologist to pursue a more active lifestyle. At that time phrenologists were using the now discredited practice of estimating the relative strengths of a person's mental faculties and their suitability to different careers by calculating the size of bumps on different parts of their cranium. In what sounds like a *double entendre*, Galton's phrenologist concluded that Galton had one of the 'largest organs of causality' that he had ever seen. Unfortunately, this experience did not give Galton the blinding realisation that a career in animal welfare was not for him, because he was soon back on his travels. He joined the Royal Geographical Society on a noble two-year trip to South West Africa applying his 'organ of causality' to the mapping of previously unexplored territories.

Galton managing to shoot a half-starved lion in the buttocks, before one of his party finished it off. On yet another blunder, he agreed that the mules and horses should be released into a canyon to feed freely. On release, the animals were promptly devoured by a pack of delighted lions. Fortunately, the lions, replete from their feast, left the now starving and distressed team of pioneers a few prime chunks to keep them going. All other game and grazing animals had been previously wiped out by other gung-ho Victorian adventurers.

Starvation and the consumption of their animal transportation were not the only perils the adventurers were facing. The Namibian Damara and Nama tribes who surrounded the travellers were engaged in low-level conflict since their displacement by Dutch and British colonists. The balance of power had suddenly shifted towards the Orlam people, descendants of the illegitimate children of Nama slaves and their Afrikaner masters. The Orlam were brutal, hacking off the feet of women and gouging out the eyes of infants. Galton's pressing issue, however, was not the well-being of the local women, but more to do with the Orlam Chief, Jonker Afrikaner, preventing his travel through Damaraland. With all the usual Victorian formalities and pleasantries, Galton penned an indignant letter demanding that Jonker gave passage and then waited, and waited, for a response. While he waited, he became interested in applying his most prized navigation instruments to the mapping of a different frontier; the breasts and buttocks of the local tribe's women.

Jonker remained indifferent to Galton's travel plans, and so, Galton constructed a flamboyant response. Resplendent in a scarlet coat and a hunting cap, Galton mounted an ox (the horses having been eaten) and charged to Jonker's hut. At the last moment, the confused animal bolted, then somehow managed to jump the moat in front of Jonker's hut, propelling itself through the air with Galton clinging to its back. The beast and Galton landed head first through the door, startling the living daylights out of Jonker, who had been quietly smoking a pipe. The sheer madness continued as Galton proceeded to give the astonished Jonker a 'piece of his mind'.

This ham-fisted intervention was a success. Junker agreed to cooperate and behave in a more peaceful way. Galton, energised by his success in peace negations, appointed himself as ambassador and began travelling around all the other local villages forewarning chiefs and setting up a moral code of conduct. Then finally, having concluded that he had solved peace in Africa, Galton continued his journey 'taking out' the odd giraffe as he went. On his return to England, he published his first book *Narrative of an Explorer in Tropical South Africa* (1853) and, for his pioneering work on mapping the Namibian interior, was awarded the Royal Geographical Society's gold medal for the encouragement and promotion of geographical science and discovery.

Francis Galton was now famous, his reputation as a geographer and explorer was established and it was time to turn his attention to marriage. We know very little about his marriage to Louisa Butler, even in his autobiography, which has an entire chapter dedicated to the topic of marriage, there is little mention of the circumstances around his relationship with his wife. They were married in 1853, honeymooned in Europe and according to Galton, led a life that their social group would envy.

By 1854 Galton was writing again; 'Hints to Travellers' which was so popular that it ran to several editions. Galton expanded the text to include survival information, and this revised *Art of Travel* appeared in 1855. This highly detailed book became a key survival text. It contained information about the storage and transportation of instruments, the art of surveying and the storage of specimens, but it also included such gems as what was best way to roll up shirt sleeves so they remain in place for hours, and the burying of valuables in your arm: Make an incision into your arm, pop a jewel into the open flesh, once it heals over you will always have a pot of ready dosh for an emergency. Galton was soon giving lectures on survival to the War Office, and his work is generally acknowledged, even today, as contributing to saving the lives of many soldiers.

By 1860 the scientific revolution, triggered by Charles Darwin, had gathered energy. Social Darwinism and 'the survival of the fittest' drove arguments for all manner of reforms in the name of supremacy and Galton was posed to consider what might happen if the subjects for improvement were human. On his previous geographical pursuits, his interest in the variation among people had been piqued. He was now further inspired by his cousin Charles and the philosopher Herbert Spencer. His geographical pursuits would now take an anthropological direction; the study of individual differences at a societal level and the idea that more advanced sensory acuity was related to superior intelligence (decades later, Arthur Jensen went on to show a relationship between general intelligence and measures of sensory acuity).

In what would seem to be short-sightedness regarding his own sensory capabilities, Galton argued that sensory superiority was a function of genetic inheritance, and thus, intelligence should run in families. Intelligent people have more superior adaptive traits, and therefore, reputation, eminence and societal superiority was a valid indicator of intelligence. This led to Francis measuring the children of accomplished individuals and comparing them to others.

Galton's approach was purely statistical, which was groundbreaking for his time. His explorations had exposed him to the ideas of the Belgian astronomer, sociologist and pioneer statistician, Adolphe Quetelet, whose methods inspired him to approach the study of intelligence in a systematic way. Quetelet's work was the precursor to what we now call the bell curve: plotting, for example, the heights of a population on a chart will create a large bulge in the middle corresponding to the average height. There will be fewer people with shorter than average and greater than average on either side of the bulge.

Galton introduced the concept of 'reversion', which would later become what we now know as regression analysis. He used this technique to demonstrate what statisticians call regression to the mean. For example, when the children of very tall parents have children, their offspring are not taller, instead they tend to produce children of average height. These calculations led to the development of the first regression line, which went on to become the correlation coefficient.

By 1864 he had crafted an outline to what would go on to become the theory of eugenics which argued that mental characteristics were, just as physical characteristics, subject to hereditary control. By 1885 he was confounding abstract ideas on the nature of intelligence and character. The Negro he argued, had impulsive passions, whereas the North American Indians were cold and melancholic. The American was tolerant of fraud and violence. The peoples of every country were characterised in this way, even peoples from countries he had never been to and knew very little about.

Galton completed the results of his study of excellence, and these were published in *Hereditary Genius* (1869). Eminent parents, who were motivated to encourage their children, had children who were more likely to have children who would make exceptional contributions to society. The government should provide funding to both scientifically pair and support superior individuals to have more children. He argued that such decisions should be formed through the inspection of family records and that those records would eventually form a national genealogical database which would be used to classify families and individuals.

Races did not escape Galton's new statistical enthusiasm. Negros, he argued, were significantly less intelligent than whites. His evidence was predictably circular. He could think of no eminent Negros, we never hear of travellers meeting tribal chiefs who are better men, and, he had met large numbers of half-witted men on his African travels. Australian aboriginals were, he argued, even worse.

His ideas did little to influence the policies of the British Government, although he did manage to bolster white supremacy in countries such as America and Australia. Galton's extreme views were mostly unchallenged and when they were challenged, his scientific approach to answering those questions uncovered additional differences of interest. When challenged by the French philosopher Alphonse de Candolle that environmental climate, government and a flourishing economy were every bit as important as inheritance, Galton developed what was possibly the first psychological questionnaire. He surveyed 200 of his fellow scientists at the Royal Society, asking them if they felt their scientific callings had a genetic basis. He was struck by the number of

Scots who completed the questionnaire. They, however, attributed their personal success not to inheritance, but to the liberal education system they had been born in. This data persuaded Galton to soften his ideas on the importance of inheritance to intelligence and he began to petition for the reformation of English schools.

By 1875 his nativist position was once again bolstered by the publication of 'The History of Twins'. This paper was the first detailed account of the respective role of inheritance and environment, where Galton estimated the relative influence of inheritance and the environment (nature–nurture). He concluded that monozygotic or identical twins are like one another, even when they are reared apart. Conversely, non-identical (dizygotic) twins appeared to be dissimilar even when they grew up in the same family environment.

By the late 1870s, Galton was measuring the facial features of criminals and connecting appearance with character. Photographs of murderers, burglars, fraudsters and sex offenders were organised into piles and then scanned for palpable differences and similarities. He devised a composite measure, whereby the faces could be overlaid onto one another and an average facial profile derived. The composites, were of course, undifferentiated, and the failure of this experiment challenged Galton's long-held perspective that the face will change in line with mentality. He realised he would have to move deeper into the psyche of the criminal. Drawing on the work of psychologists such as Wilhelm Wundt, he began to experiment with introspection and word association tasks.

First responses to such tests tended to be the same for most people, but responses were often strongly psychologically significant in their pairings. For example, mother-father would occur less often than say, father-fear. He also found that responses were connected to the law of errors (the early bell curve), but that many of the people he considered to be most intelligent were not terribly good at forming the images required to complete the task. This work, published in *Inquiries into Human Faculty and its Development* (1883), represents the first systematic use of the word association task and the beginning of the testing movement and the first anthropometric laboratory for the study of human body measurements at London's International Health Exhibition in 1884. It took Galton about a year to gather together the measurements of some 9337 visitors. These included head size, arm span, length of the middle finger, visual acuity and so on. Such was the volume of data that full analysis did not take place until new calculating machines could handle the task. Those analyses demonstrated that people from lower socio-economic backgrounds experienced developmental progress at a rate different to the more privileged.

However, so much in love was Galton with his own ideas, that he continued to pursue dead ducks and blind alleys. His 1889 book, *Natural Inheritance*, was statistically rich, but flawed. He had become so sure of his regression models that he began to reject Darwin's theory of evolution. He could not couple the randomness of nature and the gradualness of change, with the pull of monotonic improvement. Galton had, however, one more discovery to make.

His work in the anthropometric laboratory had provided an archive of rich information, and Galton was hunting the mark of superiority. He had failed at the physical profiling of criminals and held fast to the idea that character held physical manifestations when his attention was drawn to finger ridges. He began smearing ink to decipher hand and fingerprints, something that Asian cultures had been using to identify for decades. The work was pioneered by the amateur scientist William Herschel and the Scottish doctor Henry Faulds, and Galton sought to systematically demonstrate that it would be possible to use fingerprints (hands were too messy) to identify and convict criminals.

The 1880s and 1890s were spent analysing vast numbers of fingerprints and classifying them. Galton's intention was to identify the shapes that were related to criminality. He had amassed such an indexing system that by 1893 the Home Office was exploring how fingerprints could be used to overhaul the system of criminal identification. Galton received the glory, and in the process, the work of Herschel was promoted heavily. This was much to the indignation of Fauld, and a feud ensued.

The later years of Galton's life were mostly unproductive, unsettled by his increasing deafness he became progressively withdrawn from society. He and Louisa were persistently troubled by ill health, but they did at least continue to travel together touring Europe. In August 1897 Louisa became ill in France. What seemed to be an upset stomach quickly advanced and she died within a few days.

A change being as good as a rest, in the autumn of 1899, Galton was in Egypt with his new nurse and companion Evelyne Biggs. He was back on top form and, following the publication of Gregor Mendel's ground-breaking work on inheritance, Galton was ready for one last scientific hurrah. In recognition of his inestimable contributions, Galton was awarded the Royal Society's Darwin medal in 1902. The news was quickly sullied by the news that Charles Darwin had died.

The couple returned to England the following year, and Galton turned his scientific writing towards social change to improve the nation: eugenics, its definition, scope and aims. Galton had an audience that stretched through the Sociological Society, to Karl Pearson, H. G. Wells and George Bernard Shaw. The University of London established a eugenics lab, and the University of Oxford appointed its first eugenics fellow. The drive for eugenic discrimination was taking hold, and all that remained were some moral obstacles. By 1907 branches of the London-based Eugenics Education Society were sweeping across the United Kingdom. By 1909, the now frail Francis Galton received a knighthood. In Europe he was appointed to the council of the German Eugenics Society, and his work became popular across the globe.

Galton penned one last fantasy propaganda book which was rejected by publishers, and he died on January 9th, 1911. To this day, the scientist and explorer Sir Francis Galton's tremendous achievements remain over-shadowed by his eugenics work.

Major works

Galton, F. (1869). *Hereditary Genius*. London: Macmillan

Galton, F. (1874). *English Men of Sciences: Their Nature and Nurture*. London: Macmillan.

Galton, F. (1877). Typical laws of heredity. *Proceedings of the Royal Institution*, 8, 282–301.

Galton, F. (1883). *Inquiries into Human Faculty and Its Development*. London: Macmillan.

Galton, F. (1886). Regression towards mediocrity in hereditary stature. *Journal of the Anthropological Institute*, 15, 246–263.

Galton, F. (1888). Co-relations and their measurement, chiefly from anthropometric data. *Proceedings of the Royal Society*, 45, 125–145.

Galton, F. (1889). *Natural Inheritance*. London: Macmillan.

Galton, F. (1892). *Fingerprints*. London: Macmillan.

Bibliography

Brookes, M. (2004). *Extreme Measures: The Dark Visions and Bright Ideas of Francis Galton.* New York: Bloomsbury.

Galton, F. (1908). *Memories of My Life.* London: Methuen.

Chapter 2

Sigmund Freud

'I can most highly recommend the Gestapo to everyone'

May 6th, 1856 to September 23rd, 1939

Sigmund Freud was born in Pribor (Freiberg), Czechoslovakia on May 6th, 1856. His 37-year-old father Jakob had taken his third wife, the 17-year-old Amalie Nathansohn, 12 months before Freud's birth. Sigmund was now the eldest of eight. His father Jacob had two adult sons, Emanuel and Philipp, from his previous marriage to Sally Kanner (who died prematurely in 1852). There is some suggestion of a third wife between Kanner and Nathansohn called Rebbecca; however, little is known about her. There are reports that Freud's birth date was recorded as March 6th on official documents but that the family reported the May date to conceal the fact that Amalie was pregnant. His mother largely home-schooled Sigmund until he entered formal education at the Leopoldstaedter Realgymnasium in 1865 and the children of his step-brother Emanuel, Jon and Pauline, became Freud's playmates and confidants.

Freud's mother was widely considered to be both beautiful and austere. The family was traditional, patriarchal and authoritative, Freud's sister had to give up her piano lessons because they were disturbing Sigmund's concentration, but it was also united with strong bonds of affection and the light-heartedness of their father. The family was financially stable; there was always enough money for books, music lessons and theatre tickets and they would summer at Moravian resorts.

Freud was a bright student, by the age of 20 he had an aptitude for ancient history and the classics. He spoke fluent French, German, English and Spanish. Inspired by a lecture by the physician and anatomist Carl Brühl on Goethe's aphorisms on nature, Freud entered Vienna University in 1873 to study medicine and physiology under the German physician and physiologist Ernst von Brücke. Brücke's influence in what was known as dynamic physiology, an approach in which organisms are treated as part of a system of forces that keep it alive but ultimately lead to its demise, was possibly one of the most formative in Freud's career. Freud spent several years in Brücke's lab in comparative study (1877) carrying out brilliant, scientifically precise research, comparing the brains of vertebrates, invertebrates and humans. This was a brief but fruitful period of research. Freud's work on the nervous tissue was the first to help establish the evolutionary continuity between all organisms as well as being the first to describe the structure and function of the medulla oblongata which is the portion of the hindbrain that controls autonomic functions such as breathing, swallowing, heart and blood vessel function. Work which proved seminal for the discovery of the neuron during the 1890s.

During this period, Freud also studied philosophy under Franz Brentano. Brentano reintroduced the concept of intentionality from scholastic philosophy as well being one of the first to differentiate between genetic and descriptive psychology. Parts of his work are directly observable in the development of psychodynamics which emphasises the forces that underlie human behaviour and the dynamic relationships between conscious and unconscious processes (Gay, 1988).

In 1881, he qualified as a Doctor of Medicine and became engaged to Martha Bernays. The main obstacles to an immediate marriage were Freud's practical concerns about money, his annoyances of what he felt to be Martha's unreasonable expectations for a family home and pressure on both fronts from his future mother-in-law. Thus, their five-year engagement was tinged with long periods of separation and letter writing. Their endearment to one another is apparent in their passionate letters to each other where Freud's terms of endearment to his fiancée have child-like, submissive characteristics; *sweet, passionately loved child, little princess*. Unsurprisingly his infantilization of his sweetheart was shaded with controlling, possession and jealousy to the point of absurd behaviours. The slightest suggestion from Martha's correspondence of indecisiveness or neglect for correctness would cast shadows of doubt over the relationship, violent outbursts and unprovoked jealously. Freud's jealousy extended outside of his perceived love rivals, to people who were more attractive than himself and towards Martha's mother and brother Eli. This behaviour placed considerable strain on Martha, however, her good sense made Freud reconsider much of his unreasonable and illogical behaviours. Here we can see the emergence of Freud's thinking on emotions and reason. Freud, ever the rational thinker, was dissonant to Freud the future husband. There was a perpetual struggle between the competing needs of jealousy, possession and reason; the intensity of the base instincts that must be repressed so that the powers of reasoning can win through.

Freud's relationships with his mentors and peers were similarly volatile. He would develop deep and intense friendships, but this unconditional regard would soon cool and end in overt hostility. Freud was fully aware of this tendency but explained it as a rebellious streak which he had developed through the admiration and burning rivalry that he felt for his nephew John; an intimate friend and hated enemy.

Freud's competitiveness, his need to assert and his ambition to make a universally significant discovery were constant preoccupations but when he experimented with cocaine in 1884 on his friend Ernst von Fleischl-Marxow, the consequences resulted in death and justifiably bitter criticism. Fleischl-Marxow was a brilliant and talented doctor who had accidentally cut his right thumb with a scalpel whist researching with a cadaver. The wound would not heal, it became infected and required amputation, but the second wound also failed to heal. Neuromata, nerve tissue growths which can cause excruciating pain, formed and to manage his distress Fleischl-Marxow self-medicated with morphine eventually becoming an addict.

Freud was convinced he could cure Fleischl-Marxow with cocaine. It was a time of optimism about cocaine, there was no great concern about its use, and it was commonplace in drinks such as the tonic wine Vi Mariani and Coca-Cola. That year Freud published his monograph on cocaine, *Über Coca*, quickly becoming the authority on the drug. Freud's understanding was, however, limited. As a young doctor, the drug was financially beyond his reach. He managed some minor uneventful self-experimentation, including sending some to his fiancée Martha Bernays, a gift to 'give her cheeks a red colour' (Freud, as translated in Byck, 1974, p.7), before becoming her regular supplier. Freud was fully aware of the pain-killing properties of cocaine but had failed to report on its analgesic properties. For a man in search of notoriety, this was something of an own goal because the critical acclaim went to the ophthalmologist, Carl Koller, when he ended decades of suffering by introducing it as a local anaesthetic for eye surgery. *Über Coca* had not brought Freud the acclaim he had hoped for, but he was sure cocaine would cure Fleischl-Marxow's unbearable neuralgia. Fleischl-Marxow was, however, suffering from morphine poisoning and his protracted agony elicited stronger and stronger doses of cocaine from Freud until death finally followed. As cases of cocaine addiction began to spread across Europe, Freud faced bitter criticism. He was labelled a public menace, and by 1887 he was advising the abandonment of injected cocaine in the treatment of nervous or medical disorders. Both Freud and Martha, however, continued to take cocaine in small quantities with no reported adverse effects or addiction.

Fortunately, Freud's fortunes began to change. When backed by Brücke, he secured a position at Theodor Meynert's laboratory of brain anatomy where he began to examine what would become his passion, psychiatry. Freud won a scholarship that allowed him to study under Jean-Martin Charcot at the Pitié-Salpêtrière in Paris.

Charcot greatly influenced Freud. They shared a love of history and art, and Charcot was a brilliantly lucid writer who, like Freud, spoke several languages. At the laboratory, Charcot was a defiant character who trained Freud in the controversial use of hypnosis to treat hysteria and 'dispel' paralysis by suggestion and demonstrated that hysteria is more common in men than women.

Even before working with Charcot, Freud was fascinated with hypnosis and its capacity for the study of the unconscious and this collaboration reinforced Freud's attitude that the scientist must have the courage to explore even the most questionable scientific methods. His work in this area met with persistent resistance. His account to the Society of Medicine in Berlin on male hysteria was met with scepticism:

> One of them, an old surgeon, actually broke out with the exclamation: 'But, my dear sir, how can you talk such nonsense? Hysteron [sic] means the uterus. So how can a man be hysterical?' I objected in vain that what I wanted was not to have my diagnosis approved, but to have the case put at my disposal. At length, outside the hospital, I came upon a case

of classical hysterical hemianaesthesia in a man and demonstrated it before the 'Gesellschaft der Aerzte' [1886]. This time I was applauded, but no further interest was taken in me. The impression that the high authorities had rejected my innovations remained unshaken; and, with my hysteria in men and my production of hysterical paralyses by suggestion, I found myself forced into the opposition. As I was soon afterwards excluded from the laboratory of cerebral anatomy and for terms on end had nowhere to deliver my lectures, I withdrew from academic life and ceased to attend the learned societies.

(Freud, 1925, pp.15–16)

The typical Freudian response was that society was not ready for his work because it had taken a direction which was in opposition to the prevailing culture of observation of the physical, chemical or anatomical. The unobservable was not worthy of scientific investigation. Always the rebel, Freud hunkered down with the dissenting ranks. We can also see, however, the footprints of contemporary codes of ethics in Freud's attitudes forming. For he felt passionately that if individuals were to make a profit from the distress of others then they ought to be able to do something to help them. As it stood, the prevailing medical model did nothing more than to assign a variant of pathological symptoms to conditions which, in many cases, would have had underlying causes. The treatments of which included purging with toxic antimony, 'vapouring' with mercury, or hydrotherapy of the uterus.

On returning from Paris, Freud opened a private practice specialising in nervous diseases and was appointed to the directorship of the neurological section of the Max Kassowitz Institute for Children's Diseases. His improved position meant that he was finally able to marry Martha Bernays. To further develop his skills in hypnosis, Freud travelled to Nancy to work with the French physician and neurologist Hyppolyte Bernheim and the now ageing physician Ambroise-Auguste Liébeault. Both men were formative to the development of Freud's professional practice. In particular, Bernheim's experimental rigour and Liébeault's commitment to the needs of his patients triggered a recognition in Freud regarding the value of free talk as a therapeutic technique. The Viennese physician Josef Breuer had treated several patients diagnosed with hysteria and found that when he encouraged them to talk freely about the earliest occurrence of their symptoms the latter often declined. Freud further developed Breuer's thinking on free talk by suggesting that many phobias and hysterical symptoms originated from long-forgotten traumatic experiences. Freud sought to bring such experiences into conscious awareness and then systematically confront them; thus, it followed that distress would disappear. Their mutual study on this topic was circulated in the renown *Studies in Hysteria* (1895) which consists of a joint introduction, followed by five case studies including Anna O, a theoretical essay by Breuer, and a practice-oriented piece by Freud (the text first appeared in English in 1936).

For Freud, Bertha Pappenheim (Anna O was Freud and Breuer's pseudonym) was a fascination which led him to make significant theoretical assumptions regarding the symptoms and causes of hysteria, leading to the conclusion that early childhood events have a substantial impact on our adult personality and lives. Traumatic experiences may remain hidden from consciousness and the 'inability to remember' is supported through powerful mechanisms of self-deception. Here the terms repression and transference emerge in the Freudian lexicon.

Freud described these times as the 'groping' years, when the struggle towards his goal was anything but strident. Sometimes his clinical work confirmed his assumptions, and sometimes it did not. As was a predictable pattern in Freud's male relationships, Breuer and Freud parted company. Breuer considered Freud's emphasis (*obsession*) with the sexual origin and content of many neuroses both excessive and unjustifiable. Freud, however, was fully committed to the idea that early sexuality was a component of the child's developing personality. He had difficulty reconciling that mental health problems could have been caused by the trauma of a perverted adult's acts. Rather there was a developmental process which had become interrupted in some way.

By 1891 the Freuds had three children, Mathilde (b. 1887), Jean-Martin (b. 1889) and Oliver (b. 1891) and had moved to an apartment in the newly erected Berggasse 19 where Martha gave birth to Ernst (b. 1892), Sophie (b. 1893) and Anna (b. 1895), to whom Freud became firmly attached.

Freud began to nurture a small group of elite intellectual friends, including Alfred Adler, Wilhelm Stekel, Max Kahane and Rudolf Reitler. He founded the Wednesday Psychological Society (re-established as the Vienna Psychoanalytic Society), now the oldest psychoanalysis society in the world. Again, it was not long before fractions occurred between Freud and members of the group. Alfred Alder eventually left and founded his Society for Psychoanalytic Research (later called the Society for Individual Psychology), but the disagreements persisted, this time with Wilhelm Stekel about the editorial committee of the journal *Zentralblatt für Psychoanalyse*. Freud founded his own psychoanalytical journal devoted to interdisciplinary research in mental life, and Stekel responded by resigning from the Vienna Psychoanalytic Society.

The most well-known friendship-estrangement cycle was Freud's relationship with the Swiss psychiatrist and psychoanalyst Carl Gustav Jung. Correspondence between the two began in 1906 when Jung sent Freud a copy of his published works, triggering six years of correspondence between the two. Freud treated Jung as his heir apparent. They travelled together delivering lectures, visiting retreats, hunting and fishing. During a visit to Freud in 1907, Martha's younger sister, Minna Bernays, who was living with the Freud family after the birth of Anna, confessed to Jung that she was engaged in a very intimate relationship with Freud. Jung claims to have agonised over this secret. There is, however, very little additional, corroborating evidence to support an affair other than some letters to his friend Wilhelm Fliess, where Freud had declared that his sex life with his wife was over.

Towards the end of their relationship, Jung had diverged from the Freudian perspective of sexual drives towards a new conception of libido. Jung also felt that Freud's thinking on the unconscious was unnecessarily dark and that he tended to treat his followers as patients. Whereas, Freud felt that Jung's exploration of religion and myths was unscientific and that Jung himself had little insight into his own neurosis. In 1913 Freud published *Totem and Taboo*, partly as a riposte to Jung's interest in mythology. In the end, their ideological differences were all-consuming and, by 1912, their personal relationship was abandoned. Freud remained convinced that Jung harboured anti-Semitic feelings and a death wish toward him. The stress of which caused fainting fits on at least two separate occasions. These episodes prompted an apology from Jung. Freud's response, however, was to draw on Jung's libido theory artfully. In a less than subtle put-down, Freud wrote to fellow psychoanalyst Ernst Jones describing his fainting spell as an unruly homosexual feeling at the root of the matter (Donn, 1988, pp. 154–156). Jung was furious at the mockery; that somehow their relationship troubles were a homosexual spat, and he exploded in rage. During their intense conversations, Jung had discussed with Freud his experiences of being sexually assaulted by a trusted adult as a child. This had caused sexual confusion in Jung and he had confided to Freud that he had what he described as a religious crush on Freud. Freud had used this information against Jung in mockery of him and his theories. A series of angry letters followed before Freud proposed that they abandoned their personal relationship entirely.

The Freud–Jung association concluded in 1913 and the following year, a greater war began. Like many Europeans, Freud was initially excited by the outbreak of World War I: war was terrible, but also glorious and patriotic. His initial animation quickly turned to disillusionment. In his essay, 'Thoughts for the Times on War and Death' (1915), he argued that civilised nations knew so little of one another that their primitive instincts meant that they could turn easily against each other with hate and loathing.

The war had significant financial implications for Freud. His entire fortune, invested in Austrian State Bonds, was lost. His patients were in a similar reduced state, and he struggled to make a living through his clinics. Temporary assistance came from Anton von Freund, a Budapest manufacturer, but inflation was high, and the money was rapidly consumed. After the war, Freud spent less time in clinical observation, focusing on the application of what would eventually become his 'grand theory' applied to art, literature, anthropology, war and history.

By 1919 Freud, a long-time smoker, presented with the first signs of oral cancer. The Austrian stomatologist Hans Pichler began treating Freud for a painful swelling in his left palate and between 1923 and 1938 Freud went under some 30 surgeries. Many of these surgeries were successful, but recovery was difficult, and he could barely endure the prosthesis he was eventually fitted with.

By the 1930s, psychoanalysis had a firm foothold as the 'talking therapy' that offered a powerful treatment to a range of psychological disorders. Freud was world famous, treating an array of famous and colourful characters; Napoleon's great-granddaughter, Princess Marie Bonaparte, who, in a bid to cure her frigidity, asked

Freud whether she should sleep with her own son; the American poetess, Hilda Doolittle, who documented her experiences with Freud in such detail that we have an almost complete account of Freud's methods, and the mother of Prince Philip, Princess Alice of Battenberg. To cure her religious delusions, Freud had her ovaries x-rayed. He believed this process would accelerate her menopause, kill her libido and her religious delusions would cease.

As Nazi restrictions on Jewish business increased, and Nazi sympathisers mobilised their aggression towards the Austrian Jewish population, Freud's practice became a target. His work was of such importance the Nazi regime was reluctant to destroy his practice. Freud was similarly reluctant to leave. In 1933, his books were burned by a mob of Nazi sympathisers, along with other works considered to contain un-German ideas (Einstein, Marx, Heine). When Freud heard the news, he dryly quipped 'What progress we are making ..... In the Middle Ages they would have burned me. Now they are content with burning my books' (Letter to Ernest Jones, 1933).

By 1938 the Nazis were no longer content with book burning. They seized what remained of Freud's money and property, but Freud was still determined to stay. It was only when his daughter Anna was arrested and detained by the Gestapo on March 22, 1938, that Freud finally agreed to leave.

President Roosevelt, the French ambassador to Paris, and Princess Marie Bonaparte, whose wealth and patronage supported the advancement of the popularly of psychoanalysis, interceded on Freud's behalf. Princess Marie brokered a deal with the Nazis that permitted Freud to salvage his couch, sculpture collection and library, then leave Vienna for London. Freud was permitted to travel on the condition that he wrote a statement swearing they had treated him well. According to Freud's son Martin, Freud wryly wrote at the bottom of the statement: '*Ich kann die Gestapo jedermann auf das beste empfehlen*': 'I can most highly recommend the Gestapo to everyone' (Jones, 1957, p. 217). The official documents, however, suggest that this was more of an amusing retell of the events, than actual fact (Freud, 2007).

Freud died the following year from a verrucous carcinoma, known as Ackerman's tumour. He had suffered from this tumour for 16 years and had more than 30 surgical procedures and endured primitive radium therapy. Finally, he persuaded his physician that he had had enough and asked him to make an end of it. When the time was right, Freud's doctor Max Schur gave him 21 milligrams of morphine and Freud died within hours. Freud's sisters were not so fortunate. Mitzie (81) and Paula (78) were murdered in the Maly Trostenets extermination camp in 1942. Dolfi Freud (82) died in Theresienstadt from advanced starvation and Rosa (82) was killed at Treblinka.

Despite his long illness, Freud wrote 20 books and articles and directed the international advancement of his field. He advanced the medical perspective on psychology much further than his contemporaries by demonstrating how the science of medicine could be extended to the problems of the unconscious mind in a humane and comprehensible way. To Freud, the symptoms of problematic behaviour were attempts to manage unconscious forces and desires; the analyst would then work to restore balance to the patient's struggles by creating awareness which would help them keep their struggles under control. The id is the Freudian structure of personality that consists of drives, it has no contact with reality and is driven by the pleasure principle, always seeking pleasure and avoiding pain. The ego is a structure that develops during childhood as the developing individual must manage the constraints of reality. The ego is the executive branch of personality because it coordinates and mediates, making rational decisions to bring an individual's pleasures into the boundaries of what is real and acceptable. For example, the id may be driven towards, aggressive or sexual statements. Humour and wit enable these forbidden expressions to be placed into common conversation in socially sanctioned ways. The id and ego have no sense of morality. The superego considers whether something is right or wrong.

How does the ego resolve the conflict between its demands for reality, the wishes of the id and the constraints of the superego? Through defence mechanisms: unconscious methods used by the ego to distort reality thereby protecting the person from anxiety. In Freud's view, the conflicting demands of the personality structures produce anxiety. The anxiety alerts the ego to resolve the conflict by means of defence mechanisms. The process of psychoanalysis also involves the patient expressing their thoughts, in an uncensored way, using free associations and describing fantasies and dreams in which the therapist infers unconscious conflicts which are causing the patient's symptoms, often confronting the patient's pathological defences with the aim of increasing insight and improvement. Repression is the most potent and pervasive defence mechanism. It works to push unacceptable id impulses out of awareness and back into the unconscious mind. Repression was to Freud both a general construct and one which is also the foundation from which all other defence mechanisms work.

Other important defence mechanisms are: displacement – the defence mechanism that occurs when feelings are shifted from one object to another; projection – the defence mechanism used to attribute our own shortcomings, problems and faults to others; and sublimation – the defence mechanism that occurs when an individual replaces a socially distasteful course of action with a socially acceptable one.

Freud's theory suggests that development of the person is associated with an orderly progression through five psychosexual or libidinal stages: oral, anal, phallic, latency and genital. These are referred to as psychosexual or libidinal stages because of the primacy of the different erogenous zones during the development of the child. The adult personality is thought to be determined by the way conflicts between the early sources of pleasure – the mouth, the anus and then the genitals – and the demands of reality are resolved. When these conflicts are not resolved, the individual may become fixated at a specific stage of development. Fixation is a defence mechanism that occurs when an individual remains locked into an earlier developmental stage because needs are either under- or over-gratified. For example, the Oedipus complex is a hypothetical construct which proposes that the young child develops an intense desire to replace the parent of the same sex and enjoy the affections of the parent of the opposite sex. How is the Oedipus complex resolved? At about 5 to 6 years of age, children recognise that their same-sex parent might punish them for their incestuous desires. To reduce this conflict, the child identifies with the same-sex parent. If the conflict is not resolved the theory predicts that the individual may become fixated at the phallic stage as illustrated by an adult whose personality is characterised by self-assured recklessness, vanity and exhibitionism.

The healthy person is characterised by a dynamic balance between the forces of the ego, concerned with reality and mostly conscious; the superego, dealing with morality; and the id, the storehouse of drives and unacceptable repressed wishes and entirely unconscious. Neurotic individuals are thought to be ruled by their superegos. Psychotic individuals have had their ego defences penetrated and are ruled by their id. Thus, in the case of psychotics, therapy aims to replace id activity with that of the ego.

Psychoanalytic theory embraces every aspect of the human mind and seeks to explain every aspect of human behaviour. All aspects of human behaviour, no matter how small or trivial, have meaning. Therefore, psychoanalysis is both a collection of theories and a therapeutic method. A process whereby clinical experience is cross-referenced back to clinical theory, and thus Freud's work was constantly in a state of evolution. As we have learned more about the structure and function of the brain and its diseases, there has been a considerable backlash against the Freudian unconscious.

Hans Eysenck, one of the most vociferous critics, argued that Freud's work had a baleful influence on the progress of psychological science not least because many concepts cannot be defined in ways that allow them to be measured. In fact, some, particularly those relating to the unconscious, are so formulated that they can never be measured. Moreover, the theory makes very few accurate predictions about how someone will behave but always claims to provide a satisfactory explanation for everything a person has done in the past. Others have argued, however, that the current medical perspective does little to understand the everyday life of individuals, and the role that power plays in our lives. Until Freud, every sick woman was neurotic and every masturbating child a sexual deviant (Roudinesco, 2016).

At the time of his death, Freud was regarded as one of the significant scientific thinkers of his age receiving 13 Nobel prize nominations: 12 times for Medicine and once for Literature . In 1937, Freud was nominated by 14 prominent scientists and Nobel Laureates, to no avail. In 1938, he was again blocked, this time by Albert Einstein. Freud was wounded by the continual rejection by the Nobel committee, but he understood that psychoanalysis was already under considerable attack. He also seems to have harboured little resentment towards Einstein. The two went on to publish their personal correspondences in 'Why War', which were letters discussing violence and human nature.

Freud's work continues to be developed throughout the world. Its continuing popularity may be due in part to the fact that its core ideas appear to be widely perceived to concur with everyday human experience and to offer the promise of a coherent explanation that cannot be matched by more mainstream psychological frameworks. For example, much of the language of psychoanalysis has become the dominant idiom in which most of us explain why we think, feel and behave as we do. However, Freud never believed that psychoanalysis was the last word in psychological explanation, and he assessed its shelf-life to be limited by the rate of progress in biochemistry which, he considered, would provide a level of explanation of human behaviour to which psychoanalysis could hardly begin to aspire.

Major works

Freud, S. (1925). *An Autobiographical Study* (J. Strachey, Ed. 1963). New York: Norton.

Freud, S. (1966). *The Standard Edition of the Complete Psychological Works of Sigmund Freud*. London: Hogarth Press and the Institute of Psychoanalysis.

Bibliography

Appignanesi, L., & Forrester, J. (2000). *Freud's Women*. London: Penguin.

Byck, R. (1974). *Cocaine Papers by Sigmund Freud*. New York: Stonehill.

Donn, L. (1988) *Freud and Jung: Years of Friendship, Years of Loss*. New York: Scribner.

Ellenberger, H. F. (1981). *The Discovery of the Unconscious: The History and Evolution of Dynamic Psychiatry*. New York: Basic Books.

Freud, S. (1915). *Thoughts for the Times on War and Death, Zeitgemäßes Über Krieg Und Tod*. Zürich: Internationaler Psyoanalytischer Verlag.

Freud, M. (1957). *Sigmund Freud – Man and Father*. New York: Vanguard Press.

Freud, S. (2007). *Living in the Shadow of the Freud Family*. Westport, CT: Praeger Publishers.

Gay, P. (1988). *Freud: A Life for Our Time* (1st ed.). New York & London: W. W. Norton.

Grünbaum, A. (1984). *The Foundations of Psychoanalysis: A Philosophical Critique*. Berkeley, CA: University of California Press.

Hall, C. S. (1999). *A Primer of Freudian Psychology*. New York: New American Library.

Jones, E. (1957). *Sigmund Freud. Life and Work*. New York: Basic Books.

Roudinesco, R. (2016). *Freud, in His Time and Ours*. Translation, Porter, C. Cambridge, MA: Harvard University Press.

Chapter 3

Alfred Binet

The constructionist

July 8th, 1857 to October 18th, 1911

Alfred Binet was born Alfredo Binetti in Nice on July 8th, 1857. His parents were wealthy, his father was a physician and his mother an artist, but the marriage was not a happy one, and they divorced when Alfred was quite young. Alfred lived with his mother in Paris after the divorce. His father was a harsh man who viewed his son as weak and cowardly. To toughen him up he used to make Alfred view and touch corpses, which only made matters worse. Alfred developed a life-long fear of his father, and his career was fraught with difficulties and conflicts which circled cadavers and his estranged father.

Binet attended the Lycée Louis-le-Grand, Paris, which was named for King Louis XIV of France in 1682 and to this day plays a vital role in the education of elite French society. Alfred was a competent student, receiving several awards during his time at Louis-le-Grand in areas such as literary composition and translation. He obtained a degree in law in 1878, obtaining his practicing licence at the age of 21. He began studying for a Doctorate but found he detested the discipline, describing the law as 'the career for men who have not yet chosen a vacation' (Binet, 1904, cited by Wolf, 1973, p.3).

Like his father and grandfather before him, Binet turned to medical studies at the Sorbonne. Studying botany and zoology in the embryological laboratory of Edouard-Gérard Balbiani, he developed skills in systematic observation and experimental methods. His Doctorate was awarded in Natural Science in 1894, and he married Laure, the daughter of Edouard-Gérard. Laure and Alfred went on to have two children: Madeleine and Alice. Binet described Madeleine as a 'reflective' child, whereas Alice was more impulsive. Throughout their lives, Binet continued to observe differences in their developmental style and document their mental processes in his laboratory.

His pursuit of psychology was not through formal education, but self-directed through the study of articles and books by the British philosopher John Stuart Mill, and the philosopher, biologist and sociologist Herbert Spencer.

In 1892, after several years of self-study, Binet was introduced to the neurologist Jean-Martin Charcot. Charcot soon became his mentor, and the two began working together at the Pitié-Salpêtrière Hospital in Paris. The position was unpaid, but Binet had independent means, and this supported him to study and give over his time as he pleased. Under Charcot's guidance and inspiration, Binet commenced on one of the most productive periods of his career. Charcot's work on hypnosis, however, caused Binet considerable embarrassment. Charcot had claimed to present evidence that hypnotic states could be influenced using magnets and Binet was a forceful supporter of Charcot's position. Charcot's work did not, however, stand up to scrutiny and was soon discredited. Binet had to retract his position and ultimately severed his connections with Charcot over the fiasco.

Binet's work explored several areas; fetishism, hallucinations, perception and suggestion, visual imagery, memory, chess performance, music, fear and religion, depression, deaf-mutes and mental fatigue. He was establishing himself as a prolific writer when he began working, as Associate Director at the first French psychological laboratory, the L'École Pratique des Hautes Études at the Sorbonne in 1889. At that time, Henri-Étienne Beaunis was the director. His philosophy was in the introspective model of Wilhelm Wundt, but he gave Binet licence to study as he wished. Binet became Director in 1894. This was a productive year for him. He produced a book on experimental methods and a book on expert calculators; four papers that studied childhood abilities; two papers on dramatists and one on spatial orientation; a methodological piece on recording piano-playing techniques and he founded the first French journal dedicated to the study of psychology, L'Année Psychologique.

The following year, Binet began collaborating with Victor Henri on a series of studies investigating the abilities of Parisian school children with the intention of developing a battery of tests that would permit more systematic examination of ability. Binet and Henri were convinced that a fuller understanding could be arrived at by studying the abilities of children outside of the normal range of abilities, particularly those who were below average ability.

Termed 'Psychologie Individuelle', Binet became the most powerful promoter and advocate of study of individual differences, and by 1899 was collaborating with the physician Théodore Simon. Both became committed members of of the Société Libre pour l'Etude psychologique de l'enfant (Free Society for the Psychological Study of the Child). Profoundly sceptical regarding the utility of so-called objective assessments by parents, teachers and doctors, Binet set about trying to convince its members that systematic observation and the experimental method were the way forward for the study of child development and steered the organisation towards the psychological training of teachers and research into educational psychology.

By 1901 Binet was heading the French Ministerial Commission in Paris, which aimed to track underperforming or 'abnormal' children with the aim of identifying those who would not benefit from formal State education. In May 1905 Binet and Simon had established the first Laboratory of Experimental Psychology in a Parisian school. Here they could refine their work into a test battery which would evaluate all levels of abilities testing digit span retention, vocabulary, paper folding, comprehension, block design reproduction, similarities and differences. The sample sizes, however, remained small and unrepresentative, which is surprising given Binet's standpoint for the importance of sound experimental methods and robust research design. What made the test unique, however, was its capacity to increase in difficulty. It ranged from using simple tracking tests, to the more advanced analysis of older or gifted children through testing with complex sentence completion. The test would, in theory, enable assessments of children which would determine what mental age that child was performing at, permitting comparisons between a child's mental age and the average performance of children in a chronological age group.

The first Binet-Simon test was published in 1908, and the later 1911 revision helped answer some of the issues around representation. The groups tested were more diverse both in age, intellect and socio-economic status. Binet's intention was that the test could help him advocate for the education of all children and to better help teachers understand their individual needs and he spent much of his professional time and research efforts on educational reform. The test, however, remained largely ignored in France. It was Henry Goddard, the prominent American psychologist and eugenicist, who discovered Binet's work and translated it into English. Lewis M. Terman administered the test to North American children with the intention of understanding the genetic basis of intelligence. The test then went through further revisions at Stanford University, where Terman was working as Assistant Professor in the School of Education; resulting in the Stanford-Binet intelligence test.

Binet died unexpectedly in 1912. He was only 54 years of age and his wife was also in poor health. We know very little about the personality or personal life of Binet, few records exist. His daughter Madeleine described him as a

> lively man, smiling, often very ironical, gentle in manner, wise in his judgments, a little sceptical of course. ... Without affectation, straightforward, very good-natured, he was scornful of mediocrity in all its forms. Amiable and cordial to people of science, pitiless toward bothersome people who wasted his time and interrupted his work. ... He always seemed to be deep in thought.
>
> (cited in Wolf, 1973, p.36)

Binet is described as happiest when he had a blank sheet of paper to fill and outside of the psychology laboratory, he had a passion for the theatre, attending plays and sharing his home with playwrights, actors and directors. He wrote, co-authored and produced dramas, four of which were performed in Paris at the Grand-Guignol and Sarah-Bernhardt theatres. These plays, typically had a dark, morose, psychological side, examining the grave consequences of greed, pompousness and stupidity.

Binet mostly resisted theoretical speculations about the inherited or theoretical nature of intelligence. From 1908, he was advocating a constructionist perspective but was hampered by a lack of understanding about the structure of complex intelligence. The closest Binet came to a theory of intelligence was a manifestation of comprehension, memory and good judgement, and that a complex number of specific processes combined into a whole.

In his study of judgement, Binet distinguished between direction, adaption and criticism. Direction was the strength of task focus and problem-solving strategy. These operated to support idea generation in the face of distractions and failure. Adaptation was the extent to which an individual could make appropriate choices from alternative options and their capacity to refine their solutions to fit any task constraints. Criticism was the internal monologue which provided feedback to help evaluate potential solutions to a problem. Binet's work on this area relates closely to modern-day ideas about the role of metacognition in intelligence, particularly current thinking on learning to learn as a predictor for academic performance. Binet's study of his children and their differences in temperament also laid out the blueprint for future work on cognitive styles and the work of psychologists such as Howard Gardner who argued for different patterns of strengths and weaknesses in ability.

Binet's legacy is in his contribution to psychometric testing through the development of an easy-to-use test that examined mental functioning. The nature of intelligence, for Binet, was what his test could measure and the scale embodied ideas that are still relevant today. The best way to understand performance is to reference it against what is normal or typical, and, rather than observing simple processes, that the most substantial differences between individuals will reside in complex mental functions. To measure these processes accurately, it was necessary to assess children a variety of ways; intellect would then be the sum of those measures.

Binet did not, however, consider the impact such labels would have on children who performed poorly on the test. He believed that intellectual potential was malleable. Whilst inheritance might place a ceiling on potential, special education, simulation and support would compensate for any deficits. For Binet, the value of his test was in the opportunities it provided to children because they could be reliabily measured and reliably supported. The test was, however, heavily weighted towards scholastic experience, particularly verbal ability. The sampling of children included in the study remained too narrow to usefully record performance at higher levels, it was too easy at lower levels and too difficult at the upper end. There were several technical problems with the test including misplacements of test items relative to mental age, the same number of psychological functions were not always assessed at each age level and because mental age could be arrived at differently from person to person. In particular, when a child was expected to be developmentally verbally developed, the test began to disproportionately favour verbal test items, to the point at which at the top end of the scale the test only measures verbal ability. Test takers with poor verbal ability, or for whom French, or in the English, was not their first language, were automatically penalised. The test was doubtless a significant improvement on previous processes, but it was still inadequate. Binet was aware of at least some of these problems and did make attempts at improvements. It would be Lewis M. Terman who would ultimately go on to make the most substantial improvements revising the test into a more comprehensive and more accessible.

Major works

Binet, A. (1890a). *La Suggestibilité*. Paris: Schleicher Frères.

Binet, A. (1890b). Perceptions d'enfants. *Revue Philosophique*, 30, 582–611.

Binet, A. (1891). *Études de psychologie expérimentale*. Paris: L'Harmattan.

Binet, A. (1892). *Les Altérations de la personnalité*. Paris: Alcan.

Binet, A. (1893). *L'Etude expérimentale de l'intelligence*. Schleicher Frères.

Binet, A. (1898a). *La Fatigue intellectuelle*. Paris: Schleicher Frères (with V. Henri).

Binet, A. (1898b). La mesure en psychologie individuelle. *Revue Philosophique*, 46, 113–123.

Binet, A. (1908). Le développement de l'intelligence chez les enfants. *L'Année Psychologique*, 14, 1–94.

Binet, A., & Simon, T. (1905). Sur la nécessité d'établir un diagnostic scientifique des états inférieurs de l'intelligence. *L'Année Psychologique*, 11, 163–190 (with Th. Simon).

Bibliography

Fancher, R. E. (1985). *The Intelligence Men*. New York: Norton.

Wolf, T. (1973). *Alfred Binet*. New York: Norton.

Chapter 4

Charles Edward Spearman

The intelligence factor

September 10th, 1863 to September 17th, 1945

Charles Spearman had auspicious roots. His grandfather was Sir Alexander Young Spearman, a baronet and a senior official in the British Treasury. His father (also called Alexander) did not succeed to the baronetcy because he died in 1865, aged 33. Alexander married twice, and Charles was the younger son of his second wife, Louisa Anne Caroline Amelia Mainwaring. Louisa remarried Henry H. Molyneux-Steel in 1870. Molyneux-Steel held a position in the College of Arms in London, and the family lived in Leamington Spa, Warwickshire where Charles attended school from 1876 until his stepfather Henry died in 1882. During his school years, Charles reported having an intellectual devotion to philosophy but decided to embark on a period of military service in the hope that it might ripen his experience and help him 'unriddle university'. Family circumstances may also have contributed to Charles's decision to join the army. His mother, widowed again, had two children to support and such circumstances would have ruled out further study. Charles went on to serve with the Royal Engineers, obtaining a commission to the Royal Munster Fusiliers, eventually joining the 2nd Battalion in India and serving in Burma before finally returning to England as a decorated captain in 1897. We know very little about Spearman's decision to abruptly change his career, except that he describes military service as the mistake of his life.

Charles described his army service as wasted years. They did, however, equip him with remarkable leadership and organisational competencies, and a working knowledge of modern languages. More critically, whilst studying at the officer college in Camberley, Spearman began to learn about an experimental approach to psychology that was emerging in Germany. He became convinced that if philosophy was ever to make a genuine advance it would come mainly by way of psychology, a conviction that would later lead him to study at Wilhelm Wundt's psychological laboratory in Leipzig in eastern Germany.

Whilst at Leipzig in 1897 Spearman immersed himself in the experimental tradition, not only by working with Wundt but also with Felix Krueger and Wilhelm Wirth. They shared many professional differences, particularly around the analysis of fundamental sensations, however, Krueger, Wirth and Wundt had an indispensable influence on what Charles felt was critical to the study of psychology.

In 1900, after only a few years of study, the Boer War necessitated a recall back into active military service. Charles was made Deputy Assistant Adjutant General and sent to Guernsey. France was politically ambivalent towards the war, so the position of the militias in Guernsey was politically significant. Stationed in Guernsey for two years, it was here that Charles met and married Frances Henrietta Priaulx Aikman who was 16 years his junior.

After the war, the couple would settle briefly in Appleton, Berkshire before moving to Leipzig with their 3-month-old daughter, Fran Caroline (b1902). The couple would go on to have four more children, Alice Louisa Jean (b1903), Ivy Joy (b1912), Alexander Louis Charles John (b1916) and Anne Mainwaring (b1918). The children described their father as a remote person who would demand silence whist he worked and embarrassed them by giving their friends intelligence tests, but a kind man who was a passionate supporter of their career development.

In 1904, Spearman returned briefly to Berkshire, and published his first and possibly most influential papers in the *American Journal of Psychology*; 'The Proof and Measurement of Association Between Two Things' and 'General Intelligence Objectively Determined'. During the early 20th century, much research effort in psychology was directed towards the study of general intelligence and devices that could measure the construct. Galton's approach to measurement, was not, however, widely influential. Spearman was convinced that Galton's work was inspirational, and it became the blueprint for his work on General Intelligence where he set out the case for correlational psychology;

> for the purpose of positively determining all psychical tendencies, and in particular those which connect together the

so-called "mental tests" with psychical activities of greater
generality and interest.

(1904b, p.205)

Following publication, he returned to Germany where he stayed
for five years, moving between several institutions. He completed
his Doctoral thesis, with Wundt, in 1906 on spatial localisation,
with minors in history and political economy. Wundt admired
Spearman, describing him as combining intensive knowledge of
philosophy with an uncommon mastery of psychology.

After graduation, Spearman moved to Würzburg to study with
Oswald Külpe, one of the great structural psychologists of the time.
It was Karl Bühler, one of the founders of the Würzburg School of
psychology, who had the most significant influence. Bühler's
approach was phenomenological in nature, focusing on examining
conscious experience whilst avoiding the influence of preconcep-
tions. This was followed by a period working with George E. Müller
in Göttingen, as well as encounters with Carl Stumpf and Hermann
Ebbinghaus who would later become a supporting influence for his
work on general intelligence.

Spearman returned once again to England in 1907 to take up
the position of Reader at University College London. The position
seems to have been vacated for him by William McDougall, who
was at that time the custodian of Sir Francis Galton's anthropometric laboratory. McDougall may have been hopeful of some
help, and the London School of Psychology was formed. Few of
Spearman's predecessors or peers had made headway into the
experimental study of human ability and with McDougall stepping
aside, the pathway was cleared for Spearman to make his mark.

Drawing on his years of military expertise, Spearman would
draft in students and research assistants to work on his projects.
The entire laboratory would be mobilised as a unified whole.
After only four years, Spearman was designated as Head of
Department and appointed to the Grote Chair of the philosophy
of mind and logic. As psychology became more formally established, Spearman was appointed President of the British Psychological Society (1923 to 1926) and, following the formal split
between philosophy and psychology in 1928, the title of Professor of Psychology was awarded.

In 1909 Spearman was asked to examine results reported by two
Oxford students, Cyril Burt and Jack Flugel, on human intelligence

applying factor analysis. Spearman had long held an interest in this area, arguing that evidence from his work on school children suggested a hierarchical model of intelligence with a common factor 'General Intelligence' being explained by the inter-correlations between other mental activities. His work on this topic was remarkably like that of the Norwegian psychologist Thomas Parr who published results in 1897 showing the relationship between handwriting achievement and grades in other areas and that children with superior handwriting performed well in all other subjects.

Burt and Flugel's work demonstrated the utility of the approach and Spearman was at last able to demonstrate his competence and sophistication and now sought to strengthen the theory underpinning the mathematics of the two-factor theory of 'g' for General Intelligence and 's' for Specific Ability. By this model, intelligence behaviour requires a combination of 'g' and 's'. Regardless of the situation, 'g' is available to the same extent, but 's' will vary between situations. Thus, it is possible to predict performance from one task to another. From performance data on a task that requires a given level of 'g', it becomes possible to predict performance on a different task that requires a similar level 'g'. Predictions become more problematic when tasks have high levels of 's' factors, but because 'g' is the pervading force, the prediction would still be better than chance. Therefore, to understand a person's intellect, it was necessary to estimate their 'g'.

His work, however, put him almost immediately at odds with Edward Thorndike who fundamentally disagreed that a complex construct such as intelligence could be simplified in such a way. Other psychologists similarly attacked Spearman's theory on the basis that because there was a hierarchical arrangement in test data, it did not follow that the nature of intelligence was also hierarchical.

The accumulated evidence behind the two-factor theory was published in 1927 in 'The Abilities of Man' and was savaged by statisticians such as Karl Pearson and Edwin B. Wilson who argued that the patterns that Spearman was reporting could be explained by several different models, and therefore there could be no single index. Spearman was a remarkable statistician and advocate for his work and in a protracted series of communications, he vehemently and ingeniously defended his position which ensured the survival of the model. The study of Factor Analysis by Louis Leon Thurstone would ultimately eclipse Spearman's work by arguing that Spearman's g was merely a hypothetical construct.

Thurstone argued that despite the capacity of Spearman's factor analysis to reduce volumes of data to smaller patterns, there was still a large proportion of the variance which remained unexplained. Thurstone went on to develop what are generally considered to be superior methods which enable the maximisation variance loading and when he applied this technique 'g' disappeared. These findings suggested that intelligence was, in fact, a group of many independent abilities.

After his retirement, Spearman dedicated more time to travel and writing, including a two-volume history of psychology. He made several extended visits to America, India, Egypt and Europe, combining public talks with intelligence research. During World War II the family were evacuated to Chesterfield where Spearman continued to write papers and books in the vigorous defence of g. His son, Alexander Louis Charles, a naval engineer, was killed in 1941 during the airborne invasion of Crete. This was the first time that German paratroopers were used en masse during the war, and the first time the Allies could use the intelligence garnered from the decrypted Enigma machine. However, Crete fell, and Alexander was killed as the allied forces withdrew to the south coast. The impact on the now 78-year-old Spearman was calamitous. His health declined, leading to pneumonia and believing that everyone had the fundamental right to decide when they should die, Spearman took his own life, falling to his death from the window of his hospital bedroom on September 17th, 1945, aged 82.

Spearman will always be associated with success in operationalising methods for correlational and then factor analysis. His theory and statistical procedures enable large numbers of data to be analysed for latent structures therein. These procedures evidenced his two-factor theory of intelligence by enabling the reduction of data into underlying dimensions (or factors). Spearman found that various tests of intelligence could be correlated into what he referred to as the positive manifold, which is the factor on which all other tests converge. This process enabled the detection of the first factor, 'g'. For example, results on a test of verbal reasoning will correlate with tests of numeracy because they are both tapping into general intelligence.

Spearman's work was later supported by others at the London School, including Cyril Burt, Raymond Cattell and Arthur Jensen. As techniques developed, others such as Louis Thurstone,

Joy. P. Guilford, even Cattell, offered alternative arguments for a multi-factorial model of intelligence, and David Wechsler (Wechsler Adult Intelligence Scale) argued that Spearman was overlooking the role of personality and motivation.

It was Hans Eysenck who eventually added some closure to the multiple versus two-factor intelligence models. The two approaches were in effect mathematically similar, and the only reason for choosing one over the other was that it fitted with whatever the prevailing view of intelligence was. Eysenck reanalysed Thurstone's data and reported evidence for Spearman's g and as such concluded that there were no inherent contradictions between the two approaches.

Major works

Spearman, C. (1904a). The proof and measurement of association between two things. *American Journal of Psychology*, 15, 72–101.
Spearman, C. (1904b). 'General intelligence' objectively determined and measured. *American Journal of Psychology*, 15, 202–293.
Spearman, C. (1923). *The Nature of 'Intelligence' and the Principles of Cognition*. London: Macmillan.
Spearman, C. (1927). *The Abilities of Man, Their Nature and Measurement*. London: Macmillan.
Spearman, C. (1930). *Creative Mind*. London: Nisbet.
Spearman, C., & Jones, W. L. (1950). *Human Ability*. Oxford: Macmillan (published posthumously).

Bibliography

Burt, C. (1940). *Factors of the Mind*. London: University of London Press.
Lovie, P., & Lovie, A. (1996). Charles Edward Spearman, F.R.S. (1863–1945). *Notes and Records of the Royal Society of London*, 50(1), 75–88.
Spearman, C. (1930). C. Spearman. In C. Murchison (Ed.), *A History of Psychology in Autobiography*, vol. 1. Worcester, MA: Clark University Press.

Chapter 5

Henry Herbert Goddard

As luck would have it

August 14th, 1866 to June 18th, 1957

Henry Herbert Goddard was born into a revivalist Quaker family. He was the fifth child of Sarah Winslow Goddard and Henry Clay Goddard. The couple had lost two of their children before Henry's birth, and Henry describes himself as having all the devotion that the couple could not give to their lost children, heaped upon him, particularly from his kind and gentle father. He lived his life with the feeling that his life had always lacked direction, and if he ever completed his biography, he would call it 'as luck would have it' because everything that had happened of consequence had very little to do with thought and planning (Zenderland, 1998, p.1).

Henry's childhood, however, was impoverished and isolated. During the 1850s, Henry Clay was a prosperous New England farmer, but after being gored by one of his bulls, he became disabled. By the 1870s he had lost his farm and was working as an agricultural worker. Whist he was ill his mother mostly depended on her older married children for support. The Quaker Society offered support under such hardships, but Sarah was reluctant to ask for help.

When Henry died in 1875, Sarah found a new passion, she was awoken by the revivalist movement and soon became a lay preacher. By the time Henry was six, the local community had established that Sarah was gifted in the ministry. She began to travel to Canada to spread the good work in jails, prisons, reformatory institutions and holding public meetings and then on to the Holy Land. Herbert was left behind.

Henry's education started locally with country teachers. At the age of 11, his formal education commenced when he entered the local Vassalboro academy, Oak Grove Seminary. In 1883 he began studying at Haverford College where his poverty and his mother's religious commitment prompted a Quaker scholarship for his board and tuition: 'Quaker Jail' as Herbert would go on to describe it. Herbert's studies were dominated by mathematics, one of the few subjects that were unlikely to corrupt young minds. Between meals, there were strict recitations. Students were always on duty, studying, marching, eating or in bible study. Goddard was tortured by the cruel nature of his Latin teacher who forbade him to read even one more book until he mastered his Latin. He did manage to make time for the school newspaper and to be Vice President of the YMCA but concluded that he had no abilities, or those abilities were about as nil as could be.

Oak Grove Seminary was a harsh regime, but Goddard performed well, graduating sixth in his class and winning the Athenaeum Prize for Declamation and the Alumni Prize for Oratory and Composition. These achievements led some biographers to conclude that his more bitter reflections were not necessarily a lived reality, but reflections informed by his advanced understanding during adulthood and a long career in education and psychometric testing. Goddard never criticised his mother, such an action would question her religious calling, but within a few years, he was giving her and her new itinerant husband Jehu Newlin, money.

Henry borrowed just enough money to get himself to California in 1887 and could find no employment, so he headed north to Oakland answering 'help wanted' adds for three months. Nobody wanted him. Finally, in the spring the University of Southern California offered him a temporary position teaching history, botany, coaching the sports team (he became the first official coach of what would become the USC Trojans) and teaching the much-despised Latin. When that position ended, Henry had to borrow again to go back to Haverford to study for his MA in mathematics.

He still had no life plan when he met the strong-willed school teacher, Emma Florence Robbins. One week before his 23rd birthday they married and their union was a long, close and happy one. After some 40 years of marriage, the two would write as many as three letters a day to one another. Newly married, Henry still had no idea about what he was going to do in the world, but with the pressures of family life upon him, Henry had to find a position. Then he had a 'lucky break'. Emma taught at the primary department of the Damascus Quaker School, and in 1899 Henry was able to take up the post of Principal, teaching mathematics, moral and mental science and conducting prayer services. He stayed for two years, until an old friend Rufus Jones, offered him a post at Oak Grove where Henry eventually became Principal.

Like many teachers of the time, Henry was inspired by the speeches of the educational reformist G. Stanley Hall, who argued that schools needed to change the emphasis of their practice and focus on the child; 'the school is for the child, the child is not for the school' (cited in Zenderland, 1998, p.28). Hall was a pioneering psychologist, later founding the American Psychological Society, who called teachers to work with him in the scientific study of child development and to work towards educational reform. Henry was hooked. He borrowed enough money to study at Clarke University where Hall was president, eventually gaining a Doctorate in Psychology in 1899.

Clarke campus was qualitatively different to anything that Henry had previously experienced. Hall had no interested in feeding the spiritual needs of its students, rather the university incorporated German ideals of freedom to teach, to learn and to develop intellectual independence. The educational environment did not dismiss the role of religion; rather Hall was more focused on driving a wedge between psychology and philosophy. Teachings focused on the systematic application of the experimental method to all things human, and as such, Henry Goddard settled on a research topic which explored the scientific evidence behind faith cures and sought to put some scientific reason into the subject. As Goddard turned more to psychology, he moved farther away from his mother's interpretation of God and the role of religion. He never entirely rejected religion but felt that he could in some way fuse the two; the advancement of Christian ideals through the study of science.

Henry's career in psychology finally commenced when in 1899 he was appointed Professor of Psychology and Pedagogy at the State Normal School, West Cheshire, Pennsylvania. By the time Henry joined State Normal the membership of societies dedicated to the study of the child had reached 500. The environment encouraged the enthusiastic exploration of learning, through the recording of thousands of observations which would, it was hoped, help scientists understand the evolution of the child's mind. However, the movement was not without its critics. After decades of research, there was very little to show. Many argued that the movement was a fad at best, and at worst it operated in the same way as the vivisectionists. The study of the child should only be performed by trained professionals. Teachers had no such special training. The German-American psychologist Hugo Münsterberg went farther by dividing such amateurs into 'people who know they do not know psychology' and those 'who don't know even that' (Münsterberg, 1898, p.162). Henry had an uphill battle if he wanted to set up his own society.

Whilst arguments between psychologists and the child-study movement rattled along, the American school population was changing dramatically. Communities were becoming more urban and racially diverse. Most states now had a legal requirement for children to attend school and the rapid increase in children overwhelmed the education system and the large numbers of children suddenly appearing in school caused waves of illness. Children who were blind, deaf, seriously ill, sickly, suffering from epilepsy, tuberculosis and cardiac conditions were lumped together in classes of 50 or more. School became synonymous with suffering, even death. Of course, the methods employed by the child study movement didn't evolve in step with these significant societal changes either.

Eventually, school doctors began to get a grip on children who were clearly too ill to attend school, but whilst those doctors could help with the sick, they could do nothing to help improve the lives of children whose problems they did not understand. Few states had facilities to support children, and where they did, they were often crammed with over 1000 children with special needs. Elsewhere, all that was on offer were special classes.

More enlightened institutions supported children using what was known as the principles of physiological education, the idea being that learning difficulties were caused by poor brain development. To promote brain development children were educated by methods thought to stimulate the sensory organs; clay, wax, patterns, photographs, painting and books.

Edward Johnson, a schoolteacher at the Vineland Special Education School in New Jersey, and pioneer of such methods, invited Goddard in 1900 to visit his institution. Goddard was impressed by the institution's home-like structure and Johnson's radically different pedagogical approach. The two met the following year at a Child Study meeting, and the Feeble-Minded Club was born, with the aim of bringing scientists and educators together in an attempt to help address the inadequacies in special needs education. By the standards of today, the title is distasteful, but the movement was revolutionary. The club supported teachers to spend time in institutions where they had concentrated time to experience different degrees of learning disabilities and the interventions which could improve children's lives. Whilst some teachers marvelled at Johnson's ability to manage the 'repulsive' children with whom he worked, others credited the team with helping to remove the stigma that came with teaching special needs education. For Goddard, Johnson's work epitomised the Christian spirit that ought to scaffold education, but also the merits of the scientific principles of trial, error and careful observation. Goddard also became convinced that such children were no different from others. All children started out more or less the same, and developmental difficulties presented themselves as the child progressed. At a time when many still believed that such children were of no value to society and that the most that could be done was to keep them comfortable until they died, these were progressive ideas.

As his thinking on the subject developed Goddard argued that far too much emphasis had been placed on mindless rote learning and memorisation. Being able to repeat without thought and understanding did not constitute intellectual growth. Goddard argued that the focus should be on developing perception and action, because the mind would take care of itself. However, even the Feeble-Minded Club was at the limits of what was possible when they were asked to help diagnose developmental and learning disabilities. The movement was raising more questions and supplying fewer solutions. A psychological laboratory could provide answers, but the trustees of Vineland were in opposition to such an idea. The well-known educator and professor, Earl Barnes, attempted to reassure that the humanitarian mission of Vineland was not in conflict with the scientific in his address to the board of trustees in 1903, declaring that Vineland was already 'a human laboratory and garden, where unfortunate children would be cared for, protected and loved while they unconsciously whisper to us syllable by syllable the secrets of the soul's growth' (Barnes, 1932, cited in Zenderland, 1998, p.66). Three years later, Vineland had their laboratory and the trustees were ready to hire a psychologist, and Henry H. Goddard set about the enormous task of diagnosing the feeble-minded.

Initially, Goddard focused on medical diagnosis, but soon realised that such information provided little in the way of classification because children varied extensively in appearance, medical history, behaviour and learning aptitude; some children had mental disabilities, and some children had both psychological and physical problems. Other children perhaps ought not to have been there at all because they were suffering from disabilities, injuries, deformities, paralysis or problems that merely had social stigmas attached such as speech impediments, cleft palates and others had physical disfigurements. In some cases, there seemed to be nothing manifestly different about the child at all. One child admission was based on them hitting other children in his class, another, in a country with limited gun control, had been brought in by his family because he had shot his sister. Educational ability ranged from 'idiot savants' to children who, despite years of schooling, made no progress. Undeterred the doctors continued to search for patterns and clusters of symptoms shared by groups of this population.

Goddard began to gently and tactfully encourage physicians to shift the problem towards psychology. What use were classifications such as microcephalic and 'Mongol' in helping us understand better how to help children? Studying what a child could not do, and what their deficits were, was futile. Psychology could help explore if such children could recombine their mental processes in other ways. The job of the psychologist was to encourage fruit from a plant that is unusually slow in its growth. Medics, teachers and psychologists were dealing with a generally healthy organism that in some way lacked something, but it did not follow the child lacked so much that it could not develop at all. The feeble-minded child was trapped in a foreign land; psychology could find a way to establish communication. These striking arguments are in direct contradiction to later accusations relating to Goddard's eugenic motives and conduct.

After two years of exhausting work, Goddard had, however, achieved very little and he left Vineland in search of new ideas in Europe. He travelled through France, Italy, Germany, Austria, Switzerland, Holland and Belgium seeking new ideas and inspiration from medics, teachers and psychologists. In Brussels, Goddard had a breakthrough when a series of mental tests by Alfred Binet were given to him by Ovide Decroly. Decroly was a doctor and special educator and impressed by Goddard's work which his wife had translated for him into French. Decroly had invited Goddard to meet with him and by chance mentioned the Binet tests which rested on the idea that chronological age should be compared with mental age to how a child differed from what was typical or normal development.

Initially sceptical that intelligence could be measured, Goddard set about translating Binet's works, then trialling them on the Vineland children. He communicated regularly with Binet, exploring the findings, becoming increasingly convinced that the test was valid. The results corresponded precisely with what was being recorded through clinical judgements, and it had the advantage of being fast. Children need not be admitted into an institution for diagnosis and support.

Finally, the American Association for the Study of the Feeble-Minded asked Goddard to submit a report on his findings. The report included not only his results but also his systematic attempts to validate the results against clinical reports from institutions. This process was crude, but it convinced the panel that Goddard's findings could be trusted. Institutional diagnosis became grounded in Binet's work, and the diagnosis of mental deficits became reconceptualised. Goddard had established the value that psychology could bring to society, his work could not, however, prevent 'unprincipled charlatans' from adopting the test for broader use.

Described as a gentle and kind man, with a passion for mountain climbing, Henry Goddard undoubtedly helped popularise an alternative strategy to the study of mental ability and the diagnosis of feeble-mindedness. Much early evidence suggests that he had humanitarian motives that were radical for the time and directly aimed at improving the lives and prospects of institutionalised children. For Goddard, it was essential to discover and develop what a child could do, not segregate them on what they could not.

However, as the eugenics movement gathered pace in America, the test initially developed by Alfred Binet to support educational development, began to be used as evidence to justify the segregation and sterilisation of those considered defective in some way. Goddard was a strong advocate of eugenics, particularly segregation and his controversial work 'The Kallikaks' published in 1912 presented a sensational case for human degeneracy. The study claimed to provide extensive genealogical data from several generations of the same family. The book, depicting unattractive people, living in impoverished surroundings showed what social disasters would follow if the genetically defected were not prevented from having children. No matter that the data was based on a combination of the Binet test, personal opinion and impression, it was an instant best seller, and the term 'moron' entered the common vernacular.

In 1913 Goddard turned his attention to the migrant population. Large numbers were arriving from eastern Europe, and these new immigrants were considered to be entirely different from the Germans and British who had emigrated during earlier periods. These Jews, Poles and Italians, were mostly young males who were motivated to make money to improve their standard of living at home. They had no intention of settling permanently, but their arrival was still unwelcomed. In an attempt to manage the influx, the US government introduced quota policies which would prioritise the hardworking, intelligent and skilled. A testing programme was established on Ellis Island with the objective of controlling those considered inferior, unskilled and feeble-minded.

Goddard arrived at Ellis Island with his Binet tests, with the intention of evidencing their practical value. Once testing began, it was not long before he was reporting, unsurprisingly, that many of the emigrants had mental ages lower than 12 years old. There is some evidence that he understood that his data was likely to be impacted by the emigrant's lack of education, cultural differences, impoverishment and in many cases, their lack of English. Goddard recognised that his results were not truly representative because he had only been able to test immigrants travelling in steerage. Nonetheless he concluded that many Europeans were unquestionably feeble-minded and would degenerate American lineage. This was powerful propaganda. As the Immigration Act of 1924 was debated, Goddard and other principle eugenicists were called to advise Congress.

Scientifically, Goddard added very little to the nature versus nurture debate, and much of his data could have been explained equally well by both genetic and environmental influences. There is good evidence that in later years, he recognised that many of his ideas were both unacceptable and out of date and throughout the remainder of his career he was a powerful advocate for educational reform and improved child-rearing. Despite the many controversies surrounding his work and motives, he set the scene for the American testing movement, and his work was subsequently built upon by Robert Yerkes and Lewis M. Terman. Towards the end of his life, Henry H. Goddard developed Alzheimer's disease. He died at his home in Santa Barbara in 1957, and his ashes were interred in Vineland.

Major works

Goddard, H. H. (1913). *Standard Method for Giving the Binet Test.* Vineland, NJ: Vineland Training School.
Goddard, H. H. (1914). *Feeble-Mindedness: Its Causes and Consequences.* New York: Macmillan.

Bibliography

Münsterberg, H. (1898). The danger from experimental psychology. *Atlantic Monthly*, 81, 159–167.
Zenderland, L. (1998). *Measuring Minds: Henry Herbert Goddard and the Origins of American Intelligence Testing.* Cambridge: Cambridge University Press.

Chapter 6

Alfred Adler

The individualist

February 7th, 1870 to May 28th, 1937

Alfred Adler was born in Rodolfsheim, near Vienna, Austria. Alfred's father was a Jewish grain merchant, a job which provided only a modest income to support his seven children and those children were sickly. Their diets were poor and low levels of vitamin D and calcium thwarted normal bone development, resulting in rickets. Alfred could not walk until he was four years old and suffered from spasms of the epiglottis, a condition which can be caused by infection or injury. If Alfred became even slightly agitated, he would suffer from acute shortness of breath. At the age of five, Alfred almost died from pneumonia. His little brother had died the year before, and the experience was so traumatic that he attributed the experience as formative in his decision to become a doctor.

Alfred found academic competition a struggle. He was popular, outgoing and active, but was persistently failing in his examinations. His father, by way of 'encouragement', threatened to remove him entirely from school and make him an apprentice to the local shoemaker. Immediately, Alfred's grades improved, but never to a level that would enable him to obtain his certification.

Despite his poor grades, Alfred was accepted into the University of Vienna to study medicine in 1888. His ambitions of becoming a doctor were strong. Such a career would bring the much-needed opportunities to his family, but Alfred found the training uninspiring. He was bored by the long hours of study, experimentation and diagnosis. These were distractions from what he wanted to do, socialise in the cafes of Vienna with friends, one of which included the young Leon Trotsky. Constantly distracted, Alfred barely passed his examinations, only scraping to graduation in 1895. His first position was as a volunteer at the Poliklinik, a clinic that focused on supporting impoverished patients suffering from disorders and diseases of the eye. Ophthalmology was an interest Alfred shared with the Sherlock Holmes author Arthur Conan Doyle. Doyle had left Vienna only a few years previously, having spent an unproductive 3 months studying ophthalmology.

Vienna was now awash with writers, philosophers, artists and musicians who were encouraging experimentation. As the century drew to a close, the Hapsburg Empire began to fragment, and new liberalist demands for rights were emerging. Activists such as Else Jerusalem were lifting the lid on Viennese hypocrisy and the poverty, suffering, prostitution and high suicide rates which hid behind the opulence. The old ideas of morality and high culture were being broken down, and café society was central in shaping ideas about human nature, equality, social relationships and the future of Viennese culture. In this bohemian atmosphere, Alfred met Raissa Epstein, whose deep thinking impacted on the development of Alfred's thinking. Raissa was a radical force, a Russian socialist and feminist who came to Vienna because women were not permitted to study topics such as biology and zoology in Russia. She helped Adler identify the contradictions that surrounded them, and then to embrace socialism as the answer to poverty, oppression and lack of equality. Their political passions linked their hearts, and in 1897 Alfred and Raissa married.

By 1898 Adler was formalising his position on the psychology of the human condition, publishing his holistic arguments in *The Health Book for the Tailor Trade*. This book was one of the earliest occupational psychology books that made links between the environments in which tailors worked and constructs such as workplace justice, respect, equality and co-operation. Adler would argue that the effective management of disease would come about if equal consideration were given to social, economic and psychological factors. Aligning his professionalism with his values, Adler moved his practice to one of the lowliest parts of Vienna. At the end of the century, the Wiener Prater, a large public park in the Leopoldstadt District, was a long way from the beautiful Danube landscape of today. The Prater amusement park (today the oldest amusement park in the world) was establishing itself with cafes, swings and carousels and a giant Ferris wheel. Nearby the Barnum and Bailey Circus advertised: 'the greatest aerial feats and shows of strength, sword swallowers, expanding and contracting men, human pin cushions, armless and legless humans, and other things and amazing sights that could be seen nowhere else' (Neue Freie Presse, 1900). These acrobats and artists, capable of such extraordinary acts, would come to Adler in their sickness and weakness. Grounded in his convictions for the mutual respect of all, Adler was inspired by their strength of mind and stamina. It was in this, surrounded by human exploitation and suffering, that Adler began to develop what would later become his theories of over-compensation, the inferiority complex and their roles in human personality development. In 1917 he published *Study of Organ Inferiority and its Psychological Compensation*. This book was a study of people's self-regarded tendencies to judge themselves as deficient in some way or another, and how those inadequacies would drive their behaviours, in what Adler described as a minus or plus action.

Adler's work piqued Freud's attention. Initially viewing Adler as a potential disciple, Freud invited Adler to come and visit with him in Vienna and join his Vienna Wednesday Society (which eventually became the Vienna Psychoanalytic Society). Freud, known for the cultivation of his devotees, until they had ideas of their own, quickly entered into a tormentous relationship with Adler. Adler disagreed with Freud on the importance of sexual development. For Adler, sexual development was only a minor influencing factor in the tapestry of developmental experiences that a child was exposed to. As the second sibling in a family of six, birth order was a significant clue to a child's socialisation and goals in life. When Adler was 4 years old, his baby brother Rudolf died in bed beside him of diphtheria. This harrowing experience led to the polarisation between Adler and Freud on the notion of the death wish. For Adler, there was no death wish. The human psyche strove for significance and worth in the eyes of others, for Freud it was a battle to return to an inanimate state.

These were more than differences in scholarly opinion. The two had fundamental differences in politics and temperament. Freud's temperament was to dominate, if not in fact to bully. For Freud's version of the psychoanalytical movement to advance, there had to be a complete consensus from his followers. To ensure acquiescence, Adler was expected to commit to continual self-examination with his peers. Any deviation from absolute compliance to Freud's theories was heavily criticised and could result in expulsion from the society, but Adler was rebellious and insubordinate. The environment was intolerable and by 1904 Adler had decided to leave the Wednesday Society. Perhaps feeling that it was better to have the rebellious Adler contained within the Wednesday ranks, Freud somehow persuaded Adler to stay, but he was now seeing Adler's work as a serious threat to his dominant theories of psychosocial development and the basis of personality.

The polarisation continued to escalate and fester in other areas. Fritz Wittels, Freud's friend and biographer, gave a presentation to the group on the 'natural' position of women in society. Adler found Wittels' gendered opinions objectionable and in response gave a talk on the psychology of Marxism and the class struggle. The move resulted in Adler being viewed as a radical socialist. Hostilities within the society were barely contained, and in 1912, in another attempt to keep Adler within the society, Freud offered to step down, suggesting Adler as his replacement. The group, however, voted Adler down.

Adler could not face another argument and left, taking with him a small following of dedicated 'Adlerians' who then started their society for the study of individual differences 'The Psychology of the Undivided Whole', what would become the Österreichischer Verein für Individualpsychologie (Austrian Association for Individual Psychology). Freud would later write that Adler had let him down and he found people who had let him down to be the most hateful people of all. Consequently, he hated Alfred Adler for over 25 years.

Having put the Wednesday Society aside, Adler's fresh approach set him apart from other psychologists and soon he was enjoying success, building a movement that directly argued for holistic psychological treatment, well-being and social equality. At a time when Carl Jung was developing his ideas about psychological types, Adler had a small number of personality types that he felt were heuristic devices, that moulded personality. People who tended toward the domination of others, 'the ruling type', were governed by energy forces that sought to overpower others. When their ungoverned ruling energy was turned inwards, they may be drawn into self-harming behaviours, such as addiction or suicide. When the energy source was directed outwards, they would become oppressors or sadists.

The learning type is more likely to use their energy to protect themselves, and they will insulate themselves from the threats and challenges of life and of others. They lack energy and, to survive, will sap the energy of others. This inability to lead a useful life leads to anxieties, obsessions and depression.

The avoiding type typically presented signs of such low energy that they would avoid life completely, perhaps even retreating into themselves. They may end up in the most extreme situations developing psychosis.

The most useful type was the social type; healthy, energised, outward-looking individuals who show an interest in others. This was the 'type' that individuals should strive towards and to support his patients on their development Adler would design treatments that encouraged effective social development. At its core, the Adlerian method would seek to create equity between the client and the therapist. Both would work together in a collaboration to gain insight, and, to encourage a sense of community and responsibility as the mechanism by which to effect change. Methods that would be familiar to most modern psychologists today.

The Bohemian Viennese life was interrupted in 1914 with the outbreak of World War I. Alfred was called to work as a doctor with the Austro-Hungarian Army while Raissa unwisely took the children to Russia for a holiday. They had hoped the impending war would be delayed until after their return. Russia invaded Eastern Prussia, and, with two further Russian armies ready to fight against the Austro-Hungarian forces, Raissa and the children were promptly arrested as possible traitors. They were held for 5 months until Raissa somehow managed to convince the Czar that she was a loyal Russian citizen who had been forced to marry Alfred Adler.

At the end of his military service, Alfred began to apply his 'individual psychology' in the treatment of children with behavioural problems. He established child guidance clinics to support early interventions and school involvement as the mechanisms to manage the sources of 'backwardness, delinquency, criminality and neurosis'. By 1927, 27 clinics were established across Vienna. Staffed by Adler's trainees, the Adlerians would work with children, parents, teachers, doctors and social workers, building a support community to help children with emotional problems. Adler then began giving lecture tours across Europe and America with the aim of increasing global awareness of his individual psychology and the role that therapy, encouragement and pedagogy can play in improving outcomes for children.

His work was a tremendous success; he published *Understanding Human Nature* which rapidly sold over 100,000 copies in America alone and in 1929 Adler received an invitation to Columbia University as an adjunct professor. Raissa, however, was not keen to move to America. She was now an influential member of the Communist Party in Russia, and a move to America was not, to her mind, a politically neutral act. Raissa's position caused tension in the Adler's marriage. Adler viewed her attitude as behavioural domination, something he did not condone politically nor in his relationship with his wife. Political changes in Europe would, however, intervene to settle the matter for the Adlers.

The Jewish-Austrian population had enjoyed a period of prosperity under Franz Joseph I. The Emperor's belief that civil rights were not contingent on a people's religion had created a more equal society, but by the 1930s conservative-fascism was making life increasingly harsh; Jews were being expelled from political, economic and social life. Adler's pioneering child guidance clinics were closed, and individual psychology was at a standstill. As active socialists, Raissa and Alfred feared imminent imprisonment, so the family left Vienna for Rotterdam, where they obtained passage to America.

In America, Adler set about the promotion of his Individual Psychology. When not working as a professor of medical psychology at the Long Island College of Medicine in New York, he was touring internationally, delivering talks to mass audiences. By 1937 Adler had published more than a dozen books. He had, however, only been enjoying life in America for two years, when he suddenly died on a European lecturing tour. He was unwell before he left for the trip, potentially from exhaustion from his persistent self-drive, and he died on the streets of Aberdeen from a suspected heart attack. This tragic event was compounded further when Adler's remains were lost and remained so for over 70 years.

The Vienna Individual Psychology movement set about trying to resolve the mystery lobbying the Austrian consul to Scotland, who eventually tied Adler's cremation down to one of only two possible sites and Alfred Adler's remains were eventually recovered from the Warriston Crematorium in Edinburgh. In 2007 Adler's remains were eventually returned to Vienna for burial.

Adler's principles and values were egalitarian. He favoured equality and the right to well-being and fairness for all. He had a strong commitment to the ideas of socialism and the well-being of others, but he never became a staunch follower of communism. In later life, he was vocal in his disagreement with the oppressive and cruel tactics of Lenin and his one-time friend, Leon Trotsky. His egalitarian viewpoints had led both to Alfred's exit from Freud's Wednesday Society, and also developed the feminist ideology of their daughter Alexandra, who went on to become an even more committed socialist and the first female neurologist in Vienna and America. In 1935 Alexandra was appointed to Harvard but only added to the contract research staff list as no women were given faculty positions.

Influenced by the writings of the South African philosopher and statesman Jan Smuts, Adler believed that people are not a collection of disparate elements. To be understood people are more effectively treated as unified wholes within the context of their physical, social and economic environments. For Adler, personality related to the 'style of life' which is our style in handling interpersonal relationships, challenges and ourselves. How you live your life is your personality;

> The style of life of a tree is the individuality of a tree expressing itself and moulding itself in an environment. We recognise a style when we see it against a background of an environment different from what we expect, for then we realize that every tree has a life pattern and is not merely a mechanical reaction to the environment.
>
> (Adler, 1929, p.45).

Adler's holism was not as thrilling or sensational as Freud's work, but Adler's approach was practical and adaptable to the realities and complexities of the human psyche. He succeeded in a world dominated by psychoanalysis in promoting an alternative perspective. Work that would ultimately influence psychologists such as Karen Horney, George Kelly and Carl Rogers.

Major works

Adler, A. (1917). *Nervous and Mental Disease Monograph Series. Study of Organ Inferiority and its Psychical Compensation* (S. E. Jelliffe, Trans.). Washington, DC: The Nervous and Mental Disease Publishing Company.

Adler, A. (1924). *The Practice and Theory of Individual Psychology.* Oxford: Harcourt, Brace.

Adler, A. (1927). *Understanding Human Nature*. New York: Greenberg.
Adler, A. (1929). *The Science of Living*. Oxford: Greenberg.
Adler, A. (1931). *What Life Should Mean to You*. Oxford: Little, Brown.

Bibliography

Grey, L. (1988). *Alfred Adler, the Forgotten Prophet: A Vision for the 21st Century*. London: Praeger.
Neue Freie Presse (1900) Barnum & Baley, Grosste Schaustellung der Erde, Circus advertisement: Sunday 25 November: Retrieved, January 2nd, 2009 from www.beeston-notts.co.uk/barnum_bailey.htm

Chapter 7

Carl Gustav Jung

'We cannot change anything unless we accept it'

June 6th, 1875 to June 6th, 1961

Karl Jung (he would later change his name to Carl) was born June 6th, 1875 in Kesswil, which is in the municipality in the district of Arbon in the canton of Thurgau in Switzerland. His father Paul Achilles Jung and mother Emilie were the thirteenth children from their respective families, something considered auspicious in Swiss culture, possibly connected to the Old Swiss Confederacy which expanded to Thirteen Cantons, but also through the superstition that would manifest itself in the marriage through Emilie's developing eccentricities. The Jungian lineage was impressive, traceable back to the 1650s where the earliest records show a Carl Jung (Dr. Med. Dr. Jur) as the Catholic physician, lawyer and university president. His grandson Franz (1759–1831), a physician in charge of a field hospital during the Napoleonic wars whose wife, Sophie Jung-Ziegler, is alleged to have had an affair with the German statesman and writer Johann Wolfgang von Goethe. This union resulted in the birth of Carl Jung's grandfather Carl Gustav 1 (1794–1864).

Paul Achilles' union to Emilie was not so auspicious or scandalous, nor happy for that matter. Their first child Paul died shortly after his birth and his sister Johanna Gertrud was born when Jung was nine years old in 1884. The Jung family lived in modest circumstances, Paul was Lutheran pastor of limited income, in the most conservative part of Switzerland where the interfering town folks took delight in tracing their lineage back to German Roman Catholicism. Jung in his later writings describes Swiss society as full of resentments and defence mechanisms. He likened Swiss society to being in a chronic state of mitigated civil war, with its aggression directed inwards.

The Jungs' marriage was a microcosm of Swiss society and not a happy one. Publicly, Paul Jung was self-effacing and quiet, in private he was irritable and quarrelsome. Emilie was depressive, unpredictable and she was eventually hospitalised when Carl was three years old. This environment fostered a solitary, lonely and unhappy childhood. Carl was sent to live with his aunt, the trauma of which was acute; he developed eczema, became distrustful of his mother, developed a morbid fascination with corpses, saw ghosts in the house at night and became unusually accident-prone. By the age of 4, such was his state of mind, he was considered to be suffering with childhood schizophrenia triggered by the trauma of familial instability. In later life, he would attribute his destructive behaviour in infancy to an unconscious urge to accommodate death and that it was never his mother who saved him.

Financial fortunes and social opportunities improved when the family were appointed the more prosperous parish of Laufen. There were more children of Carl's age, but his father's status in the clergy still set them apart from others and Carl was described by a school friend as a 'social little monster' who would emerge only to stir up trouble. His relationship with his mother and his behaviour further deteriorated following the shock arrival of his baby sister. Carl carved himself a manikin 'god' from the ancient world, dressed it in a coat, hid it in the beams of their home and took secret pleasure in the fact that only he knew it was there. There is any number of interpretations of what this wooden object meant to Jung, the occult was prevalent in Swiss society during the 1880s, or it may have been merely a transitional object like a soft toy. Whatever the process, undoubtedly, young Carl was turning in on himself and away from a loveless mother and a powerless father.

Carl was at least studious at home. His father had introduced him to Latin at an early age, triggering a lifelong passion for language. He developed a secret language to communicate with this sister Johanna, and as an adult, could read most European languages and several ancient languages, including Sanskrit. Carl's aptitude for learning and scholarship continued to develop mostly at home; he did not enjoy school, particularly any activities which involved competition. A farmer's boy unrelentingly bullied him. Carl never pushed back against his tormentor; instead he sought to distract attention through pranks or feigning illness, but in the end, this strategy failed, and he left school accomplished but feeling alienated.

His interest in ancient languages directed Jung towards archae-
ology, but in the end, he enrolled to study medicine at the University of Basel. Jung was influenced enormously by the neurologist
Richard Krafft-Ebing, an expert in forensic psychiatry and sexual
pathology and it was while working under his instruction that he
settled on a career in psychiatry. His first position was in the Zurich
Burghölzi Mental Hospital with Paul Eugen Bleuler, who reclassi-
fied dementia praecox as schizophrenia. Bleuler was instrumental in
shaping Jung's examination of unconscious thought, as it was he
who proposed that Jung used Galton's word-association techniques
with people diagnosed with psychosis with a view to revealing their
unconscious thought processes. Jung's first published paper,
a psychological analysis of supposed occult phenomena, was the
basis for his doctoral thesis. In 1903, he received his PhD from the
University of Zurich: 'On the Psychology and Pathology of So-
Called Occult Phenomena'.

In 1896, Jung met his future wife and co-analyst, Emma 'Sunny'
Rauschenbach. Sunny was only a school girl when they met but as
the daughter of Johannes Rauschenbach, the industrialist and the
CEO of the luxury Swiss International Watch Company, she was
the second richest heiress in Switzerland. By 1903 Jung and Sunny
were married and the couple went on to have five children;
Agathe (b1904), Gret (b1906), Marianne (b1910), Franz (b1908)
and Helene (b1914). Emma had a limited education, but became
central to Jung's work, acting as his assistant and eventually
becoming a psychoanalyst in her own right. Their working relationship was robust, but the marriage was strained. Emma suffered his bouts of bad temper, boorishness and narcissism,
possibly worst of all his perpetual affairs explained away by his
opportune belief in polygamy.

Jung had several mistresses, one of the most notorious was the
patient, the student, then lover Sabina Spielrein. Between 1908
and 1910 they had an affair, which for the most substantial part
favoured erotic play over intercourse. Jung had been able to support a substantial improvement in Sabina who had entered the
hospital in a complex, compulsive state. She apparently developed a crush, if not an obsession with Jung. He was fully aware
of this and shared his insights and reflections about Sabrina's
desire for him in his communications with Sigmund Freud. Sabrina improved quickly under Jung's care and within a year was
able to attend university, but the two continued to communicate

until the predictable happened and they became lovers. Whether the relationship went as far as the sadomasochistic affair portrayed by Fassbender and Knightley in the film *A Dangerous Method* is difficult to determine, by the standards of today, Jung would appear to have been opportunistic, if not, in fact, treating Spielrein as a sex object.

By 1911 Jung had turned his attention to Antonia Wolf. Another one-time patient who went on to become an analyst as his mistress. Jung belligerently refused to give up either woman, calling 'Toni' his 'Anima' or second wife. This initially caused tensions in his marriage, but eventually, some arrangement was reached because Jung would regularly turn up to events with both women, describing them 'affectionately' as his polygamous components. This triangle was surprisingly resilient, lasting until Emma's death, but Emma's refusal to engage in alchemy (she was Christian) remained a significant barrier to Jung's desire for polygamy bliss.

From 1906 Jung and Freud shared intense, interminable discussions through correspondence. Freud's pattern of spotting talented, exciting people, developing intensive relationships with them and then cooling, is most well documented in the case of Jung. Jung was a long-time admirer of Freud. They met in Vienna in 1907, and although Freud retained dominance, they had significant influence on one another's work. Their friendship lasted over 13 years before Freud became increasingly detached to the point that he was convinced that Jung harboured death wishes towards him.

In this instance, however, Jung's increasing antagonism was undoubtedly the major influencing factor in the deteriorating relationship. Jung saw his role as the saviour of psychoanalysis; he wanted to ensure its lasting place as the leading psychotherapeutic method. The primary source of their intellectual disagreement lay in their respective positions on the libido (a life-force energy). Alder had already left the Wednesday Society through similar disagreements, and like Alder, Jung was unconvinced that libidinal energy was sexual. Instead, Jung saw libidinal forces as a more creative life-force that embraced not only the sexual but also the spiritual needs of the individual. Freud in his later works moved closer to the Jungian perspective on life energy, but it was too late. Jung felt that Freud inhibited his scientific freedom, that he was paralysing psychoanalysis through a 'reductive interpretation' of the human psyche and he vehemently objected to any suggestion that he was, in any way, exhibiting neurosis.

By 1912 the relationship was at an end, but both men struggled with the finality of their complicated professional relationship and firm friendship, suffering bouts of depression over the loss. Freud had seen Jung as his successor, his heir-apparent who would lead the psychoanalytical movement, but he was also frustrated by what he felt to be Jung's abnormal behaviour and his inability to accept that he had any neurosis. The impact on Jung was acute. He was at his most creative developing his own distinctive theory of personality, but he became increasingly isolated and depressed nearly to the point of psychotic breakdown. None of which could have been helped by his now very public emotional triangle with his wife and Toni Wolf. Jung was inward-looking but perhaps not necessarily introspective.

World War I interrupted psychoanalysis as a field, and the world and Jung became focused on an apocalypse. Jung was never short on imagination and became convinced his dreams and visions were premonitions to World War I, and that the key to understanding the mental condition was to decode the mythology that permeated culture and society and he began to develop his dimensional approach to psychology. He was drafted as an army doctor and given the command of an internment camp for British officers and soldiers. The camp was in neutral territory, and as such, the personnel were obliged to intern soldiers from either side of the conflict. Jung worked to improve both the physical conditions in the camp and the education of its interns.

This period of isolation lasted until 1920. Jung began to publish and, in 1923, published his most influential work *Psychological Types*, which put forward the two major attitudes or orientations of personality – extroversion and introversion and their four essential functions (thinking, feeling, sensing and intuiting) which yield eight pure personality types. This was work which would be built upon by psychologists such as Hans Eysenck and Raymond Cattell.

In 1928 Jung joined the International General Medical Society for Psychotherapy – the same year as Herman Göring's cousin, Mathias Heinrich Göring. Jung was elected Vice- President in 1930 and president 3 years later. *Zentralblatt für Psychotherapie*, the society's journal, was reorganised about this time, the intention being to publish an international edition under Jung's editorship. The German version was under the management of Göring who publicly appealed for the adaptation of Hitler's *Mein Kampf* as a basic reference text and the journal carried the appeal alongside Jung's signature. This was the only source of a widely-held suspicion that Jung was a Nazi sympathiser and that his presidency was part of a plan to impose a Nazi ideology on the business of the Society.

Jung had not helped himself. In his paper 'The State of Psychotherapy Today' (1934) he wrote feverishly on the difference between Jewish and Aryan psychology, arguing that Freud did not understand the Germanic psyche, that Jewish categories should not be applied indiscriminately to Germanic and Slavic Christendom: "The Jew was a nomad who has never created a cultural form of his own and as far as we can see never will". The psyche of the German is more than "a garbage-bin of unrealizable infantile wishes and unresolved family resentments" (Jung, 1934, p.165). Jung was presenting an Aryan alternative to the psychology of Freud, even going on to suggest that the Aryan unconscious has higher potential than the Jewish. These sentiments were a melody to the shadows of racial bigotry and bias of the Nazi regime and the German therapists who sought to associate themselves as closely as possible to Jung's work. The following year, these words reappear in Nuremberg rallies as justification for racial legislation.

Recent evidence suggests that Jung played for both sides during the war. At the International General Medical Society for Psychotherapy, he had a problematic relationship with Mathias Göring and had resigned three times from the society. Jung is also reported to have been involved in a plot to have the Führer committed as a mad-man. He worked tirelessly to help and support other Jewish psychoanalysts who were being persecuted and, towards the end of the war, played a crucial role in advising Washington war policy on how to persuade the German public to accept defeat. His influence went as far as General Dwight D. Eisenhower.

These shifts in positions show Jung to be an astute political animal. Jung wanted to secure the position of psychoanalysis within the German Reich, but when America became involved in the war, his allegiance shifted to wherever was in the best interests of the discipline.

After the war, Jung's travels took him to East Africa and India where he sought to expand his understanding of primitive psychology by spending periods in culturally isolated areas. His interests became increasingly obscure and mystical. In Africa, his insights were limited by language barriers, but he was able to engage in more productive dialogue in India which helped advance his arguments for the role of symbolism in life. The trip was blighted, however, by two weeks of illness and delirium which resulted in hospitalisation in Calcutta and on returning home he confined his travels to Europe.

On Feb 11th, 1944, the 68-year-old Jung, fell on ice and broke his fibula. While in hospital he developed embolisms in his leg and suffered a heart attack. Jung describes an out-of-body experience where only his essential self existed, whereby God told him it was not his time. He was very troubled by the experience but primarily because he reported seeing his doctor's astral spirit leave its earthly body. Jung awoke from his heart attack and in a strange coincidence, on the same day his doctor was struck with septicaemia and died shortly afterwards. Jung was convinced that this meant that the doctor's life had been taken to restore his. Respiratory and circulatory disease was now a permanent feature of Jung's health, but he continued to write and publish until his death on June 6th, 1961.

Attempts at explaining human nature in terms of typology have its roots in ancient civilisations, but the field is probably best known through the contribution of Carl Jung. The dichotomies at the centre of Jung's theory, extraversion, introversion, sensing, intuition, thinking and feeling attempted to classify people into a small group of behavioural preferences. Jung has been recognised as one of the most influential psychologists of all time, but measures that have built on his theory have been the centre of continuing controversy. Jung himself did not approve of measurement tools, describing the attempts at personality measurement as 'nothing but a childish parlour game' (1934, p.15).

Ironically, Jung's charismatic aversion to theory building, his enthusiasm for alchemy and the paranormal, has always deterred many psychologists from engaging in debates around his work. Nonetheless, Jung's approach was innovative focusing on the way in which individuals make sense of personal existence and what gives point and purpose in their lives. His interest was firmly grounded in the present and not in past unresolved conflicts and unfulfilled desires. His method, 'individualisation', focused on encouraging the patient to face their unconscious inner forces, integrate those forces into conscious awareness and develop their potential self. Jung retained the tripartite structure of the mind wherein the ego is conscious, but personal consciousness also refers to those things that are unconscious but can readily be brought to conscious awareness through attention. The collective unconscious refers to experiences that cannot be brought to conscious awareness and cannot be directly examined. For example, primordial or ancestral memory traces. These are traces experienced by all individuals of a species and populate through universal symbols such as the Tree of Life, Hell, Time, Rebirth, Darkness etc., while they cannot be directly observed, they influence our actions and the actions of others. Examples that provided particularly strong evidence of its existence would be insights from déjà vu, near-death experiences.

Jung's dynamic model of the psyche has three governing principles. The principle of opposites states that every wish suggests its opposite. He regards the opposition between states (e.g. good–bad, happy–sad, love–hate) as the source of libidinal or psychic energy. The second principle is that of equivalence and refers to the degree to which one is prepared to recognise the presence of opposite states. For example, the degree to which one recognises that our children can be both a source of unconditional love, but they can also be a source of unhappiness and often hate. Denial or suppression of this state suppresses growth and development because it critically diverts vital psychic energy into the development of a maladaptive complex. To help diagnose a complex, Jung pioneered the use of word association in therapeutic contexts reasoning that delayed verbal responses to specific words and noticeable changes in breathing or posture were symptoms of a complex.

A third principle, entropy, refers to the tendency for oppositions to come together over time. Jung argued that entropy increases with age thus accounting for reductions in libidinal or psychic energy as we get older. The goal of life is to realise the self. The self is also an archetype that represents the transcendence of all opposites so that every aspect of one's personality is expressed equally.

Jung regarded 'attitudes' and 'functions' as operating at both conscious and unconscious levels of awareness. He claimed that there are two principle attitudes: introversion and extraversion. Introversion is oriented towards subjective experience whereas extraversion is oriented towards objective experience. Jung regarded everyone as possessing both attitudes, the unconscious of the extrovert is introverted, and the unconscious of the introvert is extraverted. Both introverts or extroverts must to deal with the inner and outer worlds and Jung argued that this occurred through four functions: sensing, thinking, intuiting and feeling. He suggested that most people develop one or two of the functions, but the goal of personal development should be to use all four. One function may be more natural, but individuals could learn to use their opposites.

This combination of attitudes and functions provided the basis of Jung's eight Psychological Types. These types were subsequently developed by Katharine Briggs and her daughter the dramatist and novelist Isabel McKelvey Myers. Jung himself did not approve of measurement tools but also recognised that his renunciations would make little difference. Jung's rejection of measurement did not, however, prevent attempts at developing personality indicators, with the Jungian Type Index being developed as recently as 2001.

Major work

Jung, C. (1923). *Psychological Types*. Oxford: Harcourt Brace.

Jung, C. (1928). *Contributions to Analytic Psychology*. Oxford: Harcourt Brace.

Jung, C. (1928). Foreword to the Argentine edition, in Jung, C. (Author), Adler, G. & Hull, R. (Eds.), *Collected Works of C. G. Jung, Volume 6: Psychological Types* (pp. xiv–2).Princeton, NJ: Princeton University Press.

Jung, C. (1934). *The State of Psychotherapy Today, Collected Works*. London: Routledge.

Jung, C. (1946). *Essays on Contemporary Events*. London: Kegan Paul.

Jung, C. (1960). *Collected Works, 1902–60*. 18 Volumes. London: Routledge and Kegan Paul.

Bibliography

Bair, D. (2003). *Jung: A Biography*. London: Little Brown and Company.

Jung, C. G., & Storr, A. (1999). *The Essential Jung: Selected Writings*. Princeton, NJ: Princeton University Press.

Chapter 8

Hermann Rorschach

Faces staring back at us

November 8th, 1884 to April 2nd, 1922

The German poet and physician Justinus Kerner, was losing his sight when he invented klecksography (circa 1879); the art of dropping ink onto paper and making interesting shapes by folding the paper in half. Because of the human tendency to see patterns in randomness (apophenia), patterns often seem to resemble concrete objects. Kerner would embellish these images, turning them into people and objects then using them to illustrate his poems.

These patterns caught the attention of psychologists as early as 1885. Theorists such as Alfred Binet and Victor Henri suggested that they facilitate the study of involuntary imagination; a cognitive methodology that uses imagination as the modus for the bridge between the conscious and unconscious. From Binet, this idea spread to the intelligence theorist's practitioners who started to explore the extent to which the patterns could form an instrument for testing. By 1910 there was an 'inkblot' type test in the *Manual of Mental and Physical Tests*. It was, however, the Swiss psychiatrist Hermann Rorschach who went on to create possibly the most recognisable psychological test of all time.

Hermann Rorschach was born in Wiedikon in Zürich, Switzerland to Ulrich and Philippine (nee Wiedenkeller). Ulrich was a painter and teacher. He had a minor speech impediment which he could overcome, but it could often make him appear unusually reserved, but he was known to be kind-hearted and gentle. Ulrich's parents were embroiled in constant bickering to the point that Ulrich was convinced his parents never loved one another. Therefore, creating a loving, stable family home was fundamental to him. He married Philippine who was a warm, loving, energetic mother who was full of mirth and merriment. The couple had four children; Hermann, Anne, Paul and Klara, who died at 6 weeks old. For the times, Ulrich was an involved father. He would make extraordinary efforts to read to the children, take them on long walks explaining the history of old buildings, take them butterfly hunting and write plays in which the children would act.

Herman grew up on the banks of the Rhine in the Renaissance city of Schaffhausen. When Anne was born, they moved to a larger home on the Geissberg mountain where they lived for three or four years, and Herman grew up mesmerised by nature's surprises. Hermann attended the Schaffhausen Gymnasium from 1898 to 1904. It was German tradition that fraternity students would receive nicknames. It has been said (Paul, 2005) that so passionate was Rorschach about the pastime of klecksography that his fraternity friends called him 'Klexs', 'inkblot', however, an alternative explanation (Searls, 2017) was that Hermann was being praised for his drawing skills: '*klecksen*' also means to daub.

'Klexs' performed well at school, despite suffering from a much-reduced financial situation in comparison to his peers who were from prominent Swiss families. He began to show an early interest in transformational experiences, such as putting yourself in another's frame of mind, a process which he argued helped one understand the need for gender equality. While at school he created whimsical artworks and would seek opportunities to deliver lessons on Darwin, arguing that evolutionary theory should be actively and factually taught to children. By the end of his school years, he was already working as a tutor.

This period also saw the tragic death of both of his parents. In the summer of 1897, Philippine was found to be suffering from diabetes. In an age before insulin, treatments were largely based on a starvation diet, little could be done and his mother died after four bedridden weeks. One year later, Ulrich announced he would marry Philippine's younger half-sister and Hermann's godmother, Regina. The children did not receive the news well, but the marriage brought a brief period of happiness to the Rorschach family as well as a new baby, whom the children affectionately called Regineli. Poor Ulrich, however, was stricken by lead poisoning, probably caused by lead exposure from his early career as a journeyman painter. He was suffering from periods of fatigue and dizzy spells, which soon developed into depression and delusions. He died in the early hours of June 8th, 1903. Hermann, who was also very ill with a severe lung infection, was too ill to attend his father's funeral. Watching his parents suffering and being unable to do much to help them, was a powerful motivator that influenced Hermann's desire to become a doctor, but for now, Hermann had no time for his grief. He and his siblings were about to experience a life very different from the loving, kind family life filled with imagination and joie de vivre. Regina was widowed, and without a pension she and the children were impoverished. Her distress manifested in strictness, almost to the point of cruelty. She neither seemed to understand her step-children nor dare to appreciate their different personalities and needs. The family home was restrictive and kept deliberately cold with the children's hands turning blue on occasion. There were no play times only constant chores. Hermann was now 18 and had to grow up fast, becoming father to his siblings and an emotional crutch to his stepmother. Hermann had, however, held onto the one thing he had inherited from his father, the talent for living.

A year after his father's death, the family had finally scraped together sufficient funds for Hermann to travel to Zurich to study medicine. Zurich was a magnificent city to live in at that time. Full of multi-cultural influences, anarchists and revolutionaries. Vladimir Lenin was in exile, and the Russian influence was prevalent. Hermann had a passion for Russian culture and life and held Russian women in high esteem. Without tuition, Hermann mastered the Russian language in less than two years. He became involved with the radical pacifist group, the 'Doukhobors', befriending their leader Ivan Mikhailovich Tregubov and becoming a 'pen pal' of Leo Tolstoy.

His medical school schedule was punishing, but Hermann made time for language, for art, reading and conversation. He was a competent student, who loved life and still obtained the best academic results in his year. This was a dynamic time for the field of medicine and psychology. Zurich was the centre for work which transformed the understanding and treatment of mental illness. Advances were coming from psychiatrists such as Freud and Jung, but these revolutions were not without in-group and out-group therapeutic feuds.

Hermann Rorschach developed a pragmatic sanction towards psychoanalysis, he practised it and taught it, but always clarifying what he felt it could and could not do. He had no interested in paranormal psychology. Freud, Jung and other leading psychiatrists at the time studied séances and other spiritual mediums to attempt to bridge the unconscious, but he did revisit techniques such as word association, which had been largely left behind by Jung. The exploration of symbols and cultural phenomenon which replaced it, the myths, religions, art and the Jungian 'energy-life' were a fascination but also a technique that he found he could apply in attempting to diagnose the causes of mental illness and interpret the mind.

For Hermann, the future of psychology would be driven by the nature of perception. Zurich was in the heart of where psychoanalysis was receptive to new developments and by the spring of 1906, he was finally practising medicine there. He was, however, beginning to feel some repugnance towards the gauche, and on occasions discourteous, behaviour of his peers to their patients, who were often of inferior social standing if not, in fact, utterly impoverished.

The attitude from his peers and the increasing distrust of patients contributed to a general feeling that Rorschach had had enough. He wanted to move away and began to take advantage of the opportunities that advanced medical school students had for study in other institutions, alternating his time between Zurich, Berlin and other short-term posts across Switzerland. His time in Berlin was not entirely pleasant, he found it cold, the society dull and conformist and the spiralling metropolis unhealthy so in July 1906 he travelled from Berlin for the broader horizons of Moscow.

In Moscow, Rorschach attended cultural and political events, experienced the panorama from the Kremlin tower and the silence of 25,000 sledge rides. The Russians took him out of himself, and when the time came to return to Western Europe, it was a considerable comedown, but his developing relationship with Olga Stempelin gave him a way to live. Olga was from Kazan, in the present-day Republic of Tatarstan, Russia and had first met Hermann as a medical student in 1906. Their relationship had slowly developed, and they became engaged in 1909. Olga returned to her hometown to work with cholera patients in 1908, and as soon as his final exams were completed, Hermann followed her for a permanent life in Russia, where he could make a better income and pay off his debts. However, the process of securing his credentials proved endlessly bureaucratic, and Hermann and Russia began to fall out of love. Hermann's disillusionment was so great, he even went to the point of expressing complete disapproval of his sister's Russian love interest. Perhaps not realising that he, himself, was becoming reactionary, Hermann justified his disapproval based on what he described as the reactionary nature of the Russian State. Hermann stayed five months before finally returning to Switzerland to set up practice in the Münsterlingen Clinic. Olga remained in Russia for a further six months. They finally married in Geneva on April 21st, 1910, and went on to have two children, Elizabeth (b1917) and Ulrich (b 1919).

One year after his marriage to Olga, Rorschach started his experiments with inkblots. His first blots were not standardised in any way, he developed them afresh at each new presentation. Then gradually, he and his friend Konrad Gehring began annotating the blots, recording what had been observed. When the blots were tested on school children, the results were uninteresting. The students rarely saw much in them, but when they were shown to psychiatric patients, they saw much more. Rorschach began to explore their use as a bridge between what the patient was seeing and what the psychologist could explore. When Hermann felt he had gone as far as he could with his inkblot experiments, work was paused so that he could move forward and complete his MD dissertation.

Supervised by the eminent Swiss psychiatrist Paul Bleuler (who coined the term schizophrenia) Hermann's project focused on the study of the connections between what we see and what we feel. 'On Reflex Hallucinations and Related Phenomena' is an exploration of the cross-sensory perceptions that occur in such conditions as Proustian memories (memories triggered by tastes, smells or sounds) and synaesthesia, which is the merging of senses which are not usually connected. In 1913 Hermann was promoted and transferred to Münsingen, near Bern. Olga remained in Münsterlingen as she had her own medical career to pursue. In Bern, the focus of his work on perception began to broaden into an examination of the interplay between psychology and culture and the recognition that people see the world in different ways.

Finally, in 1914, Hermann tackled the Russian bureaucracy and was permitted to take the Russian state medical examinations. He and Olga left Switzerland for Moscow at a time when new cultural and scientific movements were sweeping across the county. He was offered a post at a leading psychoanalytical clinic in Kryukovo which treated voluntary patients suffering from nervous conditions. In this peaceful, rural setting, patients would receive treatments such as hypnosis, suggestion, rational emotive therapy and psychoanalysis. Here, Hermann brought his exploration of synaesthesia, visual art and self-expression to the study and treatment of mental illness, but he still struggled to settle in the unpredictability of the Russian culture, and Hermann left once again to settle in Switzerland, this time for good. Olga was reluctant to leave. It was almost a year before she joined her husband and when she finally returned, they moved again, this time to Herisau, in the northeast of Switzerland, where the family finally found somewhere that they could call home; their gipsy wanderings had come to an end.

His years of travelling gave Rorschach more breadth of experience than most of his peers. This had developed him into a creative problem solver who had begun, through his Russian experiences, to make connections between art and science and he had developed a deep understanding of the power of visual imagery in the exploration of psychological phenomenon. For example, he had begun to make significant breakthroughs with seriously ill patients by providing them with art supplies. For most patients, however, talking about pictures was more comfortable than making them.

By 1915, World War I and the nationalistic rivalry in Switzerland were at their height. These years brought significant financial burdens to the family and Hermann supplemented his meagre income by making furniture and toys (more often for his own children). Not all was well within the family and Hermann's late-night working would lead to repeated arguments. Olga had a fiery and violent temper, and would throw crockery to the point that the kitchen wall was permanently stained with coffee. Hermann was also frustrated by his inability to serve:

> now it's the Germans duty to kill as many Frenchmen as possible, and the Frenchmen's duty to kill as many Germans as possible, while it's our duty to sit here right in the middle and say, 'Good morning' to our schizophrenic patients.
>
> (Morgenthaler, 1965, p.86)

As asylums began to be requisitioned for the ever-growing war casualties, Hermann and Olga were eventually able to serve for 6 weeks, helping in the transportation of 2,800 psychiatric patients from the French asylums. The work was distressing. While pioneering specialist care was provided in these newly acquired war hospitals, the cost to the mentally ill and their families was terrible. Asylums that were not requisitioned became overcrowded, spreading distress and disease.

By 1917 Rorschach had returned to his obsession with improving his tests of free association. Visual imagery could go much deeper into human psychology and some recent work, although inconclusive, by a Polish medical student Szymon Hens reignited his focus. He was convinced that the way forward was better images and he started to make hundreds of images, to find patterns that made some sense; images that had something 'there'; images with meaningful spaces that would trigger description and insight, but also, images that would be devoid of craftsmanship or artistry. It was also crucial that the blots did not look like a test or a puzzle. His patients were distrustful and agitated so the blots had to elicit attention and not encourage the patient to be attentive to what they might mean. The symmetry of the inkblots was also crucial. Early blots were not constrained by regularity, they were shaped blots which were simply interesting or strangely shaped. Rorschach, however, made the crucial decision to create images that were pleasing to the eye and therefore encourage participation from the patient. To achieve this, he would hand paint ink patterns then use horizontal/bilateral symmetry to produce a pattern which mirrors the symmetry of faces. In a second break from previous inkblots, Rorschach used colour. He was long aware of the connection between colour and affectivity. He wanted his inkblots to confront the viewer, so he applied the colour red.

These blots were only blots, they could claim to be nothing more, but with imagination they became interpretations. The only issue with measuring the imagination is that some answers were imaginative, and some were not, and when dealing with psychotic patients, it is impossible to determine if they are using their imagination or if they believe what they are seeing is real. Therefore, as Rorschach designed and developed his inkblots, he had to figure out and design what his experimental work with those blots would actually do.

We know very little about the intermediate stages of the test development process because there are no surviving correspondences between 1917 and the summer of 1918 when he finally wrote up the remaining ten inkblots and their testing process for publication. The framework was detailed, with a focus on how the patients responded and with extensive data analysis. He expanded on this manual later in his career, but never changed it. The publication provided a challenge. The presentation of his findings to the Herisau medical association was poorly received, and publishers all refused it. If it were not for the intervention of the respected psychiatrist Walter Morgenthaler, the blots might never have been published. A small Swiss publishing house, the House of Bircher, agreed to print the test. The printers, however, bungled the printing process and the crisp blots were turned into shades of grey. Rorschach, resilient to this setback, decided that the spoiled inkblots presented an opportunity for further exciting interpretation. Response to the test was, however, at best indifferent and at worst, hostile. Only a few copies were ever sold, and during the German Society of Experimental Psychology conference, William Stern delivered a scathing review, denouncing the test as contrived and superficial.

On April 1st, 1922, Hermann Rorschach was taken suddenly ill and by 10 am the following morning he had died from peritonitis. It would be another 13 years before the inkblot test would be revived.

The inkblot test is more of a method than a theoretical approach to the study of schizophrenia which eventually evolved into a general test of personality. The theoretical routes are found in Freud's work on object relations which suggests that the way in which people relate to situations and other people has its roots in infancy where traumatic experiences become objects in the unconscious. The test it was hoped, would provide therapists with a route into unconsciously held motivations, beliefs, perceptions and emotions by using the clustering of responses from the test-takers. Those responses would cluster on responses related to needs, base motives and conflicts that could be traced to real-life situations.

The cards eventually crossed the Atlantic to America in 1935 where they began their superlative journey. The Jewish-German psychologist Bruno Klopfer fled the increasingly oppressive Nazi regime in 1933. En route to America, he spent a year with Carl Jung at the Zurich Psychotechnic Institute where he learned about the inkblot cards. Klopfer had an exotic, magnetic and alluring personality. Often holding the cards so close people would think he was smelling them, he was quickly surrounded by a loyal following of Rorschach disciples. Debate and conversation about the test spread. Psychology students were in love with the test; psychology professors were less excited, popularity did not necessarily equate with helpfulness.

As the Rorschach cult grew, there were offshoots in approach, differences and warring factions. In the end, there were as many as five different methods of interpretation. Even with no possibility of an agreement the test continued to triumph and gather credibility to the point that Klopfer and his colleague Gustave Gilbert were given unfettered access to test Hitler's inner circle during the Nuremberg trials.

The most comprehensive scoring system was published in 1974 by John Exner, with a growing emphasis that the test was not a test, but a method to understanding people. However, Rorschach confusion continued and, in the end, tests considered to be more objective and scientific were gaining ground. By the 1990s the method was struggling for survival. The final knockout blow was delivered by James Wood and Scott Lilienfeld in their 1999 *Psychological Science* paper. Wood and Lilienfeld attacked the reliability and validity of the test and others soon followed, some calling for a complete moratorium of its use. The test routinely generated abnormal and dysfunctional labels for its test-takers, and in no way represented ordinary people. There was almost no independent peer-reviewed evidence to support the claims of the Rorschach community yet child custody decisions, mental illness diagnoses and employment decisions were based on it.

By 2001 the public was listening. The inkblots, to the dismay of Rorschach devotees, were released into the public domain. The publication by Wikipedia was described as reckless and cynical but welcomed by those who argue that pseudoscience has no place in psychology. Today, Rorschach bashing is an ingrained tradition in psychology in Europe and the United Kingdom where there is a strong tradition for complex theoretical modelling (for example, Freud, Broadbent, Eysenck). The test/method remains enormously popular in countries such as Japan, where the labour-intensive nature of Rorschach mastery contributes to its popularity. Despite the visual and cultural touchstone that is the Rorschach test, the first complete biography of Hermann Rorschach was not written until 2017.

Olga Rorschach estimated that the family made only about 25 Swiss francs from Hermann's labours.

Major work

Rorschach, H. (1942). Psychodiagnostics: A diagnostic test based on perception, including Rorschach's paper 'The application of the form interpretation test' (published posthumously by Emil Oberholzer). Berne: Verlag Hans Huber. *Journal of the American Medical Association*, 120 (13), 1076. www.igorgrzetic.com/wp-content/uploads/2011/02/Herman-Rorschsch-Psychodiagnostics.pdf

Bibliography

Morgenthaler, W. (1921). Biographical sketch. In H. Rorschach (Ed.), *Psychodiagnostics*, 3rd ed. Bern: Heber; New York: Grune.

Morgenthaler, W. (1965). Erinnerungen an Hermann Rorschach. In K. W. Bash (Ed.), *Hermann Rorschach, Gesammelte Aufsätze* (pp. 95–101). Bern: Huber.

Paul, A. (2005). *The Cult of Personality Testing: How Personality Tests are Leading Us to Miseducate Our Children, Mismanage Our Companies, and Misunderstand Ourselves.* New York: Free Press.

Wood, J. M., & Lilienfeld, S. O. (1999). The Rorschach Inkblot Test: A Case of Overstatement? *Assessment*, 6(4), 341–351.

Searls, D. (2017). *The Inkblots: Hermann Rorschach, his Iconic Test, and the Power of Seeing.* New York: Crown.

Chapter 9

Karen Horney

Upending Freud

September 16th, 1885 to December 4th, 1952

Karen Clementina Theodora Danielsen was born to Clothilde Marie (Sonni) Danielsen and Berndt Henrik Wackels Danielsen in Eilbek, West Hamburg on September 16th, 1885. Sonni lost the great love of her life in the Franco-Prussian War and at 28, fearing a life of spinsterhood, she married the accomplished Norwegian steamship captain 'Wackels'. This possibly explains why Karen's family always believed she had been born in Blankensee; the romantic municipality to the east of Hamburg, where it was said many ships captains lived.

Wackels was one of the first to complete the Hamburg–South America route, travelling to Chile, Peru, Costa Rica and Guatemala, around the Horn and back again. He would have cut a dash with his merchant's uniform and a bushy blond walrus moustache. Wackles was a man of action. A pioneer who had both the nautical skills to pilot large ships through difficult waters and the personal agency and charisma to command a crew of 40 men in an environment which could swing from treacherous to tedious.

The marriage was a mistake. Despite his charisma, Wackels was nearly 20 years Sonni's senior, a conventionalist, a passionate Lutheran, whose four grown-up children from a previous marriage would frequently involve themselves in the couple's marital disagreements. Wackels would frequently spend long periods away from home, often up to 5 months at a time, and on his return, would make his presence felt.

Sonni probably did not help matters. She responded poorly to Wackels' piety. She became a devotee of divination; communicating with the dead and fortune-telling practices. To some extent, these interests complemented a period of Victorian religious revival; a golden age of magical thinking with advances in science and technology, intertwined with evangelicalism and the occult blurring together in popular thinking. In response to Sonni's interests, however, Wackels would invite the local pastor to deliver fiery sermons in the family home. Sonni also seems to have found it difficult to separate herself from her biological children. She naturally favoured her two very young children, Karen and Berndt, but would often subject her children to emotional abuse, reminding them that they were her only source of happiness and if it were not for them, she might be dead. The acrid air of continual family discord, the distance of Karen's father and the obligations and guilt from her mother played out 45 years later in *Our Inner Conflicts* where Horney describes the consequences to children who find themselves drawn into taking sides;

> his first attempts to relate himself to others are determined not by his real feelings but by strategic necessities. He cannot simply like or dislike, trust or distrust, express his wishes or protest against those of others, but has automatically to devise ways to cope with people and to manipulate them with minimum damage to himself. The fundamental characteristics that evolve in this way may be summarised as an alienation from the self and others, a feeling of helplessness, a pervasive apprehensiveness, and a hostile tension in his human relations that ranges from general wariness to definite hatred.
>
> (Horney, 1945, n.p.)

These feelings of hostility and isolated helplessness would later become what Horney termed 'basic anxiety' whereby children would come to see their social environment as unfair and unpredictable. Ultimately leading to the feeling that they had no power to influence their circumstances, developing distrusting and hostile feelings and behaviours towards others.

During her formative years, Karen avidly recorded her life experiences in her diaries. As her writings progressed, they evolve from marginally interesting 'chatter' towards an involved record of her self-scrutiny, intellectual and moral development that would later influence her theory of female personality. She would record events, expressing their meaning and reflecting on her thoughts and feelings. A childhood crush towards her convent school teacher, Herr Schulze, is perhaps considered a typical narrative for

adolescent diary writers. Karen went further, questioning the
double standards of patriarchal marriage conventions versus the
reality of love: giving oneself over to a man outside marriage or
over to a man in a marriage devoid of love.

A girl who gives herself to a man in free love stands morally
way above the woman who, for pecuniary reasons or out of
a desire for a home, marries a man she does not love. Marriage is something only external. It is bad – not theoretically –
but when one comes to know how few marriages are really
good ones. I know two families from our large circle of
acquaintances of whom I guess this is the case. But the one
couple are pretty limited people, the other very superficial
(Horney, 1980, p.61, February 1903).

Such writings are early validation of her perceptive understanding
of the conflicts surrounding the female role in society, establishing
herself as a progressive thinker and may also have provided an
outlet for her to unburden herself about her dislike of her father
who would at "every turn every additional penny he has to spend
for me 10 times in his fingers" (Horney, 1980, p.26, January 18th,
1901), before spending it on her education. "I can't respect that
man who makes us all unhappy with his dreadful hypocrisy, selfish-
ness, crudeness and ill-breeding" (Horney, 1980, p.22, December 1900). Wackel's zealousness coalesced with his firebrand
mentor and friend Pastor Nikolai Von Ruckteschell. Their combined belief that 'God the Father' was on their side, pushed the
limits of Karen's religious acceptance and conformity. Throughout
her journaling, Horney demonstrates herself to be a developing liberal, doubting of religion and unable to experience faith. During
a religious class examining Christ's appearance after his crucifixion
to Paul as proof of Christ's resurrection, Horney described Paul as
suffering from an overwrought nervous condition causing her
beloved Herr Schulze to slam his Bible shut. Karen's relationship
with a literal interpretation of scripture had come to an end.

Despite the rigidity of her home life and her mother's very evident unhappiness, Karen fought for the opportunity to study at
the girl's gymnasium in Hamburg and eventually secured a place
at the University of Freiburg medical school in 1906. Her mother
Sonni followed Karen to Freiburg and in so doing, achieved what
was almost unthinkable for Victorian women, she left Wackels.

Karen's conduct in Freiburg was no less shocking. Her mother's letters berate her for spending time with men without a chaperone and staying out all night. Karen also began a passionate affair with a fellow medical student before meeting her future husband Oskar Horney. The couple had a dynamic, intellectual friendship but the relationship may also have had more practical benefits for Karen in redirecting her mother's attention. She was frustrated by her mother's constant husband hunting. Oskar was ambitious, with good prospects with the Stinnes Corporation, a coal and shipping company in Berlin. He was a progressive, and in contrast to many men of that era, he was supportive of Karen having her career, but Oskar was a man who was not unlike her father. He was authoritarian, and he prized self-control.

It did not take long for cracks to appear in the marriage, Karen began to wonder about having extra-marital relationships, she was suffering from depression and her journaling peters out. When the couple started to experience sexual problems, Karen began to attend what would be life-changing sessions with Karl Abraham, the leading psychoanalyst and pupil of Freud. After their sessions, Karen realised that she had a strong desire to make a difference in the world and to work as a psychoanalyst. Abrahams seems to have been impressed enough with Horney to write to Freud about his new client, and after almost a 3-year hiatus, Karen begins journaling again. Her writing, however, is a jumble of personal anxiety over motherhood, and self-torture about her mother's sudden death from stroke, all through the lens of Freud, Jung, Adler and Rank.

In 1920 Karen became one of the founding members of the Berlin Psychoanalytical Institute. These were prosperous years. The Stinnes Corporation had come a significant supplier of raw materials during World War I, but Oskar's growing nationalist views were causing difficulties in the Horney marriage. Then in 1923, Oskar's company failed, and he became seriously ill with meningitis. Barely recovering from his illness, Oskar became morose and quarrelsome, leading some to speculate that he may have suffered brain damage. The family was in decline financially and emotionally when Karen's brother Berndt suddenly died of pneumonia. Three years later Karen left Oskar and took their children to New York.

Horney could not identify with Freud's position that neurosis was an outgrowth of an individual's ability to cope with their

sexual drives and impulses. Horney agreed with Freud that anx-
iety-provoking childhood experiences could result in personality
maladjustment, but felt that Freud's perspective was limiting
because it overlooked both the cultural and relational experiences
that surround development. Horney put forward an alternative
explanation which placed socialisation and culture at its centre,
finally freeing psychoanalysis from its strict instinctive and mech-
anistic conception.

Horney argued that neurosis is an outcome of disturbed formative relationships, particularly with parents and principal care-
givers. Broken relationships impacted on personality development
and it was this that caused impaired sexual functioning. Culture
to Horney encouraged different manifestations of fear. For
example, Western individualistic cultures encouraged feelings of
inferiority and fear of failure, whereas individuals from Eastern
cultures were more at risk of the shame that dishonour brings.
Individuals with well-developed defence mechanisms will adapt
and change, but the neurotic will find this adjustment more problematic. At the centre of Horney's theoretical position is the
warm, loving, consistent nature of parenting, respect and support
she rarely experienced as a child. This nurturing environment
supports the development of the 'real self', which is the ultimate
expression of abilities and talents, the expression of which supports the individual to feel comfortable in the world and relate
easily to others. Children whose environment fails them are
more likely to experience multiple disturbances and are therefore more likely to develop neurosis. Such children are also more
likely to rely upon defence mechanisms which may operate to
temporarily protect the child but will result in them becoming less
in touch with their real feelings and thoughts. A split occurs
between the real self and the idealised, where they will create
images of themselves that portray them as worthy, successful and
perfect persons. Horny describes this as the 'Tyranny of the
Shoulds', non-negotiable standards that if met will resolve all inner
conflicts and pain and anxiety will disappear.

The neurotic has the need for affection and approval at any
cost, which pulls them toward others while fearing criticism, particularly from those whom they value. They can be overly
dependent on others. Finding it difficult to function on their own
they rarely take risks. They do not seek mutual caring; instead,
they need a more dominant partner to take over their lives and

may work to restrict their lives in safe and inconspicuous ways. Alternatively, the neurotic may seek to present an image of infallibility, moving away from others by seeking freedom from commitment and seeking a level of perfectionism which will disguise their flaws and help them avoid feelings of self-loathing. The third theme is moving against others, whereby the neurotic will crave power, the exploitation of others, social recognition, prestige and admiration. Horney describes this as indiscriminate ambition. This ambition is unrealistic and results in resentment and hostility. As success is such a dominant driver, energy will be directed into retaining power balances in relationships and undermining others, the purpose of which is not necessarily the intention of increasing the chances of their success, but rather to ensure that others fail.

Horney mostly agreed with Freud's defence mechanisms but argued that the neurotic also developed defences to help support their inner conflicts and disturbed relationships by externalising their feelings and shortcomings onto others. These mechanisms included blind spots which allowed denial of constructs that were at odds with the person's ideal self – compartmentalisation whereby incompatible needs or beliefs were separated so that they did not appear inconsistent, for example, the separation of beliefs from actions. Rationalisation would be applied to offer plausible excuses for conduct or actions, and extreme self-control or arbitrary rightness applied when individuals cannot tolerate feelings of doubt and indecision. They may adopt elusiveness or dogma to assert their rightness in all situations. Cynicism is where the individual purports to have no positive expectations and thus cannot be disappointed.

Where Horney potentially made her most significant contribution to the field was in her stance against Freud's position on the female personality. She was one of the first to point out that men developed the assumptions of psychoanalysis through the analysis of neurotic women and she took exception with Freud's penis envy and the related construct of female masochism. These concepts suggested that all women feel themselves to be deficient and envious of men, and women who competed with men are seen to be the ultimate manifestation of penis envy. Horney contended that this was male engendered nonsense and that what women wanted was the attributes of the dominant masculine society; freedom, respect and independence. A woman's wish to be male merely represented their desire for the same privileges that men had in society. By using terms such as penis envy women were liberated from taking responsibility for their dysfunctional behaviours, it was easier to blame a sense of contempt towards husbands on penis envy, than deal with the sense of inferiority and self-denial that resided in many marriages. This female masochism was further fuelled by Freud's ideas that women were pre-programmed to derive satisfaction from pain, citing menstruation and childbirth as examples of satisfying experiences. No woman enjoyed the pain of childbirth; rather they redirect their attention to the joy of the birth of a child. The behaviour that Freudians describe as masochistic represents the caring roles that women have within society as they place the needs of others in front of themselves. Men have devalued this role by ascribing the term masochism, particularly when they themselves may envy women.

Horney's contribution was inspiring. She founded the American Psychoanalytic Institute, which operated as a platform for her voice. In the introduction to her final lectures (Horney in Ingram, 1987) her compelling theory of personality is described as triggering self-recognition in the reader. Her courage to stand against the mainstream view of psychoanalysis was ultimately a *Dolchstoßlegende* (stab-in-the-back). Fritz Wittels wrote a bitter open letter in March 1940 to the society members in an attempt to have Karen removed from her position:

> Our students come to us because of Freud's invulnerable name expecting to be taught the result of forty years of patient psychoanalytic work. Instead, we are urgently asked to teach them a doctrine diametrically opposed to Freud's findings and rejected by probably ninety-nine per cent of the experienced members of the International Psychoanalytic Association.
>
> (Fritz Wittels to Lawrence Kubie 13th March, 1940. David
> Levy Papers)

Wittels was hot-headed and passionate. A disciple of Freud, but ironically also a writer of 'high-toned' violent pornography. In his book, *The Jeweller of Bagdad*, Wittels recounts the love of Achmed the jeweller, for the beautiful Enis. He proceeds to beat and subjugate her through the entire book until she thinks on his command. Freud may well have had something to say on the connection between Wittels' pornographic writing and his behaviour toward Horney, but there is also a suggestion that Wittels' letter was in fact stage-crafted by the society's president Lawrence Kubie, a man described as tending to professionally seduce only to abandon. Wittels joined other disciples at the board of the education committee, and a Freudian stronghold was dug in and ready for war. What followed was a series of depositions, threats to withhold society membership from students who had been trained by liberal analysists, and blatant student intimidation, including one student being told that his behaviour was caused by unanalysed homosexuality.

The society took a hard stance against Karen Horney; she was singled out as a troublemaker, stripped of her status as a training analyst and removed from all teaching and supervision. Horney resigned and is reported as walking out of the meeting, followed by five members of the faculty singing 'Go Down Moses (let my people go)'. Horney and her group moved swiftly after the walkout, within weeks they had named their new institute, the Association for the Advancement of Psychoanalysis and later the American Institute for Psychoanalysis, where she remained as Dean until her death from abdominal cancer, on December 4th, 1952.

In her lifetime, Karen achieved where Alfred Alder and Carl Jung had failed. She instigated the first concrete split in the American Psychoanalytic Institute. So well thought of as an analyst and a teacher, her students pieced together their fragmented lecture notes, turning them into a book covering the lectures she gave in the final year of her life.

Major works

Horney, K. (1917). Die technik der psychoanalytischen therapie. *Zeitschrift für Sexualwissenschaft*, 4.The technique of psychoanalytic therapy. *American Journal of Psychoanalysis*, 28 (1968), 3–12. Reprinted in Paris, B. J. (ed.) (1999). *Karen Horney: The Therapeutic Process*. New Haven, CT: Yale University Press, 11–23.

Horney, K. (1937). *The Neurotic Personality of Our Time*. New York: Norton.

Horney, K. (1939). *New Ways in Psychoanalysis*. New York: Norton.

Horney, K. (1942). *Self-Analysis*. New York: Norton.

Horney, K. (1945). *Our Inner Conflicts*. New York: Norton.

Horney, K. (1950). *Neurosis and Human Growth*. New York: Norton.

Horney, K. (1967). *Feminine Psychology*. New York: Norton.

Horney, K. (1980). *The Adolescent Diaries of Karen Horney*. New York: Basic Books.

Ingram, D. H. (ed.). (1987). *Final Lectures: Karen Horney*. New York: W. W. Norton.

Bibliography

Horney, C. (1945). Our Inner Conflicts. New York: W. W. Norton, Opensource. http://creativecommons.org/licenses/by-nc-nd/3.0/us/

Horney, K. (1980). *The Adolescent Diaries of Karen Horney*. New York: Basic Books.

Chapter 10

Henry Alexander Murray

'Revealing the personal narrative'

May 13th, 1893 to June 23rd, 1988

Henry (Harry) Alexander Murray was born in New York in 1893. The America that the infant Harry grew up in was one of sharp contradictions. His life was comfortable and secure. Growing up in an affluent area, close to Central Park, the children would have had little sense of the growing societal divisions. Immigration was increasing and with it the harsh realities of low wages, exploitation and slum living.

His mother, Fannie Morris Babcock, was from New England with a long prosperous pedigree. She married Henry Alexander (Sr), a well-bred but financially modest Scot who worked in stocks and bonds. Through hard work he found favour with the Babcock family, eventually winning Fannie's heart. The couple prospered and lived in a fashionable part of New York attending social clubs with the financial elite of the day.

Harry was the middle child; he had an older sister and younger brother. Harry's mother was nervous, self-absorbed, she suffered from hypochondria and was prone to meddling. Fannie made no secret of the fact that her favourite child was Virginia. She was a demanding child, a 'terrier', whose demands probably resulted in the abrupt end of Harry's weaning aged two months. Harry fared poorly afterwards. He did not eat properly for two years and was suffering not only from lack of nutrition but also lack of maternal love. At the age of nine, he recalls coming home from school where he was confronted with an operating theatre and two surgeons in the family dining room. His mother, who was obsessed with perfection, had decided that Harry had a squint in his eye. This deviation needed adjusting there and then. The terrified boy was offered the option of a general aesthetic, or he could get

on with it, and she would buy him an aquarium. Not understanding entirely what was about to take place, Harry opted
for the aquarium. The trauma of the surgery not only resulted
in Harry developing a stutter, but the surgeons overcorrected
his eyes causing Harry to suffer from a complete lack of stereo-
scopic vision. These experiences had a profound impact on
what he would describe as his marrow of misery and melan-
choly, which would eventually manifest in a disposition which
would flip from excessive buoyancy to pessimism.

His relationship with his father and his younger brother Cecil
was much better. He describes his father as a jolly, kindly man
whom he credited with giving him rules for living and simple
self-esteem. Rather than directly protect Harry and his brother
from his mother's exuberance, his father's strategy was that they
should all find ways to keep their distance. So, he would spend
long periods reading to the boys, taking them to Central Park,
on fishing trips and trips to Europe.

After a period at private preparatory schools, Harry was sent
away to board in 1906 at Groton School, an Episcopal college in
Massachusetts. Harry worked and played hard at Groton,
becoming a positively engaged and well-rounded adolescent.
Playing sport was his passion, but as a result of his yet unknown
eye damage, he was not particularly good at it. His physical
development was still slow; he suffered from adenoid problems,
bouts of scarlet fever and mumps. Otherwise, his health was
good and he would brush the illness off and bounce back
quickly. As his adolescence developed, Harry would show more
interest in hunting, fishing, drinking (but not excessively) and
'chorus line girls'; a pursuit he reports himself to have been quite
successful at. He did well at school, emerging a stable and secure
man. Not all in his college cohort of 26 faired so well. Many
developed drinking problems and six of his peer group took their
own lives in the years to follow.

At Harvard, Harry continued his socialising, jesting that he
graduated in the three R's; Rum, Rowing and Romance. He
eventually majored, poorly, in history. Harry compensated for
his poor early performance at Columbia University, where he
studied for his MD, also receiving an MA in biology. In 1919 he
graduated, took up a position as an instructor in physiology at
Harvard and began studying for a PhD in biochemistry which he
completed in 1928. While pursuing his medical studies he met

and married Josephine (Jo) Lee Rantoul and they had a child together, also called Josephine (b1921).

In 1923 Harry met Christiana Morgan which would change both the nature of his personal life and the trajectory of his professional career. Christina was strikingly beautiful and held many qualities that may have seemed familiar to Harry. She was married to Will O. Morgan, a graduate of Harvard and an acquaintance of Harry's. They had an infant child, from whom Christina had withdrawn, giving total care over to their nanny. Depression, anxiety and inner turmoil surrounded Christina. She was beautiful, and she knew it, bold and flirtatious, but she was also destructive and the creator of drama. Harry knew she was neurotic, but he was also besotted.

It was Christina who introduced Harry to Carl Jung's significant writing, *Psychological Types*. At dinner one evening she articulately contrasted Jung's work with the writings of Freud. Perhaps to impress Christina further, or because he was sincerely interested in the topic, Harry promptly went and acquired the copy from Christina. It was a turning point, the book and Christina seemed to offer Harry direction and answers to his most scattered self. Although the relationship started as a mostly intellectual exchange on Jung's work, it was not long before an intellectual, but non-physical, affair begun.

Harry was already starting to think about a route into psychology and was due to spend a year in Cambridge, England in academic study. Christina persuaded Will that they should follow the Murrays to Cambridge. Until this Jo point was trying her level best to bend to the situation but the relationships were becoming increasingly strained. Harry still loved his wife, she made him deeply happy, but Christina was becoming more overly confident in meddling between the couple. Christina was highly critical to Harry of his wife's inability to make allowances for this vital side of Harry's psyche, and Harry did little to protect his marriage. Matters started to come to a head one night after dinner. As the Morgans left the Murray household, Harry bizarrely blurted out to Christina that she fertilised him. This startled Jo and Will, but with all the politeness of New England society in the mid-1920s, they said nothing. They could see what happening and the pain was acute, but there was always the hope that it would wear itself out.

In 1925, with this slow-burning affair simmering in his personal life, Harry took himself to Zurich to meet with Carl Jung.

En route, Harry was taken by the striking presence of a beautiful woman, Lady Winifred Gore, also on her way to visit a Swiss psychiatrist. Harry was convinced that he was having an anima experience, that their souls were somehow connected, that they had met before. Little came of the meeting, but when Jung was showing little interest in discussions with Harry on Psychological Types, Harry began to relay this experience and then, explain in detail his relationship with Christina Morgan. Jung's interest was piqued, and he began to share his own candid detours in love. The sessions continued for 3 weeks, interspersed with sailing trips, meals and talking, followed then with Jung's mistress Antonia Wolf and his wife Emma Jung serving tea. Jung's insights helped to explain away what was happening in his personal life: to reach full creative potential Harry would have to cast off his neurotic ties. He would finally abandon biology and biochemistry in favour of psychology and continue openly with both relationships.

The couples met with Jung. Christina consented to pursue therapy with Jung, then confessed all to Will and Jo. Will was hurt but stoic, and Jo felt the meeting with Jung was a complete waste of time. She concluded that Jung was nothing but a dirty old man but ironically his assessment, that her husband's affair with Christina was base, helped her eventually accept the situation. As divorce was out of the question, Will and Jo were resolved to try and make the best of an awful situation.

On returning to the United States in 1926, Henry took up a post at Harvard University at a clinic to study abnormal psychology. He was hopelessly under qualified and worse still the department was not in the least bit interested in the teachings of Jung. Harry deplored the experimental focus and measurement science and quickly became known as a difficult if not in fact openly hostile and obnoxious member of the Harvard team. Somehow, he managed to secure directorship of the clinic in 1928. He changed the direction of the clinic to focus on understanding human nature and man, and gave Christina Morgan an office in the clinic. Under Harry and Christina's leadership, the clinic became more of an intellectual salon, where the great artists, thinkers and psychologists of the time would come, to dine and share conversation. Harry never saw the clinic as being aligned to one psychological approach or another, strongly resisting descriptions of the clinic as Freudian or Jungian. Instead, all perspectives were embraced.

It was within this body of great minds that Harry began to wrestle with the question of abnormal psychology. Rorschach and the Minnesota Multiphasic Personality Inventory (MMPI) had a foothold in the psychologist's toolbox, neither provided much in the way of understanding what manifested as abnormal personality, and both were often applied in over-zealous and high-handed ways. Harry felt such techniques were superficial measures, and, quoting the philosopher George Santayana, Harry argued that human imagination and fancies were more revealing to personality. What Harry liked to call 'apperception'. Others such as Francis Galton had been down this road, exploring the relationship between word associations and thought. Freud saw slips of the tongue as the means of accessing the inner self and Rorschach's inkblots attempted to explore Freud's ideas of projection.

Harry began to create techniques for use in the clinic that would enable the mind to wander and provide the psychologist with an additional route by which to understand the patient. These were highly inventive for the time and included musical stimuli, literature, art and odour. Dozens of approaches were developed but one, in particular, was emerging as useful in the clinics, pictures that depicted 'stories' that could be interpreted and expanded upon by the viewer.

The team set about collecting large numbers of pictures from magazines, newspapers and other media resources. Those pictures were shown to students, peers and family with the aim of understanding how those considered to have normal personality functioning would interpret the pictorial messages. Henry and Christina called their test the Thematic Apperception Test (TAT). Thematic because of its capacity to elicit themes that were prevalent in the test-taker's life, Apperception because they triggered fantasy and imagination. The test seemed to do what everyone hoped.

In clinical practice, patients would share their deepest thoughts and emotions about the images, and the therapist was thus able to understand the patient quickly. TAT still did little to combat the culture of high-handed testing. The tester's nativity about the purpose of the instrument was essential to understanding human thought processes. As such, takers were often lied to and told that the test assessed intelligence or creativity. The work was not readily accepted by the scientific community and suffered several journal rejections before finally finding a home in the *Archives of*

Neurology and Psychiatry in 1935. Even then, the publication was a minor achievement, mostly circulated within the clinic's promotional material.

It was 1939 before interest in the theories behind such projective techniques gathered momentum. Harry's major work on psychogenic need theory helped to stimulate attention. The publication of *Explorations in Personality* was based on the experience and understanding that Harry had developed through his clinical practice. The theory examined the interaction between motivation and personality arguing that our personalities reflect behaviours which we control by our needs. Some needs are fleeting, others more fundamental to our nature. Primary needs are based on biological demands; food, sex, sleep. Secondary needs are psychological, for example, nurturing, achievement, love and power, the fulfilment of which are essential for our well-being and happiness. Thus, personality was a process, which was governed by the fabric of the person and their environment at that time.

Explorations also contained an overview of TAT, explaining how the test could tap into the unconscious processes that governed those needs because, in addition to using lived experience to explain the pictures, test-takers would also project their own personal, emotional and psychological existence into the pictures. The test made it possible to find the 'buried self', and finally the American press began to take notice. The TAT would eventually become be the first projective test developed and published in the United States.

Whilst the TAT was gathering momentum, war in Europe was looming. Keen to help the war efforts, Harry set about developing an effective officer selection technique. The ground-breaking tests method could be used to select the best agents behind enemy lines to work as spies and saboteurs. Harry had a yet more ground-breaking contribution to make, a psychological profile of Adolf Hitler. Commissioned by the intelligence agencies and with only the briefest of time frames to complete the work, Harry carried out an extensive analysis of Hilter's speeches and writings. He studied reports from people who were in relationships with Hitler, including reports from women who had sex with him, his childhood friendships and familial connections. By 1943 Harry had produced a 227-page analysis, including predictions about his future behaviour and how the allies might deal with him once the war ended. The extreme contradictions in Hitler's personality and the galvanising ideology that compelled him to drag Europe into an abyss presented a frightening combination of insanity and sanity. Despite high levels of satisfaction with Harry's report and its exceptional insights, the report was quickly swallowed up by the America military establishment and ordered 'destroyed'. This was a blow, but Harry moved on quickly to other war matters. The report never saw the light of day, until in 1972 Walter Langer published *The Mind of Adolf Hitler* Langer appeared to have taken Harry's work and published it as his own.

Throughout the 1950s and 1960s, Murray continued to work with the CIA on the forensic applications of his work. This included a series of controversial experiments, intended to increase understanding of stress and resilience. Harvard students were subjected to intense interrogation and humiliation. One of those students, John Kaczynski, would later blame his experiences as a participant in Murray's studies as a contributing factor to his psychological state. Kaczynski spent 200 hours over 3 years in Murray's studies and went on to conduct a terrorist campaign against anyone involved in modern technology (the 'Unabomber', university and airline bomber).

Harry's wife Jo died suddenly of a heart attack on January 14th, 1962. Despite his ongoing devotion to Christina, Murray was devastated. His relationship with Christina was also faltering. Following excruciating sympathectomy surgery, she had developed a drinking problem. Her alcoholism was an open secret, and she was now an embarrassment to him. In an attempt to help her sober up, Harry refused to marry Christina if she continued to drink. She managed to stop briefly but was soon back drinking heavily. Christina had been drinking heavily when she drowned in shallow water on March 14th, 1967. Life, however, had one more great love for Harry. At the age of 76, he married Nina Chandler Fish whom he described as the most balanced and stable person he had ever had in his life. The couple shared almost 20 years before Harry died from pneumonia at the age of 95.

In addition to his lasting impact on the field of psychological profiling, Henry Alexander Murray's creative tool has perhaps had its most lasting influence in the field of advertising. The application of TAT-like methodologies in encouraging customers to talk about what they see in an advertisement is an essential marketing technique in determining what customers think and feel, what they want and what they do not want.

Major works

Morgan, C. D., & Murray, H. A. (1935). A method for investigating fantasies: The thematic apperception test. *Archives of Neurology & Psychiatry*, 34, 289–306.

Murray, H. A. (1938). *Explorations in Personality*. Oxford: Oxford University Press.

Murray, H. A. (1973). *The Analysis of Fantasy*. Huntington, NY: Robert E. Krieger.

Bibliography

Langer, W. (1972). *The Mind of Adolf Hitler*. London: Secker and Warburg.

Novak, F. G., Jr. (Ed.). (2007). *'In Old Friendship': The Correspondence of Lewis Mumford and Henry A. Murray, 1928–1981*. Syracuse, NY: Syracuse University Press.

Robinson, F. G. (1992). *Love's Story Told: A Life of Henry Murray*. London: Harvard University Press.

Chapter 11

David Wechsler

'Factorial analysis alone is not the answer'

January 12th, 1896 to May 2nd, 1981

Born in Lespezi, Romania, David was the youngest of seven children, four girls (Anna, Eva, Freda, Anthony) and three boys (Sam, Israel). Their father Moses was a Hebrew scholar. Their mother Leah Pascal was a shopkeeper. When David was six years old, the family emigrated to America. Like many of the European Jewish immigrants of the 1920s, the family were fleeing religious persecution. New laws discriminating against Jewish working men were causing high levels of unemployment, and as the Weschler family left Romania, the right to education was removed from Jewish children as well.

The Wechslers were just one European family of 20 million immigrants arriving in America, ready to give Henry H. Goddard and the other eugenicists of the time cause for concern. The family settled in New York, but within five years of their arrival, both of David's parents died of cancer. A tragedy which would likely have provided the eugenicists with further data to back up their restrictive immigration policies. While he went through public school, David was raised by his physician brother Israel, before entering the College of the City of New York in 1913. He obtained his BA in 1916 before specialising in psychology at Columbia. David's specialism was in Korsakoff psychosis, which is the memory loss associated with chronic alcoholism.

While awaiting his army draft, David worked as a volunteer, scoring the Army Alpha and Beta tests that were being rolled out by the Yerkes testing programme. When finally appointed an officer commission, David formally joined the testing programme, administering a combination of Alpha and Beta and the Stanford-Binet intelligence tests. David began to sense that while there was apparently a relationship between what the tests measure and the capacity to function in society, the current testing models were not necessarily the best tools for capturing adult abilities, particularly when English was not the first language. Something much broader was needed.

When the war finally ended David was posted to England to study with Karl Pearson and Charles Spearman. He used this period at the University College London to deepen his understanding of Pearson's correlational work and Spearman's theory of general intelligence. For David, the notion of general intelligence was to narrow a construct. He held onto the belief that non-intellectual factors such as motivation and personality could play a key role. With his supervisor, Robert S. Woodworth's support and a field scholarship under his belt, David then travelled the University of Paris to study with Henry Piéron and Louis Lapicque, where he would spend two years exploring the relationship between emotional changes and psychogalvanic skin responses.

Returning to America in 1922, David took up a position at Psychopathic Hospital in Boston, before returning to New York City to work with the Bureau of Child Guidance. Many of the children who were attending these clinics were from immigrant families, and David began to notice patterns between those children and the army recruits he had once tested. Colleagues at Columbia were starting to wake up to the idea that culture could impact on test performance, and David's experiences as a Romanian immigrant made him particularly receptive to those ideas.

David completed his PhD under Woodworth in 1925 and continued to practice psychological testing, both privately and for the Psychological Corporation. He published a few minor articles in the area, which suggested how his attitudes were developing. The first paper demonstrated that as children became increasingly educated their tests scores became more homogenous. These findings reinforced his belief that intelligence was malleable and that it was mostly environmental factors that contributed to underperformance. His second finding was that the Army Alpha tests were more useful in the diagnosis of individual abilities and disabilities because rather than providing a unitary score that compared mental age with chronological, those tests were designed to identify where a participant was particularly good at something. In other words, average overall performance could mask exceptional performance on one construct.

In 1932 David was soon able to explore his ideas in more detail when was appointed chief psychologist at the Bellevue Hospital in New York. Bellevue was a large institution, with hundreds of patients differing in language abilities and socio-economic status. The diversity of this population convinced David that mental testing was of limited utility to such patients. The effective formulas of the day, all relied on chronological development at a normal pace which meant if a child's development was delayed, their abilities quickly hit a ceiling. Similarly, intelligence seemed to peak around the late teens, with performance decreasing rapidly after this point. For some, this was good evidence that intelligence tests could not capture the expertise, knowledge or creativity that develops in later life. For others, it merely reinforced the idea that adolescence is the period at which intelligence is at its optimum level.

Wechsler set about developing his own set of tools that would be more representative. First, the Bellevue-Wechsler Scale (1939) which offered better standardisation. His method was to apply the points-based system which focused on the prevalence of performance in the normal population, rather than age. Using this methodology, performance can vary across age, with an absolute point score reflecting where most people at a certain age would fall. This deviation IQ score expressed an individual's performance relative to the appropriate age group. The score of 100 was assigned to any result exactly at its age group average, with standard deviations of 15. This measure enabled clarity about where most people fell within the normal range of intelligence. More than two-thirds of IQs fall one standard deviation below and above the mean: between 85 and 115. IQs were then assigned percentile ranks. So successful was this technique in removing inconsistencies almost all ability test developers have adopted it. Following on from this, a system which would enable the pinpointing of each participant's strengths and weaknesses was made possible by establishing norms for 11 different sub-scales. Thus, a profile could be created of each participant's performance, and the next generation of intelligence tests was born.

The method was so compelling that it was quickly expanded from adults to children. As described by the psychometrician Lee Cronbach, Wechsler had avoided breaking into any new understanding of intelligence. Instead what was more remarkable was Wechsler's capacity to improve mental testing through the intelligent application of statistics in a pragmatic way. The tests sub-scales still, as predicted by Spearman, correlate positively and arrange themselves in a hierarchy suggestive of the g factor. These clusters have split thinking on the nature of intelligence, on the one hand, the tests may tap into 'isolated intelligences', or it may be that the test is simply constructed from g-saturated questions.

Despite contrasting perspectives on the nature of intelligence and abilities, its correlations and causality, David Wechsler's perspective was clear. In his address to the American Psychological Association following his award for distinguished professional contribution to psychology he described intelligence as:

> What we measure with tests is not what tests measure – not information, not spatial perception, not reasoning ability. These are only a means to an end. What intelligence tests measure, what we hope they measure, is something much more important: the capacity of an individual to understand the world about him and his resourcefulness to cope with its challenges.
>
> (Wechsler, 1975)

In addition to developing the Wechsler Intelligence Scales, David formed a mental health programme in Cyprus to support Holocaust survivors and helped establish the Hebrew University in Jerusalem. In addition to his intelligence and ability scales, David Weschler left a profound mark on the fields of psychometrics and psychology. David Wechsler came into the testing debacle, on the heels of Alfred Binet, Henry Goddard and Lewis M. Terman but is generally considered to be one of the most cited and eminent psychologists in the field of individual differences. We know very little about the personal life of David Weschler, other than content contained within his obituaries. He was married twice. In 1933 to Florence Helen 'Freda' Felske, but she was killed three weeks after their wedding in a car accident. David was married again in 1939 to Ruth Anne Halpern. They had two boys, Adam and Leonard.

Major works

Wechsler, D. (1939). *The Measurement of Adult Intelligence*. Baltimore, MD: Williams & Wilkins.

Wechsler, D. (1952). *The Range of Human Capacities* (2nd ed.). Oxford: Williams & Wilkins.

Wechsler, D. (1975). Intelligence defined and undefined: A relativistic appraisal. *American Psychologist*, 30(2),135–139.

Wechsler, D., Doppelt, J., & Lennon, R. (1975). *A Conversation with David Wechsler* (Transcript, Archives of the Psychological Corporation). San Antonio, TX: The Psychological Corporation.

Bibliography

Carson, John. (1999). 'Wechsler, David.' In John A. Garraty and Mark C. Carnes (Ed.) *American National Biography*, vol. 22. New York: Oxford University Press.

Matarazzo, J. D. (1981). David Wechsler (1896–1981). *American Psychologist*, 36(12), 1542–1543.

Wechsler, D. (1974a). Distinguished Professional Contribution Award for 1973. *American Psychologist*, 29(1), 44–47.

Wechsler, D. (1974b). *Selected Papers of David Wechsler*. With introductory material by Allen J. Edwards. New York: Academic Press.

Chapter 12

Katherine Cook Briggs and Isabel Briggs Myers

The indicator

Cook Briggs: January 3rd, 1875 to July 10th, 1968
Briggs Myers: October 18th, 1897 to May 5th, 1980

Isabel Briggs was born October 18th, 1897, to Lyman J. Briggs and Katharine Briggs in Columbia, South Carolina. She grew up in Washington where she was home schooled by her mother, whilst her father Lyman worked as a doctor.

In her heart, Katherine was an author. She had driving ambition, but her schooling had equipped her inadequately. She is quoted as saying that whoever had taught her to read and write had done so badly. At a time in history when it was still believed that excessive education would diminish a women's fertility, Katherine still managed to secure a college degree. She developed an academic career, studying geology with the emerging field of psychology, but then sacrificed it to support her husband's medical career. Katherine remained an avid reader and writer throughout her life, keeping a detailed diary of Isabel's development so that in the future they would, together, explore the ideas and ideals, the influences and the methods of their lives which would inevitably shape little Isabel's character. When baby Albert died at 18 months, Katherine's grief is recorded in this leather-bound diary. She failed in her later attempts to publish novel called *The Life of Suzanne*, but was able to turn her writings into a series of 300-word editorials in the *Ladies Home Journal* and some feature articles under the pseudonym, Elizabeth Childe. Her writing career was unorthodox for a woman of that time, but it was a grounding that enabled Katherine and her husband to evolve a new educational system for their surviving children, Isabel and Peter.

Katherine's bond with Isabel was intense. Isabel was, throughout her early life, her mother's project. Isabel's nurse was promptly dispatched after advising Katherine that the child's feet were ill matched and that they should never feed her hog meat as it would make the child abrasive. These attitudes were incompatible with Katherine's permissive child-rearing beliefs, attitudes which quickly changed when she discovered her infant child waving a carving knife around the kitchen and lessons in obedience commenced. Katherine's exhaustive efforts with Isabel meant that by the time Isabel was entering kindergarten she could read. Following a bout of measles, however, Isabel was not returned to school and remained at home.

Public school education was, to Katherine, plagued by rules, definitions, drill, confusion and haste. Katherine also had a very modern philosophy that the knowledge that a child has, does not make them clever. Rather, it is their attitude to what they do not know that supports their intelligence. Katherine wanted to encourage curiosity in Isabela so that she would try out her own ideas about her education without interference. Nobody was needed to intercede between the knowledge seeker and where the knowledge existed. Isabel's school days were not fixed or planned, there was a great deal of independent reading, arithmetic and writing. By the age of seven, Isabel had kept a sophisticated log of a month-long journey to Costa Rica, by the age of eight she was learning German, Latin, French and studying classics such as Cicero and Virgil.

Katherine's writing success was soon followed by Isabel who, from the age of 14, began submitting editorials and letters to magazines. These were mostly muses on the irritations of school life, poems and short stories. The only subject Isabel did not seem to thrive at was music, but she was partial to some dancing, particularly throughout her college years. Despite her mother's close supervision, Isabel was turning into a well-socialised young woman with an array of hobbies and interests. By her pre-college years, she was managing the attentions of five men, before she met Clarence Gates Myers at the co-educational institution Swarthmore College. Clarence, known to his friends as 'Chief', was to Isabel splendid 'on strength and control and the moral code' (IMB to KCB letters 16th December, 1915, cited in Saunders, 1991, p.29). The couple soon became 'secretly engaged' but the imminent threat of conscription to join the fighting in Europe, triggered Chief into making an application to the army aviation service. Draft would give no such choice. The couple publicly announced their engagement and while they awaited Chief's orders, they returned to study. Isabel remained in Swarthmore, but Chief went to Princeton, which had placed its resources at the disposal of the government to support the war effort. Chief went on to train as a bomber pilot. Eventually the couple secured a brief window of time in which to marry and Isabel became a war bride on June 17th, 1918.

Katherine began to struggle in 'letting go' of Isabel. She had been a formidable influence in her life, but her affections were now usurped by Chief. In an attempt to continue to exert influence, Katherine began to encourage Chief to write to her and then, supply her daily letters of advice to Isabel. This constant stream of advice was causing strain on the relationships between Chief, Isabel and Katherine and the young couple soon started to create more distance. This move did not, however, prevent detailed lifestyle comments arriving from mother.

Regardless of her mother's continued intrusion, Isabel returned home to her mother's care for the birth of her first child. This was a solid decision because her baby boy was delivered still-born. This tragedy was followed by the premature birth and death of her second child; a little girl. Chief, clumsily, wired her a message: 'third time is a charm' (CGM to KCB telegram July 8th, 1924, cited in Saunders, 1991, p.74). The couple finally returned to their now new Swarthmore home where Isabel eventually gave birth to a healthy boy in April 1926. 'Peter-baby' was joined the following year by baby Isabel-Ann.

Whilst Isabel was growing her family, the avid reader Katherine had begun directing her attention back to her own education. She started by trying to analyse and understand the basic components of human behaviour by keeping notes on the characters she had read about, such as Benjamin Franklin, General William T. Sherman, Henry Adams (autobiographical accounts of women were a rarity). Then in 1923 she came across Carl Gustav Jung's Psychological Type and is alleged to have said 'this is it'.

Katherine's attempts at turning her ideas into fiction were however failing. She could find no publisher prepared to take on her works which were stories untangling the secrets of the psyche but relied so heavily on the work of Jung and Freud that they were simply over the heads of the average reader. It was Isabel who was to rise to acclaim as an author. In 1928, in response to a newspaper advertisement, Isabel wrote in the space of 5 months, her first manuscript. This book won several literacy prizes, eventually leading to further books and work as a playwright. Katherine never wrote fiction again but something else had piqued her interest.

In 1926 *The New Republic* ran an article which suggested how personality type could be used both for profit and for pleasure. This was just before the great stock market crash of 1929 and by 1931 America was amid the Great Depression. Katherine's husband Lyman was unexpectedly promoted, his director died of a stroke at his desk and Lyman inherited a workforce that was inflicted with cutbacks and wage cuts. The difficulties of his position were further compounded by Isabel's belief that they could make money on the wayward stock market and they all lost heavily.

Following his publication of psychological types in 1937, Katherine had begun corresponding with Carl Jung. She finally met Jung at the Terry Lectures at Yale University and explained how she had, on reading his work, burned her own notes about the human psyche. Jung must have taken her reasonably seriously because he expressed disappointment at what she had done. He then proceeded to send her his seminar notes. Katherine continued to pursue her interest, gathering momentum in 1942 writing a *Reader's Digest* article entitled 'Fitting the Worker to the Job'.

Such measures had been in circulation since the early 1900s. Popularised by the Taylorism movement, the search for efficiency and a tidy solution for people sorting, but quality in industry was widely variable, if not completely fraudulent and prejudiced. As the world prepared for World War II, developing a code that could identify the human psyche, in particular the facets of resilience and personality constructs that would help make the world a safer place was becoming a national infatuation. Isabel discovered the Humm-Wadsworth Temperament Scale and hoped that the test would prove efficacious in helping match people to the right positions, but the tool was a failure. Katherine's response to her daughter was that she should develop her own tool.

The 'indicator' was born from Katherine and Isabel's ideas about Jung's personality types, funded by their family and driven by Isabel's passion. Never deterred by lack of knowledge on a subject, Isabel studied everything she could about statistics and psychology, she then drew up some preliminary questions in a forced-choice format and began testing increasingly larger samples of people. The basic premise was that 'the indicator' would identify the personality profile of its takers, profiles which would be differentiated on the dimensions of sensing versus intuition; thinking versus feeling; judging versus perceiving and introversion verses extraversion. These dimensions assigned 16 personality types, and it was intended that those types would further diverge from one another by the extent to which they were dominant or auxiliary drivers; one is the driver and one is the helper.

Jung was still in sporadic correspondence with Katherine and had historically expressed dislike of the theory and rationale behind the measurement device and he made it clear Katherine's work was in no way aligned to his. A letter does exist, signed by Jung, which seems to contradict his usual position. The letter states that the 'The Type-Indicator will prove to be of great help' (Jung letters to Briggs Myers, 1950, in Saunders, 1991, p.121) which would completely contradict his usual stance, that this type of measurement device was nothing but a parlour game. There is strong evidence, however, that the then 75-year-old Jung, was not in effect writing his own letters and that the content represents little more than the platitudes of his secretary Marie-Jeanne Schmid. It is not difficult to imagine that this was the encouragement that Isabel needed.

In 1956, the Educational Testing Service's (EAS) interest was piqued. They were already the publisher of the Standardised Assessment Tests (SATs) that were being implemented for college admission. The SATs were highly profitable, and the indicator offered an opportunity for expansion into personality and, by 1962, the newly titled 'Myers-Briggs Indicator' was being printed for research purposes. The publishing staff, however, were less enthusiastic, deriding the test as unscientific rubbish. The supporting manual was produced by a young test developer, Larry Stricker, and contained a harsh critique of the test. This was not something that Isabel was going to passively accept, and she penned the trademark of the academic feud; a 24-page missive to the publishing house and filed the manual in a folder labelled 'Larry Stricker, Damn him'.

Then, much the way as her mother had helpfully supplied a constant stream of advice, Isabel began to make daily (and nightly) visits to the publishing offices in a bid to gather evidence to support the re-writing of the manual. Fuelled by what she described as the perfect energy drink (milk, yeast and Hershey bar), victory was assured. Stricker was replaced and a new version of the manual was finally published in 1962. This achievement is even more remarkable when we consider that from 1956 Isabel was fighting a malignant tumour in her lymph glands, even delaying surgery so that she could give a symposium.

Isabel had turned into a formidable character. The EAS was, however, losing money on the project and staff, and those who did not ask for the day off or hide when Isabel was in the office, were voicing discord with her nocturnal reconnaissance missions. At the end of 1965 EAS terminated any consulting arrangements with Isabel and, after 10 years of losses, they ceased publication in 1975.

Isabel's test was in danger, but there were greater threats. In 1963 Isabel's father Lyman died and Katherine died two years later. Isabel's cancer returned in 1972 and her children were in crisis. Peter and his wife Betty were divorcing, and her daughter Ann was embroiled in an affair with a college professor. Isabel and Chief were working hard to support Ann and her children, when Ann suddenly died from a pulmonary embolism. The death of a child is a grief like no other. Seventy years earlier, in her leather-bound book, Katherine Briggs had written of Albert to Isabel:

> If sorrow comes to you, my little girl, and I should not be there to help you bear it, remember this, the message from my grief to yours. Bereavement and sorrow are as much a part of life as birth and joy.
>
> (July 19th, 1901 in Saunders, 1991, p.8)

Isabel would later respond to her mother, as she wrote a 'Credo for Living' and her search for meaning and comfort in God.

In 1975, at the age of 78, Isabel's clashes with EAS were at an end. The Myers-Briggs Type Indicator, which had started as a family affair, became the venture of Consulting Psychologists Press who would turn it into one of the most well-known personality measures in the world. Isabel spent the final years of her life continuing to support and promote her work and she died from cancer on May 5th, 1980.

Based on Jungian theory, the term 'test' is frequently associated with the Myers-Briggs Type Indicator (MBTI), but the MBTI is an indicator of personality and not a test per se. The confusion about what the MBTI does and does not do has often led to allegations of poor psychometric validity, misuse, misunderstanding and the scientific and academic community being reluctant to adopt the test in mainstream research. For example, publications citing the MBTI have progressively fallen since 2017, while trait measures such as Costa and McCrea's 'Big 5' continue to rise. The disparity in application is puzzling, given that it has been known for some time that there is significant overlap between the two measures (Furnham, 1996). The British Psychological Society Testing Centre, who offer independent reviews of psychometric tests, also provides a favourable account of the measures.

Type measures such as the MBTI have clearly fallen out of popularity in mainstream psychological research. They do, however, appear in various research methodologies 'testing' personality in diverse areas such as outcomes in heart failure patients (Gilotra et al., 2015), managerial cognitive styles (Armstrong et al., 2012) and school achievement (Munteanu et al., 2011).

Major works

Myers, I. B. (1962a). Inferences as to the dichotomous nature of Jung's types, from the shape of regressions of dependent-variables upon Myers-Briggs Type Indicator Scores. *American Psychologist*, 17(6), 364.

Myers, I. B. (1962b). *The Myers-Briggs Type Indicators*. Princeton, NJ: Educational Testing Service.

Myers, I. B. (1964). *Relation of Medical Students' Psychological Type to Their Specialties Twelve Years Later*. Gainesville, FL: Centre for Applications of Psychological Type.

Myers, I. B. (1974). *Type and Teamwork*. Gainesville, FL: Center for Applications of Psychological Type.

Myers, I. B. (1976). *Introduction IO Type*. Gainesville, FL: Center for Applications of Psychological Type.

Myers, I. B. (1977). *The Myers-Briggs Type Indicator: Supplementary Manual*. Palo Alto, CA: Consulting Psychologists Press.

Myers, I. B., & Myers, P. B. (1980). *Gifts Differing: Understanding Personality Type*. Palo Alto, CA: Consulting Psychologists Press.

Bibliography

Armstrong, S. J., Cools, E., & Sadler-Smith, E. (2012). Role of Cognitive Styles in Business and Management: Reviewing 40 Years of Research. *International Journal of Management Reviews*, 14(3), 238–262.

Furnham, A. (1996). The big five versus the big four: The relationship between the Myers-Briggs Type Indicator (MBTI) and NEO-PI five factor model of personality. *Personality and Individual Differences*, 21(2), 303–307.

Gilotra, N. A., Okwuosa, I. S., Shpigel, A., Tamrat, R., Flowers, D., Skarupski, K., ... Russell, S. D. (2015). Myers Briggs Type Indicator and Outcomes in Heart Failure Patients. *Journal of Cardiac Failure*, 21(8), S131.

Munteanu, A., Costea, I., & Palo⊠, R. (2011). Relationships between Academic Achievement and Personality Dynamics during Adolescence. *South African Journal of Psychology*, 41(4), 552–561.

Saunders, F. W. (1991). *Katherine and Isabel: Mother's Light, Daughters Journey*. Palo Alto, CA: Consulting Psychologists Press.

Chapter 13

John Carlyle Raven
Elegant design

June 28th, 1902 to August, 10th 1970

John Carlyle Raven was born in Islington, London in 1902 to John Raven, an umbrella maker, and Jane Elizabeth Martin. The couple were married in St Matthew's Church in Westminster in 1894 and went on two have three children: Phoebe Jane, Sara Edith and John Carlyle. We know very little about John's early life other than he struggled at school with dyslexia. His work was always marked highly for creativity and content, but the presentation was always poor, as such his teachers discouraged further academic study.

John Carlyle disagreed with this assessment of his future, but his father died prematurely in 1923, aged 54, leaving John with the task of providing for his older sisters and mother. To resolve this problem, John worked to convert the rooms in their Islington home into rooms for lodgers and as luck would have it, one of the lodgers married his sister. This happy event at least partially releasing him from family responsibility, John took up a position as a teacher at St. Probus School in Salisbury (1923), and he soon made Assistant District Commissioner. In 1928 the family was stabilised to the point that he could start a formal education in psychology with Francis Aveling at Kings College, London. Even as a postgraduate, John Carlyle had little contact with Aveling. As an undergraduate, he became friends with Charles Spearman who introduced him to the geneticist and mathematician Lionel Penrose. Spearman asked John Carlyle to deliver a letter to Aveling and John sold himself instead. Lionel needed an assistant to help him in the investigation of mental deficiency and, in 1928, John agreed to join his team at the Royal Eastern Counties Institution in Colchester.

Penrose's exploration into the genetic and environmental determinants of mental defect relied mostly on the Stanford-Binet test of intelligence and required extensive field work across East Anglia testing children and adults in homes, schools and in workplaces. John struggled both with the cumbersome nature of the test and the testing constraints which included noise, time pressure and the management of parents who were always keen to assist their child. He was unconvinced about the theoretical basis behind the test which lumped diverse constructs together making the results nearly impossible to interpret. The sub-scales were too short to be reliable and the overall score disguised individual strengths and weaknesses. John Carlyle also disagreed with the testing movement. It was not, he argued, the job of psychologists to measure and put people right; rather psychologists ought to be attempting to understand people and their problems.

When the work was completed at Colchester, he set about devising a different method of psychological measurement that would be more theoretically based and easier to administer and score. A test was needed that could measure intelligence throughout the life course, from early years to older adults.

To compensate for his struggles with the written word, John also had a strong preference for diagrams over words, peppering his publications with figures that have continued to fascinate students of dyslexia for decades. With his preference for images and convinced by Spearman's two-factor model of intelligence, John began developing a model which would assess the two factors of g identified by Spearman. His method for the test's development is set out in his Master's dissertation. The information is not so much a literature review in the usual sense, but a set of standards that the, then non-existent, test should meet.

He began working closely with Mary Elizabeth Wild who would later become his wife. The couple met accidentally when Elizabeth was looking for someone to help create a fountain in her garden, and a friend suggested that 'Raven would do that'. They married in Salisbury in 1923 and went on to have three sons together, John Jr, Barton and Martin. John's mother Jane Elizabeth also lived with the family in their new home in Tendring, Essex until her death.

Mary was also a key supporter of John, helping him improve the quality of his writing, which was challenged by his dyslexia. Then with a grant from the Darwin Trust, he and his wife set about developing a test based on the principles that John had set out in his Master's thesis. A test that would eventually measure the desire and the ability of individuals to make sense of 'booming, buzzing, confusion' (Raven, 2008, p.22) and make meaning; what he termed 'eductive' ability.

John Carlyle Raven produced the first experimental version of his Raven's Progressive Matrices test in 1936, publishing in 1938. The test methodology applies what is now known as Item Response Theory and analysis, which enabled researchers to improve the analysis of test results by obtaining a measure between an individual's performance on a given and that item's level of difficulty relative to the items on the test. There were two principal components to Raven's theoretical model. First, the eductive aspect of mental ability, which relates to making meaning and gaining insights from disparate pieces of information. For example, to master language, children need to progress from 'mark making' through to the complex integration of motor skills coordination, then learning and integrating different sounds and shapes. Second, the reproductive aspect of mental behaviour relates to mastery, being competent at recalling and reproducing information. The two are interactives; the ability to absorb information in the first place is dependent on being able to manage ambiguity and confusion. Test-takers would be required to integrate the ambiguous, to make meaning, but also apply sets of rules which increased in difficulty. The processes involved in problem-solving were cumulative, demonstrating that individuals with higher intelligence scores have more capacity to build on previous information, which extended their performance. Intelligence was thus a continuous process, rather than a sum on a particular test.

In 1939, John Carlyle was awarded Fellowship at the London Child Guidance Clinic and became a psychologist to the Child Guidance Council, but as war was declared against Europe, the Raven family moved out of central London and into Larkspur cottage near Elmstead in Essex. Larkspur had no electricity, gas, nor running water, but ever the outdoor enthusiast, John Carlyle set about creating a smallholding to support the family. The farm was an escape not only from the dangers of London but also the impracticalities of war.

At a time when the British Government was encouraging families that it was the patriotic thing to do to put down their beloved pets (countless pets were humanely destroyed, or just thrown in canals) the Carlyle family experienced a new world of chickens, goats and rabbits; hundreds of rabbits in different colours which would later become hats, gloves and bed covers. John, Barton and Martin, aged between three and seven, would walk the billy goats down the cottage lane each day, tethering them to where the sweet grass grew. Until one day, to their horror, the sweet green grass was replaced by anti-aircraft guns. The tranquil Larkspur was right under the German flight path. The Luftwaffe, running short on aviation fuel, would regularly off-load their cargo in the fields around their cottage. Bombs would fall so close that the fields became peppered with craters. His son, John, recalls the stench of burning flesh when they hit the nearby cattle barn.

John Carlyle was a Quaker. On the grounds of faith, Quakers were known conscientious objectors but for John Carlyle, his objections were based on his convictions that war removed autonomy and that individuals followed orders without rational thought. He was not prepared to put himself in a situation where this could happen, so he began to direct his attention towards using his professional skills to support the war effort. He could apply his skills and knowledge by studying the impact of stress and injury on human behaviour at the London Child Guidance Clinic and joining the Mill Hill emergency hospital team.

Whilst working with the sick and injured John Carlyle also began to collect additional test data that would enable him to predict success on army training courses. He began directing experiments for the Royal Army Medical Corps at Beckett's Park, in Leeds. Four thousand troops were tested in the first ever large-scale psychological investigation and testing of British Army troops. The project was a success. The test's puzzle-solving nature overcame the challenges of numeracy and literacy in the troops, and the absence of language enabled the test to be used across the world. Raven's Progressive Matrices became the army's standard psychological test, and Hans Eysenck later used this work as an example to evidence that a single psychological test could provide as much information about candidates as an assessment centre.

In 1944, one year before the war ended, John Carlyle moved his family to Dumfries in Scotland to work at the psychological department of the Crichton Royal Institution which was a mental hospital. The family lived in a roomy lodge house in the grounds of the hospital, but gradually the boys and their father constructed a three-roomed cabin for the boys. Surprised guests would often also find themselves accommodated there.

In Dumfries, John Carlyle split his time between his children, his research interests and clinical work. He continued to seek ways of thinking about and assessing the broader application of individual differences, criticising the construct of personality and lobbying psychologists and psychometricians to change their models. The department at Crichton was not a clinical department. It was largely focused on research, and so in order to create distance between the medical model, or indeed becoming drawn into clinical work, Raven had the physical department shifted into the centre of town.

As Hans Eysenck had started his anti-Freudian offensive, attacking the creditability of psychoanalysis and all who sailed in her and key psychologists at the Maudsley and Tavistock took their feud to the British Psychological Society, Raven began his own gentler offensive. Drawing on his training in the sciences, psychometrics, therapy and an appreciation of the works of George Kelly, in an attempt to reduce polarisation, he began reminding psychologists of their role as clinicians:

> It is not the clinical psychologist's function to put other people right, either by treating them therapeutically or by fitting them into appropriate social situations. By trying to understand people we also change them; at the same time, if we try to change people or even think their conduct is pathological, we are less likely to understand them. For this reason, a clinical psychologist who desires not only to understand people but also to alter them is not only in danger of being pretentious; as a psychologist, he is less likely to become successful.
>
> (Raven, 1950, cited in Raven & Raven, 2019, p.15)

In response, the board began to seek out someone who would deliberately secure this distinctive feature of psychology at Crichton. While John Carlyle Raven carried out minimal work to demonstrate that Spearman's model could be used to understand the nature of eductive ability, this work was carried on after his death by his son John Jr.

John Carlyle Raven retired in May 1964, but his retirement was brief, he died on August 10th, 1970 aged 68, he was working in his beloved garden. His wife had died two years previous. She had been suffering from a brain tumour since 1960. John Carlyle had spent several years caring for her, driving her back and forwards from

Edinburgh for brain surgery and caring for her in-between. John Carlyle had a brief year of happiness when he married Irene Hunter, his hospital housekeeper. The two would often plot together to accommodate visiting students, by concealing empty beds from NHS inspectors.

John Carlyle's work on item-response theory created a paradigm shift in testing that went on to influence leading statisticians such as Lord and Novick and Georg Rasch. In addition to his many contributions to psychological testing, John Carlyle was also a keen naturalist, particularly in human ecology. His son John, who carried on the work of his father, believes that the most pervasive motivation in John Carlyle's life was elegant design. He was motivated not only to create through the Progressive Matrices test, but also through the recreation of evolving rock gardens. A fascination which continued until his death.

Responses to Raven's test were initially cool, but following acceptance by the armed forces, the test soon gained widespread adoption throughout the world. Its cultural neutrality has driven educational systems in Europe, Russia, Asia and South America to embrace Raven's Progressive Matrices.

Major works

Raven, J. C. (1936). Mental Tests Used in Genetic Studies: The Performances of Related Individuals in Tests Mainly Educative and Mainly Reproductive. MSc Thesis, University of London.

Raven, J. C. (1948). The comparative assessment of intellectual ability. *British Journal of Psychology*, 39, 1219.

Raven, J. C. (1950). What is clinical psychology? *Bulletin of the British Psychological Society*, January, 14.

Bibliography

Raven, J. (1997). Scotland's Greatest Psychologist: J. C. Raven and Contemporary Psychology. *Bulletin* (Newsletter of the Scottish Branch of the British Psychological Society), June, 12–17.

Raven, J. (2000): The Raven's Progressive Matrices: Change and stability over culture and time, *Cognitive Psychology*, 41(1), 1–48.

For a full list of Raven's work and other related resources, John Carlyle's son has put together resources at Eye on Society. Preparation of this article was greatly assisted by material supplied by Professor

John Raven and his wife and incorporated into their article entitled 'John Carlyle Raven and his Legacy'. Raven, J., & Raven, J. (2019). John Carlyle Raven 1902–1970. http://eyeonsociety.co.uk/resources/ J-C-Raven-Biography.pdf, preparation of which was precipitated by my requests.

Chapter 14

Starke Rosecrans Hathaway

The Minnesota normals

August 22nd, 1903 to July 4th, 1984

Martin Walter Hathaway and Bertha Belle Rosecrans married in the Shaker Settlement in Union Village, Darby County, Ohio in 1900. Three years later they had moved six hours north to Central Lake Michigan where Starke Rosecrans was born before they moved south again to the industrial town of Marysville where Martin could obtain work as a labourer at the Every Day Milk Plant (later bought over by Nestle).

In this heavily industrialised town, Starke grew up around machinery, and he loved to tinker. When he was eight years old, his family let him set up his own workshop in a crate in the backyard. Here he could experiment with electronic equipment, building everything from bicycles to electronic circuit boards. This passion stayed with him throughout his life. As an adult, he would invent a device that would automatically open his garage door. He fitted a rain detection device to his patio awning; he created his own television set and even made jewellery. When the University of Minnesota was improving its psychiatric facility to reduce injury and suicide, Starke constructed a complex system of buzzers and sound-carrying conduits that would enable staff to summon emergency help.

At high school, Starke set up the boys' science club, which brought together local kids once a week to study Elisha Gray's 1900 book *Electricity and Magnetism*. This was an exciting time for children interested in science; rural Ohio was growing fast, and electricity and telephone lines were reaching the rural communities. Gray had also been embroiled in a drawn-out patent war with Alexander Graham Bell. They had both invented the telephone independently and had both lodged their patents on the same day, Bell actually filed his patent later than Gray and there were accusations of fraud, theft and bribes which were still being revived and circulated for some time after Gray's death. Elisha Gray's book is still in press today.

Starke enrolled in Ohio University to study electrical engineering but quickly changed his major to focus on mathematics and psychology. He was particularly interested in the physiological aspects of psychology, and this provided him with the opportunity to set up a workshop dedicated to the development of experimental apparatus which included the psychogalvanometer, which was the forerunner to polygraph/lie detecting equipment, and used it to assist the local law enforcement on a murder case. By 1926 Starke had become President of the Psychology Club. The organisation aimed to promote research within the student body and membership was offered to those who had obtained advance standing within the Ohio psychology department.

Stark graduated in 1928 with a Master's degree from Ohio State in Psychology and began making enough money from his inventions to marry Virginia Riddle. Two years later he accepted an Assistant Professor position at the University of Minnesota. Minnesota was establishing itself as a centre for applied psychology, particularly behaviourism. Starke spent his entire career at Minnesota, initially teaching anatomy and studying neurophysiology, gaining his PhD in 1932. He was promoted to Assistant Professor in 1937, then full professor in 1947.

Starke is described as someone who was always deeply engaged in thinking about something 'else'. A serious man, keenly intelligent, Starke would frequently forget the names of his students and colleagues, he would wear shoes that didn't match, forget to put a coat on in the freezing Minnesota winters and often turn up to class covered in grease and oil from his inventions. He was also fiercely independent and sceptical of authority.

It was while working in the University's psychiatric department that Starke had the realisation that psychology was not really considered to provide anything of use to the treatment of mental health. He realised that his peers in psychiatry were seldom interested in a psychological approach. The medics and psychiatrists were not interested in his insights. The best tools he had to offer were crude personality and intelligence tests, but neither did he feel that medicine and psychiatry had much to offer. The best options were highly dangerous insulin coma therapy or electroshock treatment.

One pressing problem was that there was no systematic system for mental illness classification and anything that did exist was wholly inadequate, with questions that elicited superficial responses, inaccurate diagnoses and could not control for the very human tendency not to be completely honest with the test administrator.

Starke joined forces with the neuropsychologist J. Charnley McKinley, and they began to collaborate, trawling the scientific literature and other personality tests, documenting the variety of signs and symptoms of mental illness. When they finally settled on a cluster of test items, they did something which had never been done before; they let the test-takers decide. Hathaway and McKinley did not assume that they knew what abnormal was; instead, the data would speak for itself. This was a revolutionary idea. For example, test items designed to tap mental illness, in tests such as the Bernreuter Personality Inventory had frequently been found to be associated with normal behaviour rather than mental illness. For Hathaway and McKinley, the data should be able to speak for itself.

Breakthroughs in statistical analysis, which enabled the handling of large datasets, had triggered the idea of the comparative norm. Abnormality could be better explored as statistical infrequency, but to understand what was infrequent it was first necessary to fully understand what the full range of normal behaviour was. The approach was a-theoretical in nature, and the test itself would be free from the prevailing theories of mental health and psychiatry of that time. The patients, however, were not free of those dogmas and were labelled and treated accordingly. A reality which would have undoubtedly influenced the way in which they thought about themselves and explained their symptoms.

While Hathaway had unfettered access to abnormal populations, normal participants were more problematic, until he had the idea to use the families of those patients attending the psychiatric clinic. What was to come about, was a data set that would define normality for the decades to come.

Hathaway's population were all white. Most were of Scandinavian Protestant descent, married with children who were either farmers, blue-collar workers or housewives and educated, on average, to age 14. They became known as the Minnesota Normals. Once he had the data from the 'normals' and the 'abnormals' in place, the question items that discriminated between each of the groups could be identified.

The first test, published in 1943, was an odd mix of test items that probed (at McKinley's insistence) medical problems: 'I have never had any black, tarry-looking bowel movements'; 'once a week, or more, I suddenly get hot all over for no reason'. Sexual preferences and concerns, 'there is something wrong with my sex organs', 'when I get bored, I like to stir up some excitement', as well as items on religion and the devil, and questions that measured normal behaviour and others that seemed wholly judgemental, if not in fact offensive. The test contained 566 true-false items and it took almost an hour to complete. Rather than commit an answer to writing, test-takers would sort the questions into true and false piles. Hathaway had the idea that removing any requirements to commit an answer to paper, would encourage users to respond more honestly. It also contained the first deception scale, a series of times that would indicate if the user was faking good on their test responses (responding to questions in ways that they feel will best serve their interests). The Minnesota Multiphasic Personality Inventory (MMPI) was cumbersome but revolutionary.

After initially struggling to secure a publishing agreement for the test, the Minnesota Press agreed to co-publish. McKinley and Hathaway were required to find a sponsor to provide 50 per cent of the funds. At a time when mental health practitioners were keen to move away from the vagaries of the Rorschach inkblot test, the MMPI offered new prospects for more reliable diagnosis across a range of psychopathological problems. The tests' following quickly grew and by mid-century they were being written about in *Time Magazine*. The market for the MMPI began to exceed supply. The Minnesota Press could not keep up, and by 1947 a new publisher had to be found. The Psychological Corporation took over publication of what had become the world's most widely used psychological test.

McKinley, however, was ill. He suffered a stroke in 1946, becoming partially disabled. Hathaway and McKinley had an agreement that if anything happened to either of them, they would facilitate each other's suicide. Starke did not have the heart to go through with it, so McKinley tried, and failed, to cut his own throat. McKinley died four years later from another stroke.

The test was also not doing so well. The predicted clear categories that Hathaway and McKinley had expected to see from the data were becoming less evident. The data was suggesting that those with psychiatric problems were elevated on several scales, but so were those considered to be normal. Hathaway was becoming increasingly reluctant to discuss the test. He disapproved of the testing culture that was forming around it. His former students, still enthusiastic about the test, suggested that these patterns were indicative of complex syndromes. Individuals could be more than the sum of a cluster of specific items, rather what the test was doing was profiling a combination of conditions that the individual in question was experiencing. These were important ideas which served to bring psychologists, psychiatrists and neurologists closer together.

The test continued to gather momentum with a new population. Before McKinley's death, he and Hathaway had already begun discussing the social applications of the test. Organisations were becoming increasingly interested in the possibility that the MMPI could be used to identify personality traits in the normal population, screening for jobs, applied in court cases, used for army recruitment and even in high schools. A test initially designed to pinpoint extremes in behaviour was being applied in areas where behaviour varied in much more subtle ways. To expedite the process, complex diagnostic dimensions were reduced to Scale 1, Scale 2 and so on. The new test barely resembled its parent, and it was applied in unsystematic and heavy-handed ways.

During the mid-1950s, with McCarthyism finally coming to an end, an argument ensued between the testing movement and the American government. The public, weary of invasive scrutiny, were rejecting the conformity that such tests imposed on its citizens. The test was considered at best intrusive, at worst immoral. A series of correctional hearings followed with the intention of banning or at least severely limiting the use of psychological tests in government.

The testers fought back, implying the ignorance of those in opposition, that their rejection of the test was merely evidence of underlying maladaptive personality constructs. Hathaway, who was normally quiet on the subject, wrote an impassioned letter insisting that his motivations were not to pry into the lives of individuals. His work was serious science, and this explained why it was not possible to alter in any way any of the test items. Decades of data would be rendered useless.

The testers won the battle and the argument dissipated. By the 1990s the MMPI and its occupational hybrids were being used by many major organisations as a principal method of selection and development. A series of successful lawsuits followed against organisations that used the MMPI and other intrusive personality tests, but the pay-out, which in cases was in the millions, did little to curb testing fever. Hathaway actively discouraged the use of his test in such contexts, calling it a personality cult. The test he had developed was becoming a 'Stone Age axe', and Starke became dismayed that psychology had failed to progress in this area, and he began to wonder if true assessment of personality was possible at all.

Criticisms about the blind empiricism behind the MMPI are difficult to counter, but Hathaway was a pioneer and a visionary. He was the first to construct a systematic measurement process and the first comprehensive, structured interview, which was self-directed, self-administered, the nature of which made it difficult for the test administrator to influence the result.

Starke Hathaway held the position of Director at the division of clinical psychology with the University of Minnesota medical school from 1951 until his retirement in 1970. Outside of the development of the MMPI, he had an accomplished career in clinical psychology and deviant behaviour and often lamented that interest in the MMPI overshadowed his other work. He died on July 4th, 1984 after a long illness.

Major works

Hathaway, S. R. (1939). The Personality Inventory as an aid in the diagnosis of psychopathic inferiors. *Journal of Consulting Psychology*, 3, 112–117.

Hathaway, S. R. (1942). *Physiological Psychology*. New York and London: D. Appleton Century Co.

Hathaway, S. R. (1964). MMPI: Professional use by professional people. *American Psychologist*, 19, 204–211.

Hathaway, S. R., & J. C. McKinley. (1940). A multiphasic personality schedule: I. Construction of the schedule. *Journal of Psychology*, 10, 249–254.

Chapter 15

Raymond Bernard Cattell

Psychology: 'describing things
which everyone knows in language
which no one understands'

March 20th, 1905 to February 2nd, 1998

Raymond Bernard Cattell was born in Hill Top, Staffordshire, England, on March 20th, 1905 to Alfred Earnest Cattell and Mary Field. His family were second-generation owners of several manufacturing plants in the United Kingdom. They were mechanical engineers and the inventors of engines and automobiles, World War II military equipment and the new internal combustion engine. Raymond was the second of three sons, and the family moved to the seaside town of Torquay in Devonshire when he was 6 years old, triggering a love of the sea that would last a lifetime. Later in his life Cattell would publish a personal account of his sailing experiences around the coastline and estuaries of Devon.

Raymond quickly demonstrated an aptitude for literature and science. By the age of ten he was reading H. G. Wells and Arthur Conan Doyle. His academic competence put him in conflict with his less able brother, but the problem was soon resolved when Raymond won a scholarship to attend Torquay Boys' Grammar School and his brother was moved to a school which could address his education outside of forthright academic study. Raymond's talent developed quickly in this new environment and he eventually became the first in his family to pass the university entrance examination to study chemistry at Kings College London. Cattell graduated in 1924 at the age of 19 with a first-class degree in physics and chemistry. Always open to the works and ideas of others, Cattell browsed far outside of his science, attending the lectures of Bertrand Russell, H. G. Wells and Aldous Huxley, who Cattell said, converted him to vegetarianism for almost 2 years.

The works of Sir Cyril Burt and of Francis Galton and their arguments to secure a better future for mankind, merged with the destructive aftermath of World War I, influenced Cattell's decision to use the new science of psychology to solve human problems and he began studying for a doctorate in psychology with the psychologist and priest Francis Aveling. His Ph.D was undertaken to resolve problems raised by Spearman's Principles of Cognition and the nature of mental energy. Cattell was closely involved in developing a new factor method to further study of Spearman's theory of general intelligence, work which would eventually lead to an invitation to work at Thorndike's lab at Columbia University.

Following the successful completion of his PhD in 1929, Cattell secured a post at Exeter University and his first son Herry was born to his childhood sweetheart Monica Rogers. Cattell was studying for an MA in education at the time, and soon moved to Leicester to organise the development of one of England's first child guidance clinics. He was awarded a Darwin Fellowship from the Eugenics Society which enabled him to conduct research into declining population intelligence. During these productive years, Cattell finally published his book *Under Sail Through Red Devon* (1937), however, unable to tolerate his consistent neglect, his wife left him after only four years.

Cattell's MA work was his first systematic attempt to articulate what would become the lynch-pin of his career, his ideas on the structure and function of personality, but it was his work on intelligence which captured the notice of Edward Thorndike and in 1937 Thorndike offered him a research position at Columbia University. The following year, 1938, he became the G. Stanley Hall Professor at Clark University, Massachusetts, which was a role primarily aimed at the study of developmental psychology.

Clark was another disappointment for Cattell. Depression ensued, largely because he felt there were limited opportunities to research. In 1941, Cattell moved to Harvard to work with Gordon Allport and Henry Murray on more serious personality research but was again disappointed. He and Allport spoke a different personality language which was near impossible to reconcile. World War II finally settled Cattell's career path; he was invited to work on psychological measurement issues for selection purposes, he caught the attention of the American Psychological Association President Herbert Woodrow and he was invited to occupy a new professorship at the University of Illinois which had the first electronic computer owned by an educational institution.

Soon after joining the faculty at Illinois, Cattell met and married the mathematician Karen Schuettler who would become instrumental in supporting him with the statistical aspects of his work. Karen and Raymond went on to have three daughters (Mary, Heather and Elaine-Devon) and a son (Roderic). The marriage ended in 1980.

At Illinois, Cattel would complete the most advanced large-scale factor analyses of his career. With his wife, he founded the Laboratory of Personality Assessment and Group Behaviour and the commercially successful Institute for Personality and Ability Testing. Cattell remained at Illinois until 1973, only leaving at the mandatory retirement age. He continued to write up results from research projects after retirement, eventually moving to Hawaii, which enabled him to pursue his love of sailing while working part-time advising at the University of Hawaii. The Hawaiian low-altitude environment also enabled Cattell to better manage his worsening heart condition.

The researcher and clinical psychologist, Heather Birkett, became Cattell's third wife. They moved to a lagoon near Oahu (meaning the gathering place) where Cattell continued to publish and sail until old age made navigation hazardous. Heather would become fundamental to the development and publication of the most robust of Cattell's tests the 16PF, which became the one of the most well-known personality tests in research, occupational selection and clinical practice for decades.

Throughout the course of Cattell's career, he authored 56 books, 500 journal articles and book chapters and 30 standardised testing manuals. He was doubtless one of the most significant psychologists of his time. Awards included the Educational Testing Service Award for distinguished service, the Behaviour Genetics Association Memorial Award for eminent research and the Distinguished Lifetime Contribution to Evaluation, Measurement and Statistics from the American Psychological Association. In 1997, the American Psychological Society named Cattell as their Gold Medal Award for a Life Time of Achievement in Psychological Science; an award which risked the destruction of his legacy. Cattell, now aged 92, was accused of supporting white supremacism and segregation.

Although an eminent and prolific psychologist, Cattell's style throughout his career was divisive and grandiose. He was so contentious, that a common belief was that the award was delayed until he was 92 years old because, by then, almost everyone he had ever offended would have died. Psychology is too difficult for psychologists, he would argue, teachers and researchers in psychology were mediocre. Cattell was also reluctant to discuss or acknowledge the works of others in his field, something noted by Arthur Jensen in his review of 'Intelligence' (Jensen, 1987). Cattell's book did not contain a single reference to developments reported in leading journals. His writing was also neologic and lacking in clarity, because he also shared an attitude with Hans Eysenck that re-writing was an encumbrance that distracted him from the next scientific endeavour. Cattell wrote faster than most people could read, but it did not always follow that this writing was good, "an assault on the English language", "an alphabet soup so thick a parenthesis drowns" (see Tucker, 2009, p.18) Perhaps seeing the irony in his own works Cattell described psychology as "describing things which everyone knows in language which no one understands" (1965, p.18). Cattell's study of intelligence had always been a branch from his study of personality. His interest largely focused on the idea that personality factors could explain why some individuals of similar intelligence, were unequal in achievement. The trait of perseverance offered fertile ground and he characterised individuals into racial categories, using hair and eye colour, stature and cephalic index, to analyse if there was a possible hereditary factor to perseverance. This work, much to his frustration, was largely ignored and he discontinued this line of investigation in favour of more empirically grounded research into personality.

He did, however, remain interested in defending the study of racial difference and saw nothing instrumentally wrong with segregation. Cattell went as far as attacking the integrity of those who were interested in the scientific study prejudice for attempting to introduce false values into science. Cattell published *Beyondism: Religion from Science* in 1972. The book described his socio-moral beliefs and his arguments against human rights, humanism and social justice because, he argued, they interfered with genetic progress. Group competition increased positive evolutionary progress. Those who were reluctant to investigate racial differences were 'ignoracists' and more dangerous than racists.

For Cattell, inter-race relationships were not the issue, instead what he called for was genetic management, where the genetically unproductive would not be permitted to have children. While not overtly racist in its central thesis, the book championed intellectual elitism even though his research into the decline of intelligence had been declared defunct by James R. Flynn. This was at a time when America was becoming a more culturally diverse and integrated nation. Unsurprisingly there was a limited inclination towards the kind of values, scientific and religious, that Cattell was advocating. Ignored by mainstream science, he began an association with *Mankind Quarterly*, a marginal anthropological journal which had been started in part as a response to UNESCO's declaration that race was not a biological construct. The journal's editorial team included a leading Nazi anthropologist and a British anthropologist who had contributed to the Nazi literature on racial hygiene. The outputs from the journal could be reasonably described as racist. Whether Cattell and the editorial team were completely ideologically compatible, remains to be seen. However, *Mankind Quarterly* gave Cattell an outlet for *Beyondism*, and he joined the editorial team, but he was now firmly tied to extremist arguments that attempted to apply scientific justification for racial policies.

Two weeks before the award ceremony, Barry A. Mehler, who was Director of the Institute for the Study of Academic Racism issued a press release about Cattell's lifetime commitment to eugenics and Cattell, who was mostly unknown to the public, became the surprise target of mainstream news. The Foundation delayed the award and began investigating the allegations.

Cattell attempted to address the misconceptions of his work in an open letter published in the *New York Times*. He attempted to clarify that his ideas had developed over the years and he now only believed in voluntary eugenics and that there was no valid evidence to support the argument that there were racial differences in intelligence. He attempted to correct the misconceptions and attacks against him by writing an open letter to the Association:

> I believe in equal opportunity for all individuals, and I abhor racism and discrimination based on race. Any other belief would be antithetical to my life's work. ...it is unfortunate that the APA announcement ... has brought misguided critics' statements a great deal of publicity.
>
> (Cattell, 1997)

Cattell was now in poor health, he withdrew his name from the nomination and died a few months later, on February 2nd, 1998, surrounded by his family and his two dogs.

Cattell was one of the first psychologists to use this 'mental model' framework to make some categorisations about the traits that make up personality. He defined personality as that which may predict what a person will do in each situation, and if we can better understand personality, we can then use it to investigate human behaviour.

Initially, Cattell started with thousands of traits, about 18,000 different trait terms in the English lexicon. This technique is known as the 'inductive-hypothetico-deductive spiral' approach, eventually condensing those vast numbers down into 16 primary traits using the statistical methods of factor analysis. The inductive approach is a cyclic process whereby theories that emerge from the data are used to generate testable hypotheses and then fed back into the cycle. At that time, it was possibly one of the first genuinely objective approaches to the measurement of personality because it broke away from what is sometimes referred to as the Barnum effect – the tendency for people to latch onto general descriptors about personality – towards the breaking of personality into useable workable constructs which were grounded in a theory of personality that could be used to interpret behaviour. This shifted thinking in the field away from 'grand theories' of personality as a state, changing over time, towards a nomothetic trait definition of personality as a constant characteristic that remains stable, more or less, over time.

In part to answer Gordon Allport's criticisms that Cattell was relying on statistical analysis over individual observations, he developed four key research methodologies; the P-technique whereby a person's scores on several measures are compared across different situations and over time; the Q-technique which correlated large numbers of different measures; the R-technique, whereby individuals are compared in terms of their scores or performance on many specific measures; and Differential-R which measures individuals on different occasions and examining changes and similarities.

Using his methodology, Cattell could present evidence for ability, temperament and dynamic traits, and surface and source traits. Ability relates to skills and intelligence, temperament to the emotional life and dynamic to the motivational life. Surface traits are the behaviours and attitudes that manifest from the source traits from which they are formed.

Despite Cattell's exhaustive efforts to map out an analytically derived model of personality, his refusal to acknowledge that personality could be represented in a smaller number of dimensions (despite identifying a three-factor model), combined with difficulties in replicating the 16-factor model, resulted in psychologists falling out of favour with the Cattellian personality measures towards a 'global' five-factor model. Cattell's extensive and pioneering work played an essential role in five-factor models of personality (Goldberg, 1990, 1993).

Major works

Cattell, R. B. (1950). The main personality factors in questionnaire material. *Journal of Social Psychology*, 31, 3–38.

Cattell, R. B. (1951). P-technique: A new method for analysing personal motivation. *Transactions of the New York Academy of Sciences*, 14, 29–34.

Cattell, R. B. (1965). *The Scientific Analysis of Personality*. Harmondsworth: Pelican.

Cattell, R. B. (1970). *Personality and Learning Theory*. London: Springer.

Cattell, R. B. (1971). *Abilities: Their Structure, Growth and Action*. Oxford: Houghton Mifflin.

Cattell, R. B. (1973). *Personality and Mood by Questionnaire*. Oxford: Jossey-Bass.

Cattell, R. B. (1982). *The Inheritance of Personality and Ability*. New York: Academic Press.

Cattell, R. B. (1987). *Intelligence: Its Structure, Growth and Action*. Amsterdam: North-Holland.

Horn, J. L., & Cattell, R. B. (1966). Refinement and test of the theory of fluid and crystallized intelligence. *Journal of Educational Psychology*, 57, 253–270.

Bibliography

Cattell, R. B. (1937). *Under Sail through Red Devon Being the Log of the Voyage of 'Sandpiper'*. London: Alexander Maclehose.

Cattell, R. B. (1987). *Beyondism: Religion from Science*. Westport, CT: Praeger Publishers.

Cattell, R. B. (1997). Open letter to the APA, December 13th. Available at: www.cattell.net/devon/openletter.htm

Goldberg, L. R. (1990). An alternative 'description of personality': The big-five factor structure. *Journal of Personality and Social Psychology*, 59, 6, 1216–1229.

Goldberg, L. R. (1993). The structure of phenotypic personality traits. *American Psychologist, 48*, 26–34.

Jensen, A. R. (1974). Review of abilities: Their structure, growth, and action, by R. B. Cattell. *American Journal of Psychology, 81*, 290–296.

Tucker, W. (2009). *The Cattell Controversy: Race, Science, and Ideology.* Chicago, IL: University of Illinois Press.

Chapter 16

George Alexander Kelly

A multi-dimensional man

April 28th, 1905 to March 6th, 1967

George Alexander was born in Kansas in the American Midwest to Theodore Vincent Kelly and Elfleda Merriam Perth. This was an impoverished community whose ideals were a double-distilled grafted product of American individualism, idealism and intolerance. Farming was as a struggle. Settlers had initially tried to replicate techniques developed in the East, growing corn and raising pigs, but these failed due to lack of water. Wheat eventually proved resilient, but export prices to Europe were widely unpredictable. Combined with tornadoes, blizzards, grasshopper plagues, hail, floods or dust bowl conditions, farmers were continually living on the knife edge of ruination.

George's parents were deeply religious. His mother, Elfleda, was born in Barbados where her father had taken the family after his trading sailing ship went out of business because of the introduction of steam. Elfleda's father became an Indian agent in South Dakota, and it was at the border town of Brown's Valley, that Elfleda met Theodore, a Presbyterian minister, who abandoned his religious career not long after George was born and took the family by covered wagon in search of free land in Colorado. This was one of many frequent moves which resulted in a sketchy, mostly home-schooled education.

No water could be found at their land in Colorado. The trip was a failure, and the family returned to Kansas. Fray Fransella argues that these early experiences helped forge the young George's imagination. If you could not imagine something in Kansas, then there would not be anything much at all. Vision and curiosity were the only way to see the world as full of possibilities. Something that George's grandfather was able to somewhat fuel with a ready supply of stories of sea adventures; the fingerprints of which can be seen in the many sailing analogies used throughout Kelly's extensive writings.

George compensated quickly for his poor education, first at the Quaker Institution, the Friends University in Wichita, followed by a year at Park College where George graduated with a degree in physics and mathematics; all the while supporting himself by teaching classes at an organisation such as the American Bankers Association or working with prospective American citizens. He briefly enrolled at the University of Minnesota for postgraduate study but found he could not pay the fees. Applying frantically for jobs, he found there were none to be had so he moved to Minneapolis and began working at three different schools. Finally, in 1927 George found a more stable teaching job at a local college which is where he met his future wife, the language teacher Gladys Thompson. Later in his career, his students would recount how he would delight in telling of his nomadic career as a penniless scholar.

With a little more security in place, George began studying as a postgraduate. Having developed his ancestor's wanderlust, he travelled to Edinburgh to study for a degree in Education, which he completed in 1930 before returning once again to Iowa to study for his PhD on reading and speech problems with Carl Seashore. After graduation, George promptly married Gladys and started seeking a position that would support family life. Gladys set about compiling the many papers he had already written in an attempt to encourage him to publish, and George began building their family home, quite literally with his bare hands.

Kelly finally started his psychological career at Fort Hays State University, and at a time when America was in the grip of the worst economic depression, started a clinic to support children in rural Kansas. It was here that George started to realise that the prevailing theories of Sigmund Freud, psychoanalysis and behaviourism, worked for some patients, but for many, they failed. He found behaviourism particularly objectionable, feeling that the approach reduced people to being nothing more than passive receptacles to life's events. The families he was supporting were paralysed by poverty and the prevailing theories did not offer any mechanism by which they could make sense of their world. Psychoanalysis was ignoring the obvious; people wanted to make sense of their lives so that they could develop the capacity to predict what might happen next, and what they could reasonably do about it. Patients needed something more constructive and relevant to the circumstances they were facing. To address this gap, George began experimenting with bi-polar adjectives to determine if there was something that he could use to help understand how people went about making decisions for their lives.

Before George could develop his thinking further, America entered World War II, and George Kelly moved to work for the Civil Aeronautics Administration on methods to select air cadets. He spent 5 years in the services, entering as an unknown, leaving with a series of publications which established him as a respected psychologist. After the war, George spent 12 months at the University of Maryland, before being appointed in 1945 to a professorship at Ohio State University. He stayed at Ohio as Director of Clinical Psychology until 1965, before his final move to Brandeis University as Distinguished Chair.

It was the publication of his personal construct theory in 1955, that changed George Kelly's life forever. He went from virtual obscurity to being one of the most widely known presences in psychology. He had initially been ambivalent about the publication of his work, believing his ideas too radical to be readily accepted. Kelly was passionately committed to his theory, believing that if it were indeed going to be accepted, it would have to survive the scrutiny of his British peers. For his theory to succeed the British would have to like it, and in 1961 he set about a world tour to convince the psychological community.

Kelly was open in identifying the philosophical works of Alfred Korzybski and the psychologist, educationalist and religious thinker John Dewey as influential to his theory of personal constructs. However, we can also see the fingerprint of Alfred Adler's work and his psychology of the 'undivided whole'. Personal construct theory is principally a theory of human action whereby the individual acts as a scientist, attempting to interpret and control the environment, thereby creating some sense of expectation about what will happen in the future. No two people share the same worldview. Each person's impressions are based on their experiences, their culture and values and for that reason, to effect change, it was vital to understand how the individual saw their world. Those different perspectives empowered individuals to explore and test out different ideas to solve their problems and could explain how people were capable of generating novel and creative solutions that were not simply based on past experiences.

This constructive alternativism moved psychological support from what was often merely a description of what was wrong with someone, or their life, and the belief that there was only one way of behaving, towards the capacity of patients be an agent of one's destiny. Personality development within construct theory was achieved through the development of systems that support knowledge development about the world. We use these constructs to make sense and make decisions when the world bombards us with information and events. The more commonality there is between our personal constructs, the easier it is for us to predict our behaviour and make sense of the behaviours of others. We continually interpret and reinterpret the world until we reach the most accurate perception possible. During infancy and adolescence this system is forming, there is little certainty about the world and the possibilities afforded to us. As we develop experience of the world, we are able to weed out inappropriate options and grow more confident of options most likely to succeed. Through this dynamic process we test out and reject our constructs of the world, our constructs become more focused until we can take control of situations and maximise our chances of the desired outcome. For Kelly, your personality is your personal construct, and personal construct theory is as much a philosophy as a psychological theory.

The theory had significant implications for clinical psychology because it provided the psychologist release from the stranglehold of psychoanalysis. Unconscious drives no longer pushed patients, instead they were making choices based on their worldview which was shaped by their appraisals of the outcomes of their previous actions. The role of the therapist was to help clients' reframing of the constructs that they were using to understand their world. For example, patients would often think and behave in a way that suggested their ideas about something were true reality, rather than merely that their ideas were just one of many possible interpretations. The therapist would explore that individual's worldview, understand how they had developed those constructs, then prepare the patient for change. In this way, patients are encouraged to become actors in their lives, not reactors. By recognising that they have freedom of choice between courses of action they can then begin to give up victimhood.

Central to this process was the idea that the patient should feel entirely accepted by the therapist. In a non-judgemental, intimate therapeutic environment, patients would feel safe to explore and analyse their personal constructs; to experiment with new possibilities and ultimately put aside maladaptive constructs, replacing them with new ways of thinking. In the days before diversity and equality, these were radical new ideas which would drive progress towards equitable and respectful psychological practice which would become the foundation of the therapeutic alliance.

Kelly was both criticised heavily and highly lorded. Visiting appointments at various universities in the USA, Europe, Russia, South America and Asia soon followed the book's release. However, after the initial flurry, things quickly died down. There was still some modest interest within the United Kingdom, but generally, the work was being quickly forgotten and replaced with the humanism of Carl Rogers. Kelly retained ambitions that construct theory would be a formative contribution to psychological theory, that his work would reconnect psychologists to the wonders of people and the truth of human relationships. He was also, however, ambivalent to many aspects of his work, arguing that the publication of his book had been a mistake. Jokingly, he proposed an additional chapter, entitled 'apologies for the book'.

What concerned Kelly most was his development of the construct repertory test, now commonly called the rep grid. This technique affords self-discovery by enabling the exploration of opposing constructs. The rep process gives the therapist an overview of their client's personal reality which can then be used to support further self-discovery. Kelly was perhaps correct in his concern that the rep test obscured his theoretical work. The test ultimately became more well-known than the rest of his work, particularly in the field of individual differences and industrial psychology. It is because the agile rep grid technique contributed so much to the therapeutic process, and also to psychological research, that people were brought once again to Kelly's personal construct theory. By the cognitive revolution of the 1980s people were ready to fully understand and appreciate Kelly's personal construct theory and over two decades after Kelly had published his seminal text, his student, Walter Mischel, appointed George Kelly as the architect of modern cognitive psychology. With his breadth of vision, Kelly was a prophet; he knew where psychology would travel in the future, before anyone else.

a very deep, original, refreshing voice was always evident to all who knew him well. What has surprised me was not the brilliance with which he first spoke but the accuracy with which he anticipated the directions into which psychology would move two decades later.

(Mischel, 1980, p.85)

But not all of Kelly's students have such fond memories of him; 'If, one were to pull away Kelly's mask, one would find Mephistopheles' (student cited in Fransella, 1995, p.27). Kelly's style with his students is well documented as problematic. There are many reports of the distress he caused. Kelly had a habit of 'slot-rattling' which is a psychological term from Kelly's own theory that explains someone who will suddenly switch from cold to warm, excited to aloof, to the point that nobody really knows where they stand with him. Kelly instilled both admiration and dread. Excited and creative he would welcome them into his world, cancelling all appointments and giving them his devoted attention, but then he would suddenly switch back to a more rule-bound rigidity and aloofness. He would be sweet, then salty, or merely polite. He was no supporter of psychoanalytical theory but would draw shrewdly on Freud in ways that would undermine and humiliate his students. He would also use non-verbal tactics to get his message across. On student described the awful silence that would indicate that you knew you had done something wrong. If he were delighted, he would blow air from his mouth and grin. If you said something he disagreed with in some way, with some theatre, he would remove his glasses and drop his head to the ground.

Kelly had control over their fates and had on at least one occasion quickly dispatched several students deemed not to be making the grade. To carry out this unfortunate task, he arrived dressed in farming clothes, remarking to the students that when you have to clean the manure out of the barn, you must be dressed for the occasion.

What was odd about this behaviour, was that it was very far aligned from the psychologist he described in his theoretical works, but he did try to change. So high were the levels of anxiety around Kelly, that in one unfortunate situation a student was rendered silent. Once Kelly realised what the problem was, he was horrified. He seemed to have had no idea of the impact he was having on his students. He went home and promptly re-wrote his role as director. At the top of the list was 'resign as director', followed by 'move out of the office', followed by, 'always have your office door open and coffee for students who happen to pop by'.

George Alexander Kelly died unexpectedly while compiling a new book on March 6th, 1967. He was survived by his wife Gladys and two children, Jacqueline and Joseph. He was the architect of one of the most potent theories to analyse what it means to be human. A man of caustic wit and breadth of vision, creative and adventurous, and someone who never settled for the pervading answers to difficult questions, the scope of Kelly's thinking continues to impact on psychology today. He was also a nonconformist, requesting that on his death all his papers be destroyed. As Fransella insightfully observes, there were two George Kellys the visionary and the one who did not want to be known at all.

Major works

Kelly, G. A. (1955). *The Psychology of Personal Constructs*. New York: Norton.
Kelly, G. A. (1969). *Clinical Psychology and Personality: The Selected Papers of George Kelly*. New York: John Wiley.

Bibliography

Fransella, F. (1995). *George Kelly*. London: Sage.
Mischel, W. (1980). George Kelly's anticipation of psychology. In M. J. Mahoney (Ed.), *Psychotherapy Process: Current Issues and Future Directions* (pp.85–87). New York: Plenum.

Chapter 17

Hans Jürgen Eysenck

The truth as he sees it

March 4th, 1916 to September 4th, 1997

Hans Eysenck was a prolific writer, a researcher with a prominent public profile and one of the most distinguished figures in the field of individual differences; 80 books or so, hundreds of papers, test manuals, even an interview with the men's magazine *Penthouse*. He is possibly the best known and most divisive of psychologists; his lasting message was that psychology should trust numbers rather than people, facts over ideology and that psychologists had a duty to speak out regardless of the social taboo. Tact and diplomacy were never his strong points, and he always felt that 'a scientist owes the world only one thing, and that is the truth as he sees it' (Eysenck, 1997, p.119).

Eysenck's blistering attack on the propaganda of psychoanalysis and the efficacy of a 'talking cure' raised ethical issues around the application of the technique, ultimately leading to its marginalisation in favour of behavioural-based therapies. Eysenck's words were clear, direct, fundamental and fierce. The psychoanalysts fought back arguing that Eysenck was simply trying to usurp Freud as the figurehead of psychology.

There is very little known about the early part of Hans Eysenck's life. He has written a biography, but the content is written in a style of self-preservation. Eysenck's parents, Eduard Anton Eysenck and Ruth (née Werner), were actors who divorced when he was two years old. His mother had a moderately successful career on the German silent screen. While she pursued her career, Hans was raised by his grandmother Antonia Werner, whom he described as loving and lenient. Hans' mother remarried the producer Max Glass. However, his production companies were shut down by the Nazi/National Socialist government, and the family had little option but to go into exile in France. This move was not, however, far enough away from the Nazis. When Paris was overrun, Ruth found herself in an internment camp. Glass spent a king's ransom on bribes to secure her release and then the couple fled to South America. Eduard Eysenck fared much better. He could trace his German Aryan lineage back through centuries. With the Jewish acting competition in exile, or worse, Eduard enjoyed considerable professional success. He remained, however, a reluctant Nazi, only joining the party when it became compulsory in 1937.

Hans entered the Bismarck Gymnasium in 1925 and then Prinz Heinrichs-Gymnasium for the next stage of his adolescent education. Some of Hans' peers describe the school as an inclusive conservative school with military connections, but Hans describes it as a being run by right-wing nationalists. His physical size, sporting prowess and combative style meant that he was mostly able to avoid being beaten up for his left-wing political views. School failed to inspire Hans; he was bored. He describes his teachers as disengaging and his peers stupidly pedantic. Matters were somewhat improved by his mother who would intersperse his German education with periods of study at a public school on the Isle of Wight and Exeter College.

Hans left Germany, via France, for England in 1934 to pursue a degree in physics at University College London. His lack of Nazi party membership had barred his entry to theoretical physics in Berlin. The worrying ideologies and political behaviours made the decision easy. He had left Germany as a principled protest at fascism, although one could argue that taking a political stance on Nazism was a luxury he was not afforded. If he had stayed, he would have, likely, joined his much-loved grandmother. Despite having few ties with the Jewish community and having converted to Catholicism, his grandmother was identified as Jewish and died in a Nazi concentration camp midway through World War II.

Things were far from straightforward in London. In Germany, students could study most topics of their choosing before commencing their physics degree. This was not the case in England, and without realising this, Hans ended up barred from the Physics programme. His only option was to enter Psychology, a discipline he openly regarded as unimpressive, unscientific and its members as rather dull-witted. So for him, it was easy to gain traction in the field, and he harnessed his 'physics envy' towards this non-robust science.

Hans eventually undertook a PhD in experimental aesthetics under the supervision of Sir Cyril Burt and his studies were a much-needed distraction from the treatment he was receiving as a German living in England. His German nationality resulted in rejection from active duty. He was excluded from service and treated with suspicion. Eysenck had little choice but to continue feverishly with his PhD studies which were now being supervised, at a distance, by Burt who had been evacuated to Aberystwyth, Wales. Eysenck could not follow Burt, because his wife was struggling with naturalisation issues. Her residence was confirmed in 1939 and then removed again once war broke out. She was facing the possibility of internment, and the couple had to stay in London.

Burt's original plan for Eysenck's PhD was the re-standardisation of the Binet intelligence scale. Working now at a distance from Burt and feeling singularly uninspired, Eysenck soon pivoted towards aesthetic preferences. The idea was that theoretical laws could be applied to aesthetic composition and analysed through the factor analytical method. His work provided some support that facets of personality, attitude and age play a role in aesthetic experience, but to Eysenck's disappointment, not with general intelligence. Despite the lack of evidence to support the role of intelligence in aesthetic experience, Eysenck's work using the Birkhoff formula was formative. He demonstrated that pleasure was a product of order and complexity, triggering new research and insights in the field of psychoaesthetics.

One of Eysenck's early impactful publications came from the development of this work. Historically psychologists had been focused on the number of questions, or test items, as the route to measuring a construct or phenomena. Eysenck was able to demonstrate that fidelity within a population was as much related to the number of persons required for an experimental study. This finding triggered Eysenck's first public spat with Bernard Babington Smith (St Andrews and Oxford Universities) who contended that Eysenck had overreached himself. Eysenck's initial response was typically adversarial, if not in fact outright insulting. Before Eysenck could deliver his offensive, Cyril Burt reigned him in, and a more moderate, evidence-based response was delivered. That was the last time that Burt was able to do much to prevent Eysenck from being 'Eysenck' and as he struck out on his own intellectual path, his signature was to deliver criticisms in the most heavy-handed style.

By the close of 1941, Eysenck had published some 11 prestigious articles, including in the journal *Nature*. Empirical aesthetics was fruitful, but Eysenck moved on to more contentious subjects and his relationship with his mentor Burt began to decline. Eysenck describes Burt as the only psychologist he ever feared. There would seem to have been some cause. Eysenck became suspicious that Burt was attempting to sabotage his career. Burt would stifle pathways that Eysenck wished to explore, advise him not to publish on specific topics and there were veiled and not so veiled criticisms of his work (a highly critical review of his work on factor analysis had significant input from Burt). Imagined or real, when the scandals around the fabrication of data by Burt emerged, Eysenck briefly jumped to his mentor's defence, only to quickly distance himself when his guilt seemed assured. Burt in turn, went on to describe Eysenck as a 'boastful Jew' and would not support his continuation as Head of Department at the Institute of Psychiatry.

Eysenck was hired to the Maudsley Hospital in 1942. This environment favoured the employment of Jewish-Germans who had suffered professionally during the war. Many of the psychiatrists who worked in the Maudsley had come in direct contact with the worst of the Nazi eugenics practices and had deep sympathy for its victims. It was hoped that Eysenck's work would establish a role for psychology as one of the basic sciences to support psychiatry.

Eysenck's appraisal of the psychiatric literature, particularly psychoanalysis, was typically critical, he began to make many enemies in the psychiatric community. For Eysenck, the works of John Bowlby, Gordon Allport and J. P. Guildford, as well as Ivan Pavlov and Carl Jung ought to be where the focus should fall. Arguably it was Donald W. MacKinnon, the Berkeley professor and director of the saboteur and spy processing 'Station S' during World War II, who was Eysenck's greatest influence. His book *The Structure of Personality* became the blueprint for Eysenck's most essential works the study of personality and the beginnings of a strident UK personality movement in a field that was primarily dominated by America and Germany.

Eysenck continued to make extensive use of factor analysis, it became the principle of his career, particularly in its application into the empirical pursuit of personality measurement to Jung's typology. Eysenck would explore what was commonly accepted, and test those ideas with rigour, objectivity and reliability. His first study demonstrated that there was no statistical evidence to support the idea that neurotics (mainly female neurotics) were highly suggestible, furthermore neuroticism had very little to do with introversion. His second study, a landmark in personality, capitalised on the punch-card data management system. Eysenck could use the factor system to analyse data from 700 soldiers diagnosed with neurosis systematically. This work eventually leads to the identification of bipolar personality factors.

The objective of Eysenck's work was to differentiate between what was normal and abnormal personality and to move psychiatrists away from using subjectivity in their decision making. He wanted to improve diagnostic outcomes for patients and to establish factor analysis as a key instrument for study. Using MacKinnon's work as an archetype, Eysenck eventually identified the two principal factors of personality; Extraversion-Introversion which is thought to tap into an individual's tendencies towards sociability/assertiveness or aloofness/passivity, and Neuroticism-Stability, which is related to moodiness/insecurity and emotional stability. Psychoticism, which indicates aggressive, cold, antisocial behaviour failed to attract widespread acceptance.

In in 1947, he published *Dimensions of Personality* and this was quickly followed up by several papers which moved the largely historical and philosophical notions behind *Dimensions* towards a more robust scientific model. This was followed up in 1952 by *The Scientific Study of Personality*, a book which presented more clarity on these arguments for a continuous dimension framework for personality. This book was explicitly critical of psychiatry and drew much more on criterion analysis. Psychologists were bewildered by his unusual approach and psychiatrists were affronted at his quantitative approach to their work, statisticians just hated it. Yet the core of Eysenck's work was soon replicated through the Cattell 16pf and the five-factor models of personality.

Eysenck, as always, was drawing controversial attention, which served mainly to spur him forward. In the search for a biological explanation for extraversion and neuroticism he drew on the work of Ivan Pavlov, associating personality to the brain's executive structures; the cerebrum, the cerebellum and the brainstem. He had much work to convince himself and his discipline that this work was valuable, but his capacity to bridge personality, genetics and biology was monumental and would ultimately pave the way for the neurophysiological research of the future.

His scientific enquiries between 1953 and 1957 into the relationship between excitation and inhibition empowered Eysenck to move from what had been descriptive accounts of the theories of others, towards causal evidence. Introverts were found to be responsive to lower levels of a stimulus than extroverts. Conditioned responses in extroverts were formed more slowly and preserved for much shorter periods of time and these insights would be the key to understanding neurotic disorders.

His work, however, was attracting increasing criticism. Eysenck was a prolific writer, but this was often at the expense of accuracy. His style was to write and publish quickly, a style which would often lead to vague methodologies that were difficult to replicate, and mistakes. Eysenck was well-aware of these problems, but rather than view them as shortcomings; he simply viewed refinement as getting in the way of the next publication. The double standard being that Eysenck was openly critical of Cyril Burt for being more concerned about the statistics than the way the data was collected and presented. However, louder voices were emerging from colleagues who argued that Eysenck had an established policy for being very selective about what he published. He would omit results that did not support his hypotheses and use diagrammatic illustrations which misled. His data was also unusually tidy suggesting that it was not an accurate reflection of the realities of human experimental testing.

His first personality model was not a resounding success, and few were able to replicate his findings, and he began to overhaul the theoretical basis for the model and revise the testing techniques. A more straightforward but more explicit application of the Pavlovian model provided the answer, and his revised theory argued that the introverted brain was operating at much higher levels of excitation than the extrovert. Humans sought optimum levels of arousal, and their personalities were manifestations of their usual activation levels. Extraverts needed more stimulation and would seek out experiences that could provide excitation gains. This was not a substantial overhaul, but it was easier to test and reach consensus about.

The problem was that the more Eysenck rose in his field, the more he was on the receiving end of intensive critical scrutiny, and this environment was choking his research and damaging his personal credibility.

Eysenck had become entangled with Sybil Rostal, a research assistant at the Maudsley hospitals. By the 1950s their affair was quite public, which was scandalising his more conservative colleagues. Loyalties were divided because many of Hans' peers were also good friends with his wife. Margaret did not want a divorce, and many saw her as a victim. However, the marriage could not be saved, and Hans married Sybil.

He was also initiating an all-out anti-Freudian offensive, directly attacking the creditability of psychoanalysis and all who sailed in her. His role at the Maudsley meant that their clinical programme 'brand' became increasingly synonymous with science and evidence-based practice, whereas the more interdisciplinary, psychoanalytical department at the Tavistock had a much narrow intellectual agenda. When key psychologists at the Maudsley and Tavistock took their feud to the British Psychological Society, Eysenck was ever confident. He had the support of most BPS psychologists, but the BPS medical section, fearing a leadership take-over, offered the Maudsley group their own separate section within the BPS. This tokenism was summarily rejected and in a cunning tactical manoeuvre, supporters of Eysenck who were not BPS members began flooding the organisation with applications for membership.

In what was potentially a bid to stop the 'Maudsley coup', many of the applications were voted down by the panel. There was an almighty argument. Accusations of vote rigging meant that the BPS had to move to suspend further membership applications until November 1956. Eysenck's scorched-earth approach did not win him this battle because the clinicians still blocked the proposed changes, holding onto their psychoanalytical power basis until the mid-1960s.

As criticism increased, Eysenck began to insulate himself within his research group and distance himself from his critics and peers. He became increasingly supercilious, only addressing his critics through his books and papers. Rather than bringing his peers closer, Hans was creating an impenetrable wall, which only served to increase what would seem at times dehumanising back-stabbing from his peers. By 1972 he was not only being denounced, but the public had also taken to punching and kicking him.

Eysenck had long been a member of the British Eugenics Society, and during his early years as a scientist, Eysenck had indeed suggested that in the UK the average IQ was decreasing. He argued that more children were being born to less intelligent, more unfortunate members of the populace. He stopped short at advising on solutions to this problem. The Holocaust was a cautionary note about the role of state-approved ideologies on procreation, but Eysenck could transcend this horror story by drawing on his personal experience as a German of Jewish descent. He made compelling arguments that politics and science are and should remain separate entities.

Then he began to weigh in on the intelligence debate. Eysenck had primarily stayed clear of studying intelligence but in 1967 he launched 'a manifesto on intelligence'. The work was designed to bring the study of intelligence closer to theory by applying the idea that speed of processing offered much promise as a proxy for intelligence measurement and 'g', but the reverse happened. In 1969 Arthur Jensen published his work on racial differences in IQ and social problems. Eysenck backed him, arguing that he had reached similar conclusions to Jensen through his own work. However, Eysenck had not raised the issue because he felt that 'The Negroes, or so it seemed to me, were having enough problems without my adding another one (Eysenck, 1972, p.80). Now that Jensen had raised the issue, science had a duty to investigate the problem and the media foray began.

Eysenck asked Jensen if he was prepared to write up his findings as a book, he was not yet and Eysenck's *Race, Intelligence and Education* soon followed. This was not a well-conceived publication. It contained no new data and omitted essential information on the segregation of children in schooling (which Eysenck was opposed to), and while there was little evidence to support genetic differences in IQ, the book tended to suggest otherwise.

The book was intended to persuade the layperson that biological and racial differences in IQ was worthy of scientific study. The book was 'low-brow' and weighted toward more towards 'Eysenckian' opinion than complex scientific evidence.

The book was largely ignored in a race-wary America. At home, the story was entirely different. Eysenck had firmly established himself in opposition to the 'environmentalists', at a time in Britain when race relations were at their worst. Far-right groups such as the National Front were on the rise. The British MP Enoch Powell gave his infamous 'Rivers of Blood' speech where he presented a vision of a dystopian Britain that was overrun with a society of dominant, aggressive immigrants. Eysenck was vilified by journalists, academics and students, to the point that his children had temporary name changes to distance themselves from their father's work. In an attempt to please the public, Hans Eysenck seemed to have lost it all.

There was growing interest from the press not only in Eysenck's work but also about what was happening on campus. His lectures were becoming disruptive events. Students would try to break up any discussion, throwing ink-bombs and being generally unruly. Matters came to a head at the London School of Economics during May 1973. A protest by the Communist Party of England went awry when the protestors invaded the lecture theatre and mounted the stage. Eysenck was physically assaulted.

Ironically this event helped Eysenck. His refusal to press charges and his immediate return to work gave him martyr status. Eysenck's detractors deplored what had happened, not only physically to Eysenck, but also what the invasion and assault stood for more broadly. This was an attack on academic freedom of speech.

Of course, Eysenck never baulked at the opportunity for controversy, and he harnessed the media frenzy that followed. He would make multiple media appearances discussing his theory of inheritability for traits such as personality and intelligence. When challenged on the social and ethical implications of his work, Hans would gently allude to his German-Jewish heritage. He himself had watched his family suffer, but such emotions and concerns had no place in a scientific argument. Thus, the audience had received this powerful personal information and were subtly challenged not to conclude that he was a de facto racist or a Nazi sympathiser.

Eysenck's ideas have had a profound influence on psychology, and the volume of his work continues to extend its impact. However, Eysenck's tendency for vague reporting, inaccuracy and overstatement is an undisputable weakness. His dogged persistence for the premier place of science and reasoning is also tested towards the end of his career in his work with the tobacco industry. In the face of developing evidence that demonstrated the link between cancer and tobacco, Eysenck persistently argued that tobacco was a minor risk factor for disease. Personality, he argued, determined longevity, not tobacco.

The biochemical mechanisms linking smoking and cancer were still poorly understood during the 1980s, but Eysenck (whose work was financed by the tobacco industry to the tune of £800,000) persistently downplayed epidemiological and animal study evidence arguing instead that nicotine was neither addictive nor carcinogenic. There is no evidence that the tobacco industry tried or could even have actually influenced Eysenck's opinion. He was very much his 'own man'. We might, however, conclude that Big Tobacco was savvy in engaging him. They knew his personal style before engaging him. Once he decided on something, Eysenck could be intractable and this personality trait made him a mighty scientific advocate for Big Tobacco.

Hans was the ultimate participant in his own personality-stress experiment. The years before his death were extremely difficult and he was known to be suffering from stress from ongoing quarrels that were often of his own making. Hans Eysenck died of a brain tumour in 1997. He was survived by his second wife Sybil, and his children Connie, Gary, Kevin, Darrin and Michael.

Perhaps still haunted by what had happened to Sir Cyril Burt, Hans followed George Kelly and ordered all of his personal papers destroyed on his death.

Major works

Eysenck, H. J. (1947). *Dimensions of Personality*. London: Routledge and Kegan Paul.

Eysenck, H. J. (1952). The effects of psychotherapy: An evaluation. *Journal of Consulting Psychology*, 16, 319–324.

Eysenck, H. J. (1964). *Crime and Personality*. London: Routledge and Kegan Paul.

Eysenck, H. J. (1967). *The Biological Basis of Personality*. Spring-field: Thomas.

Eysenck, H. J. (1979a). The conditioning model of neurosis. *Brain and Behavioral Sciences*, 2, 155–199.

Eysenck, H. J. (1979b). *The Structure and Measurement of Intelligence*. New York: Springer-Verlag.

Eysenck, H. J. (1980a). *The Causes and Effects of Smoking*. Minnesota: Sage (with contributions from L. J. Eaves).

Eysenck, H. J. (1980). *The Great Intelligence Debate*. London: Lifecycle Publications (with L. J. Kamin).

Eysenck, H. J. (1989). *Genes, Culture, and Personality: An Empirical Approach*. New York: Academic Press (with L. J. Eaves and N. G. Martin).

Bibliography

Buchanan, R. D. (2010). *Playing with Fire, the Controversial Career of Hans J. Eysenck*. Oxford: Oxford Univesity Press.

Corr, P. J. (2000) Reflections on the scientific life of Hans Eysenck. *History and Philosophy of Psychology*, 2, 18–35.

Corr, P. J. (2015). *Hans Eysenck (Mind Shapers)*. London: Palgrave.

Eysenck, H. J. (1972). The dangers of the new zealots. *Encounter*, 39, 79–91.

Eysenck, H. J. (1997). *Rebel with a Cause, the Autobiography of Hans Eysenck*. London, UK: Transaction Publishers.

Gibson, H. B. (1981). *Hans Eysenck: The Man and His Work*. London: Peter Owen.

Gray, J. A. (1981). A critique of Eysenck's theory of personality. In H. J. Eysenck (Ed.), *A Model for Personality* (pp. 246–277). Berlin, Heidelberg: Springer.

Modgil, S., & Modgil, C. (Eds.) (1986) *Hans Eysenck: Consensus and Controversy*. London: Taylor and Francis.

Storms, L. H., & Sigal, J. J. (1958). Eysenck's personality theory with special reference to the dynamics of anxiety and hysteria. *British Journal of Medical Psychology*, 31, 228–246.

Chapter 18

Arthur Jensen

A king among men

August 24th, 1923 to October 22nd, 2012

Arthur Robert Jensen was possibly one of the most contentious figures in educational psychology. During his 40-year tenure at Berkeley, he was a prolific researcher, a respected academic whose work was remarkable, but controversial. Jensen was not a natural fire-starter, but in 1969 following the publication of an article in the *Harvard Educational Review*, Jensen became one of the most divisive figures in psychological science.

Jensen's grandfather was German and his grandmother Jewish-Polish-German. The couple's parents disapproved of their union on religious grounds, and thus the couple moved from Berlin to San Diego, California to start a new life. Their son Arthur Alfred Jensen served in the World War I before becoming a lumber and building-supplies merchant in San Diego and eventually marrying Linda Mary (née Schachtmayer). Arthur (Art) was born in 1923 and his sister Lois, in Virginia the following year. Art was described as a loner with an insatiable appetite for books. Nicknamed 'the little professor' by his parents, he would often burst into an enthusiastic account of his readings at the dinner table until his sister Lois would plead for him to cease in the delivery of another one of his lectures.

Art embraced his hobbies with similar enthusiasm: hiking, swimming, classical music and the study of amphibians and reptiles. His collection of snakes was both driven by interest and a drive for the practical: he would collect wild snakes to feed the King Cobra at San Diego Zoo. The zoo keeper would trade white rats, which Art could then feed to his pet snakes.

By the age of ten, his capacity and appetite for knowledge were recognised, and his fifth-grade teacher would encourage him to study topics outside of the curriculum which he would then discuss with the class. These talks were soon favourite outside of his fifth-grade class, and Art would discuss with his peers, topics ranging from herpetology, to evolution to Gandhi.

By the age of 17, he was an able clarinettist, playing with the San Diego Symphony. Realising, however, that practice was insufficient to produce that 'special something' that he believed was necessary for greatness, Art turned his attention to finding something he could truly excel at; a case of you cannot put in what God left out. Art was, however, much more concerned with facts than religion and his interests in evolution, Gandhi and the rejection of matters of faith resulted in his expulsion from Sunday School. Arthur remained passionate about music until his death, regularly attending the opera and concerts in Europe and San Francisco. Describing music as the only certitude in his life, Art clearly had the talent to make it as a performer but, acutely aware of his own limitations, directed his focus towards the pursuit of advancing understanding in the innateness of success. This obsession of why some people make it became a life-long interest.

Art graduated in psychology at Berkeley in 1945 and began working to support himself through his MA at San Diego State College. He joined his father's business, then worked as a pharmacology technician, high school biology teacher and orchestra conductor and eventually in 1952 studied clinical and educational psychology at Columbia University's teacher's college. It was here that Art worked under the differential psychologist Percival Symonds. Symonds was an assistant of the behaviourist Edward Lee Thorndike but held tight to the psychodynamic approach and theories of free association. Jensen was a self-professed cynic and pragmatist, describing himself as having a life-long antipathy to belief without evidence. He found Symonds' interests to be of limited utility to objective science, likening the approach to measuring ability in music or sport by asking people to name their favourite artists or players.

However, Art respected Symonds, and they published *From Adolescent to Adult* together in 1961. He also drew on his council that if he wanted to be a leader in science he ought to seek out a position with a leading academic and researcher in the field. This would help Art develop a better understanding of how leading scientists structured their lives and their priorities and perhaps begin to model his own behaviour. Later in his career Art defined three things that created exceptionality; talent, unstinting energy and an intense concentration and sustained interest in what they were doing (Miele, 2002, p.29).

It was during a year's internship at the University of Maryland's Psychiatric Institute in Baltimore (1955–1956) that Art discovered the English psychologist and prolific writer Hans Jürgen Eysenck. Having read Eysenck's (1952) work, *The Scientific Study of Personality*, Art, wrote to him seeking mentorship and asking to join his laboratory. Eysenck was Professor at University College London, which was established by the fathers of measurement Sir Francis Galton and Charles Spearman and a fellowship from the National Institute of Mental Health supported Jensen to spent almost 2 years (1956–1958) working in Eysenck's lab. He was a systematic worker, who would set goals for himself, reflecting and re-evaluating on his progress at each step and he thrived there.

Art returned to California in 1958, appointed Assistant Professor of Educational Psychology at Berkeley. It was here that he met and married Barbara Jane DeLarme, describing marrying his wife as one of the two smartest decisions he ever made (the second was to become a professor). '"Barb" ... does so much that allows me to focus on my work and brings so many things into my life I would not have without her' (Miele, 2002, p.9).

Art became a full professor in 1966 at the Institute of Human Learning where he developed his expertise in human learning through the study of such phenomena as reaction time and short-term memory. His work was essential but uncontroversial. He established differences in memory processing for rote learning and recall, and abstract reasoning and problem-solving. Jensen was not, however, particularly interested in the pure study of reaction time; rather he was driven to understand how responses to stimuli could inform understanding of human abilities.

His interest expanded by the mid-1960s to the exploration of the impact that cultural disadvantage had on abilities. The psychological and scientific literature on this topic was increasing rapidly and, in an attempt to synthesise the findings Art began a comprehensive, systematic evaluation of the literature where he was struck by how easily genetic influences were rejected as a likely cause of deprivation–opportunity differences and Art could find no scientific basis for the rejection of this evidence. In 1967 gave a speech ('How Much Can We Boost IQ and Scholastic Achievement?') to the annual meeting of the California

Advisory Council of Educational Research, where he raised important questions about the role of ability in society, genetic and non-genetic factors, and effectiveness of the educational process given that ability was not normally distributed across different groups in society. This work was then published in the *American Educational Research Journal* (1968) as a tentative account of the nature of the scientific knowledge on the genetic and environmental determinants of individual differences and how those determinants could be influenced by education. His work triggered an invited paper to the *Harvard Educational Review* (1969). On publication, Jensen who had lived the 'generally quiet, cloistered existence of a scholar, burying himself with statistics, standards and students' (Edson, 1969), found himself in a firestorm.

Jensen was given the remit of providing a clear positional statement of his position on the cause of deprivation–opportunity differences concerning the role of social class, racial differences and intelligence and Jensen responded by stating unequivocally that genetic factors could not be ruled out in explaining the 15-point difference in IQ between black and white Americans. How much could education improve this difference? Jensen made three key points, (1) that compensatory education was a failure. Programmes such as Head Start had failed to boost African-American IQ; (2) 80 per cent of the variance in IQ was the result of genetic factors. The remainder was due to environmental factors. Traits may run in families because of genes, and they may also run in races for the same reasons; (3) the likelihood was that some genetic competent explained the black–white IQ difference.

The condemnation that followed was extreme; there was news coverage in the *New York Times, Time, Life Magazine, Fortune, US News & World Report,* much of which was inaccurate; student protests, sit-ins, acts of vandalism and death threats overshadowed Jensen's findings, resulting in his family being moved to a secret location. Art's childhood friend, Ellis Page, organised a two-page commentary in the *American Psychologist* (1972). Signed by 50 distinguished scientists the piece argued for free and unencumbered research because 'human problems are best remedied by increased human knowledge' (p.660) but the piece drew criticism that, in fact, the signatories were using their own political power to foster scholarly thinking (see for example, Robinson, 1973 and other commentaries). The term Jensenism to describe the belief that an individual's intelligence is largely due to heredity and racial heritage entered the common lexicon.

The challenges to Jensen's theory were moral rather more than scientific, Jensen had violated a societal taboo and tackled an area that appeared to be scientifically 'off limits'. There was a fear that racism might find a scientific footing. The MIT physicist Martin Deutsch claimed that Jensen's work was populated with errors and misstatements which maximised the differences between blacks and whites (53 in total). So shocked at the outlandish claims, Jensen wrote to Deutsch requesting a list of the purported errors but never received a response. Edson in his nine-page commentary in the *New York Times* magazine section describes how many of Jensen's peers found it unforgivable that a man with his formidable background should rock the boat and that the consequences of Nazi Germany were to make every liberal blind to any opinions in this area.

Other than the Deutsch affair, Jensen remained stoic in response to his critics, living as he described by the Gandhi principle of correspondence between inner thoughts and public pronouncements (Lubinski, 2013). He had respect for those whom he felt held religiously different views of the world but had no respect for those who agreed with him merely because it reinforced their racist ideals; 'someone who likes what he thinks I'm saying just because it seems to agree with his own prejudices' (Miele, 2002, p.15). Art was driven not by racism, but by trying to understand systematically what he felt to be society's greatest possession, intelligence. He was an opponent of social and racial segregation, supporting learning, regarding every individual as valuable by their own characteristics rather than their racial or ethnic background; 'We shouldn't make school a series of failures for students with lower learning abilities' (In Memoriam, 2012).

Jensen held a distinct lack of interest in politics, but politics it would seem was interested in Jensen. The sociologist and political advisor to Richard Nixon, Pat Moynihan, is credited with coining the term, Jensenism; 'The winds of Jensenism are blowing through Washington with gale force' (cited in Miele, 2002, p.36). Official Oval Office tapes of Richard Nixon and Pat Moynihan record both men saying that they knew the truth about race and IQ, but it was not something that they could admit to. Nixon, on discussion of the work of Jensen and the later work of Herrnstein said: 'Nobody must know we're thinking about it,

and if we do find out it's correct, we must never tell anybody'
(Nixon, 1971; phone call with Moynihan, October 7th, 1971,
10.32 to 10.58). Despite Jensen's work being politically damaging, Moynihan continued to keep the President up-to-date with
Jensen's work. Jensen visited Moynihan and his 'Jensen-assistant'
at the Whitehouse. Moynihan and Jensen had much in common,
an interest in Erikson, a passion for Gandhi and both men had
put their necks above the parapet on issues related to race, albeit
on different sides of the debate.

The furore over Jensen's work attracted eminent scientists such
as James R. Flynn to debate Jensen's argument in his book *Race,
IQ and Jensen* (1980). Flynn suggests that Jensen's ideas were
largely influenced by studies on Negro intelligence by Audrey
Shuey (whose is work widely considered to be flawed), but that
Jensen should not be dismissed because there was power and
coherence in his work. Stephen Jay Gould's (1981) stand was
more outspoken. Jensen describes *The Mismeasure of Man* as
a portrayal of 'vivid accounts of eminent but self-deluding, cheat-
ing and foolish scientific figures of the past' (Jensen, 1982,
p.121) with whom he was associated. Gould, he argued, had pur-
posefully presented expressions which were false, misleading or
grossly caricatured. Gould's 'evidence' represented hand-picked
examples which either predated 1950 and in many cases predated
1900. Such evidence was presented in such a way that the non-
specialist might accept Gould's recants as unquestionably factual.

Despite the surrounding maelstrom, Jensen continued to excel,
receiving every promotion, even to super-grades. His publication
record was impressive. Over 400 papers in leading journals, he
founded the Behaviour Genetics Association and was known as
a fair and thorough peer reviewer of every article sent to him. He
published several papers that demonstrated the extent to which
impoverished environments impair intellectual development, work
which confirmed the cumulative-deficit-hypothesis (1974, 1977).

In 1998, the exposé magazine *Searchlight* devoted a special to
race science where the social scientist Barry Mehler and his research
associate Keith Hurt contended that the funding for Jensen's work
was tainted by the Pioneer Fund (an organisation established for
the study of heredity and difference). Mehler and Hurt argued that
the organisation was 'at the cutting edge of almost every race conflict in the United States' (Mehler & Hurt, 1998). There are however strong arguments from Jensen (Miele, 2002 and others) that

the standards met by Pioneer-funded research were no different from those that were sponsored by other private foundations (see for example Weyher, 1998 and Lynn, 2001).

As Jensen's work moved from contemporary public opinion towards peer review, the higher it was valued. A special edition of the journal *Intelligence* collected articles from fellow scientists such as Philippe Rushton, Linda Gottfredson, Sandra Scarr and Thomas J. Bouchard. The articles were collected under the title 'A King Among Men: Arthur Jensen' and argued that he ought to take his place with scientists such as Sir Francis Galton and Charles Spearman.

In 2003 Jensen won the Kistler Prize for contributions to the understanding of connections between the human genome and society and the Lifetime Achievement Award from the International Society for Intelligence Research in 2006. Today the Arthur Robert Jensen memorial site supports public access to over 400 arts papers and books as well as writings about Art. As Jensen argued in his 1999 Galton Lecture and subsequent 2002 paper, 'Science deals strictly with what is, not with what anyone thinks it ought to be' (2002, p.146). If research into the three parts of 'Jensenism', could advance without political interference, then his theory would at some point be proved mostly right or mostly wrong (Miele, 2002).

Arthur Robert Jensen died in his summer home in Kelseyville, California from Parkinson's disease on October 22nd, 2012. Barbs preceded him, dying in 2007, and his daughter Bobbi survived him. The *American Psychologist* obituary refers to a second wife Justine who survived Art, but despite extensive ancestor searches, her existence could not be verified at the time of writing.

Major works

Jensen, A. R. (1967). How much can we boost IQ and scholastic achievement? Speech given before the annual meeting of the California Advisory Council of Educational Research (San Diego, October). https://files.eric.ed.gov/fulltext/ED023722.pdf

Jensen, A. R. (1968). Social class, race and genetics: Implications for education. *American Educational Research Journal*, 5(1), 1–42. doi:10.2307/1161699

Jensen, A. R. (1969). How much can we boost IQ and scholastic achievement. *Harvard Educational Review*, 39(1), 1–123.

Jensen, A. R. (1974). Cumulative deficit: A testable hypothesis? *Developmental Psychology*, 10, 996–1019.

Jensen, A. R. (1977). Cumulative deficit in IQ of blacks in the rural South. *Developmental Psychology*, 13, 184–191.

Jensen, A. R. (1980). Uses of sibling data in educational and psychological research. *American Educational Research Journal*, 17(2), 153–170.

Jensen, A. R. (1980). *Straight Talk about Mental Tests*. London: Methuen Publishing Ltd.

Jensen, A. R. (2002). Galton's legacy to research on intelligence. *Journal of Biosocial Science*, 34, 145–172 doi:10.1017/S0021932002001451

Bibliography

Edson, L. (1969). Jensenism: The theory that IQ is largely determined by genes. *New York Times* magazine section, August 31st, p. 11.

Flynn, J. R. (1980). *Race, IQ, and Jensen*. London: Routledge & Kegan Paul.

Gould, S. J. (1996). *The Mismeasure of Man*. New York: Norton.

In Memoriam. (2012). Arthur R. Jensen. https://senate.universityofcalifornia.edu/_files/inmemoriam/html/ArthurR.Jensen.html

Jensen, A. R. (1982). The debunking of scientific fossils and straw persons. *Contemporary Educational Review*, 1(2), 121–135.

Lubinski, D. (2013). Obituaries, Arthur, R. Jensen (1923–2012). *American Psychologist*, 68(5), 396–397. DOI: 10.1037/a0032872

Lynn, R. (2001). *The Science of Human Diversity: A History of the Pioneer Fund*. Lanham, MD, USA: University Press of America.

Miele, F. (2002). *Intelligence, Race and Genetics: Conversations with Arthur R. Jensen*. Oxford: Westview Press.

Mehler, B., & Hurt, K. (1998). 'Race science and the Pioneer Fund'. Revised version of 'The funding of the science'. *Searchlight*, 7 July.

Nixon, R. (1971). Talking about IQ tests and other things with Pat Moynihan. Date: October 7, 1971 Time: 10:32 am–10:58 am Location: White House Telephone www.nixontapes.org

Page, E. B. (1972). Behavior and heredity. *American Psychologist*, 27(7), 660–661. DOI:10.1037/h0038215

Robinson, D. N. (1973). The authority of reason will suffice. *American Psychologist*, 28(1), 83–84. DOI:10.1037/h0038069

Symonds, P. M., & Jensen, A. R. (1961). *From Adolescent to Adult*. Oxford: Columbia University Press.

Weyher, H. F. (1998). Contributions to the history of psychology: CXII. Intelligence, behavior genetics, and the pioneer fund. *Psychological Reports*, 82(3, Pt 2), 1347–1374. DOI:10.2466/PR0.82.3.1347-1374

Chapter 19

Walter Mischel

Oh, what a lovely war

February 22nd, 1930 to September 12th, 2018

Walter Mischel was born in Vienna, close to Freud's house, on February 22nd, 1930. Walter was the third child to Salomon Mischel and Lola Leah Schreck. The family fled Austria in the fateful year of 1938. Adolf Hitler had direct taken direct control of the German military and Austria was annexed and this was the beginning of the racialisation of the Nazi's Jewish policy. Jewish property was being seized, Jews were being expelled from Germany, or having their passports invalidated, and they were arrested, sent to concentration camps or simply murdered in the streets. Vienna had high numbers of prosperous Jewish citizens, nearly 200,000, but as the Nazis were welcomed into Vienna, the cultural, economic and social lives of its citizens were systematically dismantled. Within a week, Walter went from sitting at the front of his class, to having to stand at the back, and then to the door of the school being locked to him. Walter's father struggled to accept that the situation would not improve. In fear and denial, the family waited almost too long before exiting Vienna. They just about got of Vienna before 'Kristallnacht' when Jewish homes, synagogues and buildings all over Austria were ransacked and burned during the 'Night of the Broken Glass'.

To leave the country, Jews were forced to pay high taxes and leave everything behind. The Mischel family escaped to the United States, alive but with almost nothing. They eventually settled in Brooklyn in one of the poorest neighbourhoods. Walter reports a transformation in his parents. His father was severely withdrawn and depressed, holding on to the dream that one day they would return to Vienna. His mother Lola on the other hand, took control of their destiny as best she could. While, in Vienna, Lola was neurotic and unmotivated, in America, she was transformed. Working hard, taking control of the family and obtaining a waitressing job. Eventually, with the help of the Refugee Committee, his father opened a five-and-dime shop.

Walter performed well at school, graduating as valedictorian (top of his class) and winning a scholarship to Columbia University at a time when only 2 per cent of Jews were permitted (by quota) to enter university. However, just as Walter started at Columbia, his father had a heart attack, and he had to delay for a year, to support his father's business and make deliveries between other part-time jobs that he had taken on. When his father was mostly recovered, Walter found himself unable to get himself re-admitted to Columbia, so had to attend New York University instead. He began to study psychology but did not enjoy the subject, finding it 'ghastly'. The categorisation of humans into groups based on superficial constructs and the study of behaviourism based on rat behaviour (before B. F. Skinner's pioneering work) did not sit well with him.

Walter shifted his focus towards literature before settling on clinical psychology which he studied at City Colleague. At first, he was intrigued and fascinated by psychoanalysis, but became increasingly frustrated by what he described as 'when questions were being asked, the response was not to answer the question but to get into the dynamics and resistance of the question asker' (Mischel, 2017, interview). A turning point was when he was working as an uncredentialled social worker with impoverished children in the Henry Street Settlement House, in one of the most underprivileged areas of New York. These children were living under challenging conditions, they were very troubled. Walter recalls giving wisdom to these troubled children only to find that one of them had set his jacket on fire and recognising that he really needed to go to graduate school and get some proper training.

Walter settled on Ohio State University in Columbia mainly because their financial support was 50 dollars higher than other offerings and his first wife, Francis Henry, had received a budget to support her doctoral thesis. Francis's study of the tribes in the Caribbean Islands necessitated a move to Trinidad where Mischel found an exotic, sun-drenched haven where he could enjoy rum and Coca-Cola while exploring the locals' responses to the Rorschach test. He discovered significant cultural differences in attitudes toward gratification in the local ethnic groups. The Indians felt that the blacks were unconcerned about tomorrow and their children's futures, the blacks felt that the Indians did not know how to enjoy life. Mischel found that these differences manifested themselves at school. His work in this area was the start of what we now know as temporal economics. Do you prefer a small amount of money today or a large amount of money sometime in the future?

Walter Mischel obtained a PhD from Ohio State University in 1956. His mentors Julian Rotter and George Kelly had the most significant influence on his work, introducing him to personal construct and social learning theories, work that would later become central to his work on personality. The two psychologists operated from entirely different perspectives, but Mischel felt that between the two, there was a useful approach to the study of psychology that empowered the individual to liberate themselves from past problems and trauma. Rotter and Kelly gave Walter the signature combination that provided the context for exploration of the interaction between commitment and expectancies, with his first publications appearing in anthropological journals, marking what is often called the cognitive revolution. Later in his career, he would go on to give particular credit to George Kelly as profoundly influencing the future of cognitive psychology.

Mischel became part of the Columbia University faculty in 1956, moving to Harvard in 1958. Harvard was not a positive experience; it was an LSD 'la la land' that showed him the kind of psychologist he did not want to be. His marriage to Francis did not survive and the couple divorced in 1959. Walter married Harriet Nerlove the following year. Their relationship lasted until 1996, and they had three children together Judith, Rebecca and Linda.

Walter Mischel made a career studying self-control. The central focus of his work was the examination of the motivational structures behind the delay of gratification in children which formed a more extensive investigation into the links between self-control, achievement and well-being in later life. Ironically, Mischel had no control where cigarettes were concerned. The nicotine addiction was so strong he worked out he was craving a cigarette every three minutes and smoking as many as 60 cigarettes a day. When the cigarettes ran out, Walter had a pipe to fall back on, when the pipe tobacco ran out, he supplemented his habit with cigars. Fully aware of the damage he was causing to his health Walter repeatedly failed to stop, including making a pact with his 3-year-old child that he would stop sucking his pipe if she would stop sucking her thumb. It was, however, easy to explain away his habit as part of his professorial image and something that kept him calm and balanced.

Eventually, in 1962, Mischel could move to Stanford University. At Stanford, he found the pressure released from fast publishing towards slow thought and impact on important issues. He made Stanford his academic home for 21 years.

In the same year, in what he describes as a 'cry' against psychoanalytical theory, Mischel published *Personality and Assessment*. There was, he argued, no connection between diagnosis and treatment under the psychoanalytical model. The method was producing high levels of reliability (everyone agreed with everyone else) but zero validity, they were all wrong. The consistency of personality was not what is intuitively assumed. The environment was being overlooked as a factor in personality and behaviour. The idea that scientists could 'do personality' more simply than 'a urine analysis' was to Mischel, insane and the discipline was in crisis.

Perhaps more supported in this radically different environment, Mischel's attitude towards his smoking habit changed dramatically when, in the late 1960s, he met a man who was suffering from lung cancer. His hair was gone, his chest was bare and he had crosses on his chest which marked the points of where the radiation would go in a final attempt to manage what had become metastasised lung cancer. He never smoked again.

The response to Mischel's work was initially highly critical. The divide between social psychology and personality psychology was widening. Mischel had hoped his work would bring the disciplines closer together; the opposite was happening. The personality psychologists felt that Mischel's work was a personal attack, whereas the social psychologists misinterpreted Mischel's work, believing that he was endorsing a purely social model, rather than a person by situation interaction. In the spirit of 'don't interfere with our lovely war', his work was vilified to the point that his friends who worked in personality research refused to speak to him.

Walter Mischel died in his New York home of pancreatic cancer on September 12th, 2018. Walter was survived by his partner Michele Myers and three daughters. Among other accolades and honours, he held the Distinguished Science Award from the Society for Experimental Social Psychologists in 2001, the Personality Award of the Society for Social and Personality

Psychologists in 2005 and during 2007 he was elected President of the Association for Psychological Science. Possibly best known for his 'marshmallow study' and work on gratification, Mischel's contribution to the study of personality from an interactionist perspective is no less remarkable. The cognitive affect personality system proposed by Mischel and Shoda (1995) moved away from personality as a dichotomy by arguing that inconsistencies in behaviour, are not in fact inconsistent. Personality is therefore determined by the psychological, social and physical aspects of any given situation. How individuals interact with that environment will change depending on the determinants of that situation, but it will be relatively stable.

Despite his belief that he had failed to reconcile the gap between personality and social psychology, his theory that individuals could have agency over the stimuli that were 'controlling' them was profoundly important. Mischel sparked new methods and models to study individual differences in social behaviour and opened the door to the role of cognitive-affect processing, particularly the study of the acts, dispositions and personality factors that come together to help individuals to overcome pressure and exert self-control.

Major works

Mischel, W. (1968). *Personality and Assessment.* New York: Wiley.

Mischel, W. (1973). Toward a cognitive social learning reconceptualization of personality. *Psychological Review*, 80, 252–283.

Mischel, W., & Shoda, Y. (1995). A cognitive-affective system theory of personality: Reconceptualizing situations, dispositions, dynamics, and invariance in personality structure. *Psychological Review*, 102(2), 246–268.

Mischel, W. (2004). Toward an integrative science of the person. *Annual Review of Psychology*, 55, 1–22.

Bibliography

Mischel, W. (2017). Inside the psychologist's studio with Walter Mischel, *The American Psychological Society*, Published on December 19. Available at: www.psychologicalscience.org/publications/observer/obsonline/aps-past-president-walter-mischel-passes-away.html

Chapter 20

Lewis Robert Goldberg
The Big-5, OCEAN and the language of personality

January 28th, 1932

Lewis (Lew) Robert Goldberg was born on January 28th, 1932, at the Michael Reese Hospital in Chicago, Illinois to Gertrude Mathis Lewis and Max Frederick Goldberg. His father was born in 1899 in Globe, Arizona and raised in the small Midwest town of Danville, Illinois. He applied to Harvard University but was not immediately accepted and so spent his first college year at the University of Illinois, followed by three years at Harvard, where he was president of his college fraternity, and where he achieved his BA degree in 1922; from Harvard, he received a law degree in 1925. He practised business-related law in the famed Rookery building on LaSalle Street in Chicago's Loop, where he was revered for his honesty and integrity. He died in 1996 at the age of 97.

Lew Goldberg's mother was born in 1907 in St. Louis, Missouri, where after high school she attended the Mary Institute. She met Max on an arranged double date during a trip to Chicago, and they were married in Chicago in 1929. She was an accomplished piano player, oil painter and cook. She died in 2005, at the age of 98.

As a child, Lew was called Skipper by his parents and relatives, but deliberately changed his name to Lew when he entered high school. An only child, he lived with his parents in Chicago on Hyde Park Boulevard (across from the Poinsettia Hotel) between 55th and 56th streets, near the Museum of Science and Industry. He attended Bret Harte elementary school, skipping two semesters and graduating from 8th grade in 1944 near the end of World War II. Around that time his parents moved to the northern Chicago suburb of Highland Park, where he spent a semester at its Lincoln elementary school, graduating from 8th grade a second time in 1945. He graduated from the Highland Park High School in 1949.

His college years, 1949 to 1953, at Harvard were unusually happy, stimulating and even inspirational. Some years before he arrived, Harvard's famed psychology department had split in two, one retaining the name Psychology and the other (a fusion of anthropology, sociology and personality and social psychology) called Social Relations. Lewis majored in Social Relations, in part because its lax requirements allowed him the freedom to take elementary everything else. In his junior year, faced with the decision where to go after college, he considered becoming a physicist or a lawyer like his father but eventually settled on graduate school in clinical psychology, under the illusion that such an education would be the best training for whatever he eventually decided to do.

Accepted into the PhD program in clinical psychology at the University of Michigan, Lew developed a strong friendship with his mentor, E. Lowell Kelly, who was the psychology department head and President of the American Psychological Association. Kelly and his wife were building a sailboat in the basement of their large house in Ann Arbor, Michigan, and Lewis spent hours handing them screwdrivers and other tools. When thinking of a topic for his doctoral dissertation, he elected to conduct a follow-up survey of the participants in the Veterans Administration assessment project that resulted in the classic volume, *The Prediction of Performance in Clinical Psychology* by Kelly and Fiske (1951). The resulting Psychological Monograph was titled 'Correlates of Later Performance and Specialisation In Psychology: A Follow-Up Study of the Trainees Assessed in the VA Selection Research Project' (Kelly & Goldberg, 1959).

Although this was quite rare for graduate students back in those days, Lewis published two articles in peer-reviewed APA journals, one of which on decision-making ('The Effectiveness of Clinicians' Judgments: The Diagnosis of Organic Brain Damage from the Bender-Gestalt Test' [Goldberg, 1959]) became frequently cited and introduced him to Paul J. Hoffman, the founder of Oregon Research Institute (ORI), the institution which was his scientific home throughout his career. At the very end of Lewis' stay at Michigan, he met Warren T. Norman, who was to play a pivotal role in his later scientific career.

While writing his doctoral dissertation, Lewis travelled with the Kelly family to Washington, DC to attend the APA convention with Kelly as its president. There he was introduced by Kelly to Richard Sears, the newly installed head of the psychology department at

Stanford University, who offered Lewis a position as acting assistant professor at Stanford to fill in for a faculty member who was on leave for a year. One year later, Kelly gave a lecture at Stanford and helped arrange for Lewis to stay there a second year in his temporary position. While teaching at Stanford he became close friends with Albert Bandura and Jerry Wiggins, teaching an assessment course with Wiggins and developing the outline for what would eventually become the classic textbook, *Personality and Prediction: Principles of Personality Assessment* (Wiggins, 1973).

When it became time to secure a permanent faculty position, Kelly once again found Lewis a new job, this one at the University of Oregon. Upon Kelly's recommendation, Robert Leeper, the Oregon psychology department head, called Lewis to offer him a position as Assistant Professor, sight unseen. Almost immediately after that telephone call, Lewis received another, this one from Paul Hoffman, telling him about his new 'institute for basic research in the behavioural sciences' called the Oregon Research Institute (ORI). From 1960 on, they provided congenial homes for his scientific research (ORI) and for his undergraduate and graduate student teaching (University of Oregon). It was at the University of Oregon that Lewis met Dean Peabody, with whom he developed a deep friendship and eventual collaboration (Peabody & Goldberg, 1989).

In 1962, Kelly was appointed by Sargent Shriver, President John F. Kennedy's brother-in-law and the director of the brand-new US Peace Corps, to serve as that agency's first full-time Director of Selection. Soon after that, Kelly contacted the president of the University of Oregon (Arthur Fleming), asking him to release Lewis from his teaching duties in the middle of the academic quarter so that Lewis could assist Kelly in Washington, DC. Thus began one of the most enjoyable and fascinating adventures in Lewis' lifetime, serving the Peace Corps (PC) in a consulting capacity as one of its first Field Selection Officers (FSO).

During those early years, PC aspirants were trained in colleges and universities throughout the US, and their selection as PC volunteers took place only at the end of their typically 9-month training period. It was the FSO who made the actual selection decisions, upon the advice of a 9- to 12-person selection board, made up of persons involved in the training and assessment of the trainee cohort. Over the years between 1962 and 1965, Lewis served as the FSO for over two dozen of these training groups, most of them in the paradise-like location of Hilo, Hawaii. That permitted Lewis to fly from Oregon to Hawaii every six weeks, first to inform the trainees about the nature of the PC selection process, then to conduct a mid-term selection board meeting, and last to conduct the final selection board, followed by intense personal interviews with all trainees who had not been selected to be PC volunteers.

Back at ORI, Lewis worked with Hoffman, Leonard Rorer and Paul Slovic on topics related to human judgement and decision-making, and in 1967 he wrote a quasi-autobiographical account of that research. Knowing that the editor of the *American Psychologist* (AP) was interested in the topic, on a whim Lewis sent him a copy of the manuscript 'for his reading pleasure'. To his surprise, he immediately heard back that the manuscript was now in press in AP, and soon after was published there. The resulting article, titled 'Simple models or simple processes: Some research on clinical judgments' (Goldberg, 1968), was to become his first citation classic. Not long after, he published in *Psychological Bulletin* another highly cited article on decision-making, titled 'Man Versus Model of Man: A Rationale, Plus Some Evidence, for Improving on Clinical Inferences' (Goldberg, 1970).

Around 1965, the small group of research scientists at ORI at that time decided to apply to the National Institute of Mental Health for a 'program project' research grant, with Lewis as the principal investigator; the resulting large grant, called 'A Program Project in Personality Assessment' was used to support much ORI research for the next decade. During the 1966–1967 academic year, Lewis spent his first sabbatical as a Fulbright professor at the University of Nijmegen in the Netherlands; during the summers before and after, he and his family explored Europe, from the Scandinavian countries south to Greece, Spain, Portugal, Italy and France.

Loving the opportunity to spend substantial chunks of time in new and thus different places, during the 1970–1971 academic year he taught in the psychology department and the Institute for Personality Assessment and Research (IPAR) at the University of California, Berkeley; during 1974–1975 he was a Fulbright Professor at the University of Istanbul in Turkey (with a side-trip to visit Amos Tversky and Daniel Kahneman in Jerusalem, Israel); and in 1981–1982 he was invited to be a Fellow in the Center for Advanced Study in the Behavioural Sciences (NIAS) near the The Hague in the Netherlands. During that last period, Lewis spent countless hours with his new PhD student Oliver John commuting between NIAS, Groningen in the Netherlands (home of esteemed colleagues Willem K. B. Hofstee and Frank Brokken) and Bielefeld in Germany where John was finishing an advanced degree. It was also during this period when Lewis and John met Sarah E. Hampson, who was soon to join them at ORI. From 1960 to 1975, ORI was a fabulous place to conduct research, but over the last five years tension developed between Paul Hoffman, its founder and its permanent director, and the scientists whose research grants funded the institute; in 1975, all of the scientific staff elected to leave the institute, and many of them formed their own smaller institutes. Lewis founded the Institute for the Measurement of Personality (IMP), associated with the Wright Institute in Berkeley, California; IMP was housed along with Decision Research (DR), founded by Paul Slovic, Baruch Fischhoff and Sarah Lichtenstein, above a bank in downtown Eugene.

Lewis was fortunate to have his research funded by US government agencies, primarily by the National Institutes of Health, throughout his scientific career, the only exception being a 3-year period during the Reagan administration when funds for research in the behavioural sciences were out of favour. With no research funding, IMP could pay no rent to DR, but Paul Slovic in an extraordinary act of generosity insisted that Lewis and his research team stay rent-free in DR's offices, because he 'liked having them around'.

At the University of Oregon, Lewis worked with about 20 PhD students over the years, with four of them – William Chaplin, Tina Rosolack (later Traxler), Oliver John and Gerard Saucier – becoming virtual members of his family. Lewis had been elected to the exclusive Society of Multivariate Experimental Psychology (SMEP) during the mid-1960s, and he was elected president of SMEP a decade later. Chaplin, John and Saucier followed him as elected SMEP members, and some of Lewis' most important publications were co-authored with one or more of that trio.

From roughly 1980 throughout the rest of his life, Lewis was occupied with what he considered the single most important problem in the field of personality: the quest for a scientifically compelling structural model for organising the myriad trait-descriptive terms in the English language (e.g., energetic, warm, responsible, nervous, smart) and eventually in all of the diverse languages of the world. At first, he assumed that this scientific problem would be far too difficult for him to solve, but he continuously collected self and peer descriptions from students in his university classes and used factor analysis as a methodological technique for examining the structure of the relations among the many hundreds of personality terms to which they had responded. By the end of the 1980s, Lewis thought that he had learned enough from these analyses to settle on a provisional taxonomic structure, one that he had earlier dubbed the 'Big Five' factors (Goldberg, 1981); the article reporting these analyses and findings was titled 'An Alternative "Description of Personality": The Big Five Factor Structure' (Goldberg, 1990). That influential article became his most frequently cited publication, with well over 6,000 citations by 2018.

During the years when Lewis served as a consultant to the Peace Corps, Lewis became friends with a SMEP colleague John (Jack) Digman, who was teaching at the University of Hawaii. When Digman ended up living near Eugene, Oregon, he elected to join Lewis at ORI, where the two had daily lunches together. From 1959 to 1967, Digman had persuaded 88 elementary-school teachers to describe each of the students in her class at the very end of an academic year, using various samples of trait-descriptive adjectives. Sarah Hampson suggested that Digman try to obtain a research grant to locate those children 40-years later, now as middle-aged adults, so as to be able to relate his extraordinarily rich collection of child personality descriptions to adult outcomes.

Soon after he was notified that the grant 'Personality and health: A longitudinal study' had been funded, Digman passed away, and Lewis was asked to fill in as the principal investigator. Lewis served as the leader of this project for two 5-year periods, with Hampson serving in this role for the next two funding cycles; the present PI of what has been called the 'Hawaii' grant is Grant Edmonds. During the 21 years of the Hawaii project, the vast majority of the children have been located, and most of them have participated as adults in half-day medical-clinic visits, and they have responded to a wide assortment of questionnaire surveys. The project has been extraordinarily productive, and its many publications are becoming highly cited.

For most of his career, Lewis had been interested in measures of personality traits, and he wrote a rather detailed account of their historical development (Goldberg, 1971). He was particularly intrigued by the different methods used to measure traits, and he sought to compare these methods empirically. One frequently cited study was titled 'Comparative validity of different strategies of constructing personality inventory scales' (Hase & Goldberg, 1967), followed by the more extensive monograph 'Parameters of Personality Inventory Construction and Utilization: A Comparison of Prediction Strategies and Tactics' (Goldberg, 1972) and 'In Response to Jackson's Challenge: The Comparative Validity of Personality Scales Constructed by the External (Empirical) Strategy and Scales Developed Intuitively by Experts, Novices, and Laymen' (Ashton & Goldberg, 1973). Eventually, Lew was able to empirically compare the validity of 11 commercial inventories against behavioural acts, informant reports and clinical indicators in a sort of Consumers Reports format (Grucza & Goldberg, 2007).

Historically, developers of multiscale personality inventories such as the MMPI and CPI have used them as profit-making enterprises to be sold by commercial test publishers who deny users the right to modify the inventory in any way. Lewis had long felt that this historical practice served to stifle scientific progress. Ironically, one of the most popular recent proprietary inventories, the NEO-PI-R, was developed by individuals who worked for the US National Institute on Aging, and it achieved its fame from studies carried out in and paid for by that federal agency. Lewis had long felt that measures developed with taxpayers' money should be available to all, and he began to implement a public-domain website providing freely available personality measures, called the International Personality Item Pool (IPIP). His first publication describing this effort was titled 'A Broad-Bandwidth, Public-Domain, Personality Inventory Measuring the Lower-Level Facets of Several Five-Factor Models' (Goldberg, 1999).

Over the years, the IPIP site has been widely used for scientific studies throughout the world, becoming especially useful to students and young scientists with no funds to purchase proprietary measures. It has come to provide well over 3,000 items, and over 450 scales, which in turn have been translated into at least 40 languages, and its measures have been used in studies described in over 1,000 publications. The contents of a presidential symposium on the IPIP at a meeting of the Association for Research in Personality was synthesised for publication by the IPIP consultant, John A. Johnson; the resulting article, entitled 'The International Personality Item Pool and the future of public-domain personality measures' (Goldberg et al., 2006), has achieved well over 2,500 citations.

Lew's lessons for success include, 'shave your head, stay healthy, and outlive the competition'. He married Ruby Vera Montgomery (called Robin) while in graduate school in 1956, and they had three children: Timothy Duncan (Tim), Holly Lynn and Randall Monte (Randy). Robin has been a Wave in the US Navy, serving in the stressful role of an aviation tower operator. Tim is a businessman; Holly is a noted Hollywood scriptwriter and film director, who eventually became an acclaimed writer of young adult fiction; and Randy was a monk in Europe and India, eventually becoming an alternative medical provider. Robin and Lewis were divorced in 1978, the same year that he married his present wife, Janice Crider May (Jan). Jan had two daughters from a previous marriage: Laura Marie and Kirsten Ann, whom Lewis helped raise while Jan attended law school and later served as a partner in a business-oriented law firm, specialising in employment law. Jan and Lewis presently live on San Juan Island, north of Seattle in the state of Washington, where Lewis happily carries out scientific work most mornings and works in their forest most afternoons, an extraordinarily wondrous blend of intellectual and physical activities.

Major works

Chaplin, W. F., & Goldberg, L. R. (1984). A failure to replicate the Bem and Allen study of individual differences in cross-situational consistency. *Journal of Personality and Social Psychology*, 47, 1074–1090

Chaplin, W. F., John, O. P., & Goldberg, L. R. (1988). Conceptions of states and traits: Dimensional attributes with ideals as prototypes. *Journal of Personality and Social Psychology*, 54, 541–557.

Goldberg, L. R. (1959). The effectiveness of clinicians' judgments: The diagnosis of organic brain damage from the Bender-Gestalt Test. *Journal of Consulting Psychology*, 23(1),25–33.

Goldberg, L. R. (1971). A historical survey of personality scales and inventories. In P. McReynolds (Ed.), *Advances in Psychological Assessment: Volume 2* (pp. 293–336). Palo Alto, CA: Science and Behavior Books.

Goldberg, L. R. (1974). Objective diagnostic tests and measures. In M. R. Rosenzweig & L. W. Porter (Eds.), *Annual Review of Psychology*, vol. 25 (pp. 343–366). Palo Alto, CA: Annual Reviews.

Goldberg, L. R. (1981). Language and individual differences. The search for universals in personality lexicons. In L. Wheeler (Ed.), *Review of Personality and Social Psychology*, vol. 2. Beverly Hills, CA: Sage Publications, str. 141–165 *Big Five Factor Model, Theory and Structure*.

Goldberg, L. R. (1990). An alternative 'description of personality': The Big-Five factor structure. *Journal of Personality and Social Psychology*, 59(6), 1216–1229.

Goldberg, L. R. (1991). Human mind versus regression equation: Five contrasts. In D. Cicchetti & W. M. Grove (Eds.), *Thinking Clearly about Psychology: Essays in Honor of Paul E. Meehl* (Volume 1: Matters of public interest) (pp. 173–184). Minneapolis, MN: University of Minnesota Press. https://projects.ori.org/lrg/PDFs_papers/Human.mind.vs.pdf

Goldberg, L. R. (1992). The social psychology of personality. *Psychological Inquiry*, 3, 89–94. https://projects.ori.org/lrg/PDFs_papers/SocPsy_ofPersonality_1992.pdf

Goldberg, L. R. (1999). A broad-bandwidth, public-domain, personality inventory measuring the lower-level facets of several five-factor models. In I. Mervielde, I. Deary, F. De Fruyt, & F. Ostendorf (Eds.), *Personality Psychology in Europe*, vol. 7 (pp. 7–28). Tilburg: Tilburg University Press.

Goldberg, L. R., & Saucier, G. (1995). So, what do you propose we use instead? A reply to Block. *Psychological Bulletin*, 117, 221–225; discussion 22.

Hampson, S. E., John, O. P., & Goldberg, L. R. (1986). Category breadth and hierarchical structure in personality: Studies of asymmetries in judgments of trait implications. *Journal of Personality and Social Psychology*, 51, 37–54.

Hase, H. D., & Goldberg, L. R. (1967). Comparative validity of different strategies of constructing personality inventory scales. *Psychological Bulletin*, 67, 231–248.

John, O. P., Hampson, S. E., & Goldberg, L. R. (1991). The basic level in personality-trait hierarchies: Studies of trait use and accessibility in different contexts. *Journal of Personality and Social Psychology*, 60, 348–361.

Saucier, G., & Goldberg, L. R. (1996). Evidence for the Big Five in analyses of familiar English personality adjectives. *European Journal of Personality*, 10, 61–77.

Saucier, G., & Goldberg L. R. (1998). What is beyond the Big Five? *Journal of Personality*, 66, 495–524.

Saucier, G., & Goldberg, L. R. (2001). Institute OR. Lexical studies of indigenous personality factors: Premises, products, and prospects. *Journal of Personality*, 69, 847–879.

Bibliography

Ashton, S. G., & Goldberg, L. R. (1973). In response to Jackson's challenge: The comparative validity of personality scales constructed by the external (empirical) strategy and scales developed intuitively by experts, novices, and laymen. *Journal of Research in Personality*, 7, 1–20.

Goldberg, L. R. (1958). The effectiveness of clinicians' judgments: The diagnosis of organic brain damage from the Bender-Gestalt Test. *Journal of Consulting Psychology*, 23, 25–33.

Goldberg, L. R. (1968). Simple models or simple processes? Some research on clinical judgments. *The American Psychologist*, 23, 483–496.

Goldberg, L. R. (1970). Man, versus model of man: A rationale, plus some evidence, for a method of improving on clinical inferences. *Psychological Bulletin*, 73, 422–432.

Goldberg, L. R. (1972). Parameters of personality inventory construction and utilization: A comparison of prediction strategies and tactics. *Multivariate Behavioral Research Monograph*, 7(72-2).

Goldberg, L. R. (1993). The structure of phenotypic personality traits. *American Psychologist*, 48, 26–34. https://projects.ori.org/lrg/PDFs_pa pers/Goldberg.Am.Psych.1993.pdf

Goldberg, L. R. (2009). How to win a career achievement award in five easy lessons. *Journal of Personality Assessment*, 91, 506–517. https:// projects.ori.org/lrg/PDFs_papers/Goldberg_2009_How%20to%20Win %20a%20Career%20Achievement%20Award%20in%20Five% 20Easy%20Lessons.pdf

Goldberg, L. (2018). International Personality Item Pool. http://ipip.ori.org/.

Goldberg, L. R., Johnson, J. A., Eber, H. W., Hogan, R., Ashton, M. C., Cloninger, C. R., & Gough, H. C. (2006). The International Personality Item Pool and the future of public-domain personality measures. *Journal of Research in Personality*, 40, 84–96.

Grucza, R. A., & Goldberg, L. R. (2007). The comparative validity of 11 modern personality inventories: Predictions of behavioral acts, informant reports, and clinical indicators. *Journal of Personality Assessment*, 89, 167–187.

Kelly, E. L., & Fiske, D. W. (1951). *The Prediction of Performance in Clinical Psychology*. Ann Arbor, MI: University of Michigan Press.

Kelly, E. L., & Goldberg, L. R. (1959). Correlates of later performance and specialization in psychology: A follow-up study of the trainees assessed in the VA Selection Research Project. *Psychological Monographs: General and Applied*, 73(12), 1–32.

McCrae, R. R., & John, O. P. (1992). An introduction to the five-factor model and its applications. *Journal of Personality*, 60(2), 175–215.

Peabody, D., & Goldberg, L. R. (1989) Some determinants of factor structures from personality-trait descriptors. *Journal of Personality and Social Psychology*, 57, 552–567.

Wiggins, J. S. (1973). *Personality and Prediction: Principles of Personality Assessment*. Reading, MA: Addison-Wesley.

Chapter 21

Howard Gardner

One of a kind

July 11th, 1943

Rudolph (Ralph) Gaertner and Hilde Bella (née Weilheimer) Gaertner were married in Nürnberg in 1932. Their first son Erich was born in 1935 and the family, like Jewish families written about in this book, had to flee Germany during 1938. They eventually made it to America, settling in Scranton, Pennsylvania in 1939. When Hilde was expecting her second child, tragedy struck. Erich was playing in the snow when his sledge smashed into a stone wall, fracturing his skull. He died in January 1943, at just seven years old. Howard was born several months later, on July 11th, 1943. Neither the escape from Germany nor the death of Erich were ever discussed during Howard's childhood.

Howard's parents encouraged his intellectual development, but they provided very few opportunities for risky physical activities such as cycling or rough sports. Gardner describes discovering his secret German-Jewish history and realising that he was different from others (he is also colour blind) and that he was expected to make his mark in this new country, but that there were major obstacles to doing so. Other intellectual giants had escaped their German and Austrian origins, moving to intellectual centres in Europe, he had arrived, however, in the 'uninteresting, intellectually stagnant, and economically depressed Pennsylvania valley' (Gardner, 1989, p.22).

He was an introverted child that enjoyed writing and music, Howard reports that, despite the terrible trauma behind his parents' lives, he had a happy childhood. When he thinks of his childhood, he sees himself seated at the piano, usually next to his mother, playing Bach. His dedication to his mother continued right through his life, Howard's children describe how he provided love and tenderness until Hilde died aged 102.

Howard began to board at a local prep school where the teachers poured attention into his development and well-being. By adolescence, he had discontinued his formal pursuit of music. He believes that his true education did not start until he started his studies at Harvard College in September 1961 with the intention of studying law but focused more on a broader range of subjects including psychology. He graduated with a degree in social relations in 1965, before commencing his doctoral studies. He had hoped to pursue the study of cognition in the arts, but as there were no suitable supervisors he focused instead on developmental psychology. During his post-college year, he spent 12 months as a Fellow at the London School of Economics where he expanded his learning into philosophy and sociology.

In the summer of 1965, Gardner began working with the cognitive and educational psychologist Jerome Bruner. Bruner's work on cognitive learning theory was momentous in directing the questions that Gardner would later explore. Bruner's personal approach to his students was something that Gardner tried to emulate throughout his career. Each day Bruner's team brought delicious food from the Cambridge delicatessens, and he and his students would all sit down and eat together. He left a lasting impression that professors should learn, work and make personal time for people just out of college.

Bruner brought Judy Krieger from Berkeley to study for her doctoral degree. Gardner and Krieger fell in love immediately and wanted to get married straight away. Their parents, however, were cautious and persuaded the couple to wait a while, so they did. Judy eventually obtained her doctorate and became a cognitive developmental psychologist in her own right. The couple had three children together Kerith (1969), Jay (1971) and Andrew (1976). Howard and Judy divorced in the early 1980s. In 1994 Judith became ill while travelling with friends. She first showed signs of illness on a trek in Nepal with friends, then passed away weeks later in Jerusalem.

The early part of Gardner's career focused on children's development and neuropsychology, particularly the development and breakdown of symbol processing capacities. Gardner undertook postdoctoral studies at the Boston Veterans Administration Hospital with the eminent neurologist Norman Geschwind, while maintaining strong connections with Harvard. Howard also became the co-director of Project Zero; a research group focused on cognition and the arts.

While working at Project Zero, Gardner met Ellen Winner. Gardner was looking for an assistant to work with him on the psychology of art. Winner had no idea what the psychology of art was, but she had a background in the study of metaphor and Gardner offered her the job. Winner initially rejected the idea of committing to a post for two years but eventually felt that on balance it would improve her chances of obtaining a place to study clinical psychology. The partnership was a productive one. They were soon publishing papers together, and when Ellen eventually obtained a place at graduate-school, she continued to work with Gardner at Project Zero. By then a couple, Gardner and Winner married in 1982 and had one child together, Benjamin (born 1985).

By the late 1970s, Howard had begun to construct a theory of human intelligence which challenged many of the significant thinkers of the day. This model exposed the weaknesses in the orthodoxy of the time and provided an alternative to the belief in the salience/hegemony of general intelligence 'g'; the focus on the isolation of g overlooked the full range of possibilities that are associated with human thinking and ability.

By the early 1980s, Gardner was a leading member of the Human Potential Project. The project, funded by the Bernard van Leer Foundation in the Netherlands, was set up to examine scientific knowledge of human potential. Gardner's principal contribution, published in 1983, was *Frames of Mind*, where he set out his theory of multiple intelligences.

What was different in Gardner's approach was not a focus on test scores and correlates; instead it was the exploration of what cognitive abilities humans, in all cultures, needed to perform roles as adults. For Gardner, each discrete intelligence is like a computer that works more or less well and individuals can be stronger in some areas (and hence more intelligent) than others (less intelligent). This theory of multiple-intelligences was designed to challenge assumptions and misunderstandings, particularly in education, around traditional intelligence theory. Gardner also hoped to influence education systems which tended to favour mathematical and linguistic abilities over other competencies.

The book was ground-breaking. Its positive reception enabled Gardner to avoid the traditional 'ladder to tenure' in the academy and shift directly to Professor of Cognition and Education at the Harvard Graduate School. In his influential book, Gardner argued that as many as seven separate intelligences exist – each a discrete form of information processing. Only three are readily tested by standard psychological measures: linguistic/language skills, logical mathematical abilities and spatial understanding. There were four further intelligences; musical ability, bodily kinaesthetic; interpersonal (understanding and relating to others) and intrapersonal (understanding oneself). Gardner suggests that, rather than calling individuals more or less intelligent, one should speak in terms of being more intelligent in specific areas and less so in others. Gardner argued that these separate intelligences resided in different brain areas. His clinical observations supported this because they could be observed in isolation in prodigies, autistic savants and other exceptional populations.

Gardner's theory offered a different, rich perspective about which to understand human abilities. He argued that experimental evidence was simply one form of empirical evidence on which a theorist should draw. His work drew on a vast amount of empirical evidence, gathered in a range of disciplines from neurology to anthropology. As such, it supported a departure from the work of Spearman, Eysenck, Jensen and others.

Psychology remains split on Gardner's work, but he has had significant influence outside of psychology, particularly in the field of education. Educators argue that multiple intelligences validate not only their every-day experience of children and their abilities but also their experiences of the variety of gifted youngsters. It has helped them improve pedagogical practices and design curriculums that support development in all kinds of new ways.

Gardner responded to some of these erroneous interpretations but has moved on to other lines of research in psychology, education and ethics. In his book *The Unschooled Mind* (1991), he made it clear that he believed that the role of education was to develop deep understanding and that educators should value depth in learning, over breadth. To enable this to happen, children should have opportunities to work on a problem over an extended period using different approaches.

His vision was always a broad one and he updated his work to explore what it means to be intelligent in a digital age and how intelligence and morality can work together for a better world. With colleagues, in 1994 he established the Good Work Project which aimed to determine how those at the peak of their professions can produce work that is exemplary in nature but also contributes to the broader good of society.

The misunderstanding and misuse of Gardner's work have led to the theory being praised and damned by psychologists and educationalist alike. At the time of writing Gardner, now 75 years of age, is still involved both in the Good Work Project (renamed the Good Project) and Project Zero. His children describe him as an insanely hard-working father, whose dedication to his family surpasses his dedication to work. He cares deeply about everything he does including being a dad. What he does not care about is his personal appearance. He once turned up at an important meeting with one brown shoe and one black shoe. Marcelo Suarez-Orozco describes him as brilliant, humble, generous and deeply ethical. A man for all seasons; 'Sui generis' (one of a kind).

Major works

Gardner, H. (1983). *Frames of Mind: The Theory of Multiple Intelligences*. New York: Basic Books.
Gardner, H. (1991). *The Unschooled Mind: How Children Think and How Schools Should Teach*. New York: Basic Books.
Gardner, H. (1999). *Intelligence Reframed: Multiple Intelligences for the 21st Century*. New York: Basic Books.

Bibliography

Gardner, H. (1989) *To Open Minds: Chinese Clues to the Dilemma of Contemporary Education*. New York: Basic Books.
The good project, ideas and tools for a goodlife. thegoodproject.org
Palmer, J., Cooper, D. E., & Bresler, L. (2001). *Fifty Modern Thinkers on Education: From Piaget to the Present Day*. London and New York: Routledge.

Chapter 22

John Philippe Rushton
The incendiary device

December 3rd, 1943 to October 2nd, 2012

John Philippe (pronounced Philip) Rushton (JPR) was born in Bournemouth, on December 3rd, 1943. His family roots were Lancastrian. Rushton stated that one of his ancestors, Samuel Crompton (1753–1827), invented the spinning mule which revolutionised the yarn industry from hand-spinning to large-scale mechanisation. Crompton did not have sufficient funds to patent his invention and lived in constant fear of the Luddites, a band of workers who destroyed machinery (and their inventors) to protect their jobs. The lack of evidence for this connection is questioned and provided as evidence by Dutton (2018) of JPR's narcissistic tendencies.

JPR's French grandmother, Marguerite Adou, met his grandfather, James Anderson, who was serving in Normandy during World War I (thus contributing Philippe in the French way). Marguerite became pregnant and after the birth (of JPR's mother) her parents brought her to England and the couple eventually married in Bolton in 1918. Philippe's father, John, a decorating contractor, served in the Royal Air Force during World War II repairing battle-damaged Spitfires. His mother Andrea served with the London Fire Service and his uncle served with General Montgomery at the Battle of El Alamein. Dutton again points out that there are some glaring anomalies with Rushton's account of this time with his parents.

After the war, JPR's father became established as a private housing contractor. However, as the Labour (Socialist) Party began to nationalise many of the industries that John relied upon for his contract work, his company began to struggle. In the hope of a more prosperous life, the family emigrated to South Africa in 1948. The family returned to England in 1952, when

Philippe was due to start secondary education. JPR claims this was due to his father's struggling business, although Rushton's third wife Elizabeth Weiss claims it was really because JPRs father had an affair and his mother wanted to return home. The family settled in Poole, Dorset and Philippe passed the 11 plus examination which facilitated entry into the English grammar school education system. The family were settled for 8 years, until his father was offered a much-desired position as an artist and designer, with the new Canadian Broadcasting Corporation in Toronto. In 1956 they emigrated to Canada.

JPR recalls how the works of Hans Eysenck were significantly influential to the teenage Rushton, particularly his personality questionnaires mapping political affiliation to personality. During these turbulent teenage years JPR describes himself as growing his hair long, becoming outgoing but also utterly selfish. Finding himself surrounded by what he described as anti-white and anti-western views, JPR became interested in right-wing groups. He went about sourcing old, forbidden copies of eugenics articles that argued that evolutionary differences existed between blacks and whites. He fell in love with his best friend's sister Nina, dropped out of school and his girlfriend became pregnant. The couple married, but the relationship did not last. Rushton began a new relationship with Margaret Von Klein, and JPR retained custody of his and Nina's son Stephen. There is some speculation that Nina may have been quite young and that was one reason for the custody arrangements.

Rushton and Margaret moved to England in 1963, taking Stephen with them and both holding dreams of becoming writers. Rushton got a job as a bus conductor in South London, and in 1965 the family moved to Hackney where their daughter Katherine Marguerite was born. Rushton realised he needed more significant employment and began studying for his A-levels. The couple were living in near poverty. The combination of family relationships, stress and money worries took their toll. The relationship broke down, and Margaret returned to Canada with Katherine. Margaret fared no better in Canada, and Katherine ended up in care. She was adopted at age 4. JPR continued to live in London as a single father, living in near poverty until in 1967 he was admitted to Birkbeck College to study psychology.

Rushton obtained a first-class degree in 1973 (at the age of 27) before commencing a PhD in Social Psychology under the supervision of Hilde T. Himmelweit (a student of Hans Eysenck) at the London School of Economics and Political Science. An avid Darwinist, and at a time before Richard Dawkin's *The Selfish Gene* offered any reasoned argument on the subject, Rushton was determined to answer the question of why people help each other. For JPR, the answer was situated in social learning theory, and he planned to explore the influence of the educational system, mass media and family on altruistic behaviour. The environment at the London School of Economics was a contentious one. When Hans Eysenck was attacked at the London School of Economics, JPR was one of the students who clambered to the front of the auditorium to protect him. Rushton was also assaulted during this debacle.

JPR became involved romantically with the heiress, Felicity 'Gillian' Hammerton. Gillian was enormous support. She used her personal inheritance to support JPR, moving him and his son from the poverty of their one bedroom flat in Hackney into the more exclusive Holborn area. Although the relationship never survived, Hammerton cites JPR as a good man who supported her. Hammerton, a newly qualified barrister, was caught in a very public scandal during the 1970s when she became pregnant by David Cocks, QC. Cocks spent years fighting Hammerton, humiliating her over child support payments. JPR returned the support that Hammerton had shown him, supporting her and her son emotionally. She said that JPR made her son feel 'he was something, against his father's disdain'.

As a post-doc at the University of Oxford, Rushton continued to work closely with others in Eysenck's circle, focusing now on the question of personality development in children before returning to Canada to teach at the University of York (1974–1976), the University of Toronto (1976–1977) and the University of Western Ontario. The John Simon Guggenheim Memorial Foundation honoured Rushton in 1989 with fellowship and the University of London bestowed the DSc in 1992, which is a doctorate awarded for recognition of a substantial and sustained contribution to scientific knowledge.

It was during his tenure at Western Ontario where Rushton met his second wife, the then PhD student and future mathematician Serpil Kocabayik and became interested in evolutionary psychology. Wilson's (1975) publication *Sociobiology: The New Synthesis* argued that altruism could be observed in non-human animals and as such persuaded Rushton that there must be an evolutionary and genetic basis to altruistic behaviour; prosocial parents produce prosocial children. Rushton describes this as a personal paradigm shift; the altruism trait was not learned it was inherited.

The University of California, Berkeley appeared to be the right environment to explore further how stable individual differences in altruism were over a lifespan. From January to June 1981, Rushton worked with Paul Mussen but was disappointed by the lack of academic engagement on the role of genetics in development. This was in the years following Arthur Jensen's contentious work, and nobody was interested. However, Arthur Jensen's office was not far from Rushton's, he sought him out, and they soon hit it off. They shared mutual interests in areas related to human differences, particularly Jensen's suggestion that the three racial groups (African, European and East Asian) were situated on a developmental continuum. This work demonstrated that mean black–white differences in IQ were more pronounced on the more heritable, less cultural subtests and using what Jensen called the method of correlated vectors demonstrated that Spearman's g was the 'active ingredient' in IQ.

To further explore these relationships JPR applied Jensen's techniques to the study of inbreeding depression, the phenomenon that occurs when closely genetically related individuals have children together. On average their IQ is lower than the normal population and Rushton reported findings that suggested that the inbreeding depression phenomenon also predicted black–white differences on the same subset of tests used in the inbreeding depression studies. Further cross-cultural studies provided further evidence for the Spearman hypothesis: black–white IQ differences vary systematically as a function of a test's g loading. JPR named the phenomena, 'the Jensen Effect'. This collaboration led to another sabbatical, this time to work directly with Hans Eysenck at the London Institute of Psychiatry before returning to Canada in 1983 to fully develop his theory of racial differences using Wilson's r-K model of reproductive strategies.

Wilson's r-K is a model which maps the relationship between fertility and parental care and speed on the life spectrum (LH). Oysters, for example, produce 500,000,000 eggs per year and no parental care (fast life history, r-strategy) whereas apes provide one infant every five or six years and provide extensive parental care (slow life history, K-strategy) and have extensive social systems to support offspring development to maturity. Rushton attempted to take K-strategy one stage further and examine differences in K-strategies which could be used to predict differences in intelligence. For example, races which had more tightly knit family structures could be related to higher levels of intelligence. Rushton collected large amounts of disparate data on variables such as reproductive effort (including the size of genitalia, the frequency of intercourse, rates of sexually transmitted diseases), brain size, social organisation and muscular-skeletal differences that provided support for the three-way racial developmental continuum.

JPR's data suggested that Sub-Saharan Africans (he called them Negroids, see Rushton, 1995, p.4) had a fast r-K strategy which was designed to be functional in unstable environments. 'Negroids' are not competing against each other, they compete against the environment and to survive quantity was prioritised over quantity. This strategy works when the environment is plentiful but unpredictable (for example, predators). Energy is invested in sex, multiple children and growing up fast. There is little investment in the nurture of offspring. This strategy is successful until the environment itself reaches human carrying capacity (famine for example). East Asians (called Mongoloids) on the other hand, have a stable, predictable environment which develops a slow life history whereby people could live for the future. This environment, however, encourages interpersonal competition. To ensure children survive and thrive, Mongoloids invest fewer resources in sex, had fewer sexual partners and invested heavily in the nurture of their children. Caucasians (Europeans and those of European ancestry, North Africans, Western Asians and those from the Indian Sub-Continent) were in the middle.

This trade-off between mating effort and parenting effort impacted developmental milestones, personality type and intelligence. The more K an environment becomes, the more energy will be devoted to complex brain development. The K environment also requires additional resources committed to nurture and therefore favours prosocial, trusting and altruistic trait selection. Along with trust and altruism, agreeableness, contentiousness and lower levels of neuroticism develop. Rushton first published his theory in 1984, elaborating further in his book *Race, Evolution and Behaviour* in 1995.

Known as Differential-K, the theory was both innovative and explosive. Rushton was catapulted into the public imagination as the Canadian version of Hans Eysenck. He became the subject of an intense campaign to have him fired as a racist. He was depicted in the robes of the Ku Klux Klan, had his department invaded, his office walls emblazoned with 'pig lives here' and he had to cease giving lectures in public. There was even a police investigation to determine if there was sufficient evidence to prosecute Rushton for inciting racial hatred. Rushton was so terrified he was hospitalised with a suspected heart attack.

Undeterred, JPR continued to research contentious subjects. Working with the Pioneer Fund, he continued to survey racial differences further, circulating a questionnaire at a local shopping mall, which included collecting information on penis size and ejaculation distance. The argument is that there would be a trade-off between brain size and penis length and performance. Rushton is quoted in *Rolling Stone Magazine* as stating, 'more brain or more penis; you cannot have everything' (interview with Miller, 1994, p.106). In the days before stringent ethical approvals in psychological studies, Rushton was aghast when his university was furious with him. His work had never required approval in the past.

In 1997 JPR met Elizabeth Weiss, a Master's student, at the Human Behaviour and Evolution Society Conference in Arizona and an affair began. Weiss was 30 years Rushton's junior, but they had much in common intellectually. Rushton filed for divorce from Kocabayik and married Weiss the same day that the divorce was granted. The couple had no children, but in 2001 JPR's estranged daughter Katherine got back in touch. She had experienced a difficult life in foster care, her adoption failed and she was returning into foster care. Rushton became consumed in helping his daughter, which Weiss argued put pressure on their marriage. The couple became estranged and divorced. Weiss describes Rushton with a mixture of resentment and love. A hardworking man, who always followed the data. He had a twinkle in his eye and was always delighted to hear about the successes of others. He was, however, a 'complete jerk' and violent during the divorce (personal correspondences between Elizabeth Weiss and Dutton, June 22nd, 2018, see Dutton 2018, pp.139–141).

At the same time the marriage ended, JPR was diagnosed with Addison's disease. An immune condition, often caused by cancer, which causes low mood, thirst, weight loss and fatigue. As the disease progresses suffers experience depression, concentration problems, anxiety and even psychosis. His publications remained ever controversial, but the papers themselves became more problematic and over-confident. As the condition worsened, his weakened immune system made it too risky for him to attend large meetings and conferences and he died on October 2nd, 2012, he was 68 years old and suffering from cancer.

Shortly before his death, and in conversation with Helmuth Nyborg, JPR stated that 'Charles Darwin and Wilson were correct. Human social behaviour is best understood as part of life history – a suite of traits genetically organised to meet the trials of life – survival, growth, and reproduction' (Nyborg, 2013, p.210). Overall Life History Theory explains the interaction between reproductive strategies in animals, their individual, family and environmental characteristics. It can also be tested by evolutionary principles, it stands well enough against criticism, but there are some problems. For example, there are other principles which influence how a species evolves. Through sexual selection, those with more desirable qualities (height in men for example) are more likely to pass those qualities on through their genes. Kin selection influences the way in which close relatives will invest in those nearest to them. For example, a child from an impoverished background may benefit from the loving support and investment of more affluent relatives.

Superficially, JPR's work is no less palatable than that of Charles Darwin or Hans Eysenck, but it was his dogged application of the theory to the study of racial differences that triggered a moral and scientific backlash that he described as a moralistic fallacy and anti-reason ideology. Many eminent psychologists consider his work in the field of Individual Differences as bold, brave and thought-provoking. For example, the 2013 Special Edition on Life History Theory published in *Personality and Individual Differences* provides extensive coverage of JPR's many contributions to the field. His work, however, remains barely mentioned in undergraduate textbooks and authors such as Edward Dutton state that they have often been advised to cite someone other than Rushton. Dutton is a staunch critic of JPR but stops short at agreeing he was a racist. Rushton never claimed that one race was more superior to another, rather those that claim Rushton was a racist were over-extending the term to all those who believed that races existed at all. That because the consequences of racial differences were so awful, there was a prevailing orthodoxy that any attribution towards race was immoral. This Dutton argues is bias. An appeal to consequences should not direct scientific investigation.

In a final twist, in the final months of his life, JPR had had approximately 1.9 million dollars of research money which had originated from the Pioneer Fund. He transferred those funds to the Charles Darwin Institute (an organisation JPR had set up to support publications) and left control of those funds with his son John Stephen Philippe. The funds were to be used to establish a scholarship fund. This move was considered by some such as Richard Lynn, as a betrayal because funds were directed away from the causes JPR had fought for throughout his life. This shift perhaps also acutely reflects the conundrum that was John Philippe Rushton. Depending on your perspective he was a racist, narcissist, liar, or, pioneering scientist, decent human being, truth-seeker and enthusiastic defender of academic freedom.

Major works

Rushton, J. P. (1995). *Race, Evolution, and Behavior: A Life History Perspective* (2nd special abridged ed.). Port Huron, MI: Charles Darwin Research Institute.

Rushton, J. P., & Jensen, A. R. (2005). Thirty years of research on race differences in cognitive ability. *Psychology, Public Policy, and Law*, 11, 235–294.

Bibliography

Dutton, E. (2018). *J. Philippe Rushton: A Life History Perspective*. UK: Thomas Edward.

Miller, A. (1994). Professors of hate. *Rolling Stone* (693), 106. Retrieved from https://liverpool.idm.oclc.org/login?url=https://search.ebscohost.com/login.aspx?direct=true&db=a9h&AN=9410147504&site=ehost-live&scope=site

Nyborg, H. (2013). In conversation with J. Philippe Rushton. *Personality and Individual Differences*, 55(3), 205–211. In *Special Issue on The Life History Approach to Human Differences: J. Philippe Rushton in Memoriam. Personality and Individual Differences*.

Wilson, E. O. (1975). *Sociobiology: The New Synthesis*. Oxford: Belknap Press of Harvard University Press.

Chapter 23

Peter Francis Saville

'Global gold standard'

October 26th, 1946

Peter was born on October 26th, 1946 in Wembley, north west London. Peter's mother, Winifred (Winnie) Violet Oborne, was from Rhossilli on the Gower peninsula. This picturesque but remote small village in Wales, once inhabited by Vikings and pirates, was also the home of her mother's relative, the Antarctic explorer Edgar Evans who died with Captain Falcon Scott on the final push of his ill-fated Terra Nova expedition to reach the South Pole in 1912. It also seems likely that Peter's family (named Beynon) was acquainted with Dylan Thomas. Thomas creates Gossamer Beynon, Butcher Beynon and Mrs Beynon as characters in his classic literary work, 'Under Milk Wood' about a Welsh town called 'Llareggub' (spell it backwards!).

Winnie's mother Sarah Chalk was the daughter of sea captain John Chalk, who sailed from Swansea to New South Wales, Australia. He died of malaria and was buried at sea off Chile, South America in 1898. Life was bleak for the Chalks with a very limited infrastructure in Wales, mortality in new-born babies and children was high. The gravestones in Rhossilli are a testimony to many Chalk family tragedies.

To make matters worse, Sarah fell in love with Frank Oborne from Swansea. Her family were so against the union that they gave her money to go to London. She was to leave Wales with him and later gave birth to three daughters. The youngest was Winifred, Peter's mother.

Winifred was in Chiswick swimming baths when she met John (Jack) Edward Saville, who had matriculated from Chiswick Grammar School. The encounter was not entirely romantic, but it was gallant. Jack rescued Winnie when she almost drowned. A relationship followed, and the couple married in 1938. Jack was called up to serve in the British Army – spending most of his time in India during World War II, where he was rapidly promoted through the ranks from Private to Lieutenant. After the war, Peter's father qualified as a lawyer at the Royal Courts of Justice, The Strand, London. The couple had two children, John and Peter. Peter was born with congenital scoliosis, a curvature of the spine. From 6 months old he was treated at Great Ormond Street Hospital, London.

Treatment in the 1940s was brutal. Three times a day, Peter was swung by the neck and then placed in a rack and stretched. What caused Peter the most extreme torture, was the plaster bed. Every night he was held in place by leather straps, his body soothed with almond oil and muslin in a futile attempt to prevent sores from forming. When the sores inevitably formed, he was admitted back into the hospital for further invasive treatment. All during an age when parents were not allowed to visit, causing maternal deprivation.

For whatever comfort could be given, the family all slept in the same room as Peter. His grandmother would soothe him, singing to him in Welsh and calling him 'bach', meaning 'little, small beloved one'. Peter's cousins Janet and Barbara described Peter as having fought for his life; his early struggles helping shape his strong-willed personality. As a toddler in Wembley High Street Peter managed to knock over a bending lady with his pram that he insisted on pushing. Having legged it from the scene, Peter's father looked frantically for him everywhere, only to eventually find him sitting on the counter of the local police station. The policeman said, 'We didn't have a clue who your son was. Every time we ask his name he just replies, "Tommy Trouble"' (PS to AF, personal communication, December 11th, 2018).

The brutal treatment for scoliosis went on for some years until, at the age of seven, Peter was finally considered cured. Then he had a new battle, with dyslexia. His grammar and reading were good, but poor spelling pulled his grades down. His school teachers described him as 'highly creative and prolific with ideas but talks too much' (PS to AF, personal communication, December 11th, 2018).

In fact, he was far more interested in playing football and cricket or taking part in athletics than in school work. It was when he was first given set examinations, rather than being judged merely on coursework, that he really shone. Peter had started to use mnemonics to structure his answers in exams, coming top of his school in virtually every subject, transcending the pedantic necessity for accurate spelling.

School performance continued to improve, leading Peter to be noticed by the Surrey Education Authority. Peter was entered into Ewell High School's grammar screen. Selected from children across Surrey, he shone at mathematics, physics, English literature, history and sports. Frustratingly, when he decided to take his GCE A-Levels at Ewell Technical College (now North East Surrey College of Technology – NESCOT), students had to make arbitrary choices between art-based subjects and science. At the time, a student could study mathematics and science, but not mathematics and English literature as they clashed in the curriculum. In the end, Peter settled for an arts pathway but managed to find his way back to science and mathematics through the study of psychology, as a psychometrician.

Psychology was not Peter's immediate choice; his father had a career in the civil service mapped out for him, but Peter's school friends, on recognising his abilities, nudged him towards university. Like so many adolescents of the decade, they were also curious about the workings of Sigmund Freud's theories. Eventually, curiosity about psychology, a subject he had never come across before, brought Peter to the college library. He read many ideas and theories, that in some cases were probably nonsense, but also on topics such as human memory, personality, intelligence, child development and statistics which he found both fascinating and intriguing.

Injuries suffered while playing football for NESCOT and the then amateur Wimbledon FC, prevented his timely application to university. Peter had taken his politics A-Level examination early, and in an unusually short period of time – one year. His performance on that exam had been sufficient to attract the offer of a university place, but he had to wait for his leg to repair after a six-week stay in Epsom Hospital before he could take the remainder of his GCE A-Levels.

This injury threatened his university place, but after extensive surgery, Peter was able to take the examinations and passed the entry IQ test used at the time, so his place was eventually secured. He enrolled at the University of Leicester, supporting himself by earning money any way he could, so he could eventually buy a car. Peter took on jobs as a milkman, window-cleaner, building site labourer, hospital porter – even turning the numbers over in the local bingo hall.

The 1960s was a time when just 3 per cent of school leavers entered one of only 40 universities throughout the UK. The University of Leicester was a vibrant department, if not, in fact, one of the best psychology departments in the United Kingdom. Peter was taught by scholars such as Robert Thompson who was breaking new ground in the psychology of thinking, and Jim Reason, who developed the Swiss Cheese Model of Risk Assessment, which explained how accidents occur in complex systems. It was a young, intellectually challenging department, whose members had come together to write what became the UK's preferred undergraduate psychology textbook *Introducing Psychology*. Peter continued to excel, winning a much-coveted place on the special subject Honours Degree programme, graduating in 1969 and going on to study for a Master of Philosophy in Industrial Psychology (1974). He married his first wife Jane Johnson in 1972, whom he had met while being best man to her brother. The couple went on to have three children together; William, Frances and Christopher.

Following a scholarship from the National Foundation for Educational Research (NFER), Peter was able to pursue his PhD, gaining a job there as an assistant psychologist. A large part of his work was the adaptation of measures such as the Wechsler Intelligence Scales (WISC), writing test manuals for Aptitude Batteries, working on the publication of the first edition of the British Ability Scales and helping to take over the test range of the soon to be defunct National Institute of Industrial Psychology (NIIP). He was quickly promoted to chief psychologist for the Test Division, where he was responsible for the adaptation and standardisation of a wide range of tests for educational, clinical and occupational use. This work led to the standardisation, on a nationally representative sample of over 2,000 adults tested in their own homes, of the 16 Personality Factor Questionnaire (16PF). Professor Raymond Cattell held Peter and his work in the highest esteem, praising him for its precision and contribution to British psychology.

With Professor Hans Eysenck as external examiner, the PhD viva voce was always going to be interesting. In the PhD Peter had undertaken a Promax factor analysis of Cattell's 16PF, which could not substantiate Cattell's claimed factor structure of 16 personality scales, nor Eysenck's two- or three-factor theories of personality. Instead, what emerged as the most parsimonious solution, was essentially the Big Five Model of Personality, plus a factor of intelligence. All was well until Hans got somewhat distracted from the primary purpose of the examination and started an argument with Professor Desmond Furneaux, the internal examiner, over the nature of intelligence. Eysenck turned to Peter, asking, 'and what do you think?' Peter's answer that there may be more than just one type of intelligence did not altogether please Hans, but nevertheless, the doctorate was awarded. In that most English of ways, a glass of sherry was offered in celebration. However, Peter sat alone somewhat awkwardly in Professor Furneaux's office for more than two hours. Nobody came, and there was no sherry.

There followed an apologetic letter; Hans had managed to misplace his car, and both professors were roaming the brutalist architecture and film set of *A Clockwork Orange* that was Brunel University.

By 1977 work was coming in directly to Peter thick and fast, from organisations asking him to undertake psychological assessments and provide training in psychological testing. In 1970's England, occupational psychology as a profession was pretty much unheard of, but organisations such as Mars, BP, British Leyland, Jaguar, Standard Life, Prudential and even the United Nations, were asking Peter for professional support with the selection and development of staff. The five-day Occupational Testing Course, which Peter designed, was approved by the British Psychological Society (BPS) in 1974, and had won a number of awards based on reviews like one from Kodak Ltd, 'In every respect, one of the best training courses I have attended in over 20 years in personnel and training. Level of expertise and intellectual content very high. Justification of Occupational Testing fully and rationally ratified'. It was time for Peter to step out on his own.

Peter went to visit Roger Holdsworth, who had worked for the NIIP but for seven years had been working independently with his company Holdsworth Audio Visual Limited, to ask Roger's advice on an offer Peter had received from HTS Management Consultants to form a new company. Roger, however, suggested they form a company together, called Saville and

Holdsworth Ltd (SHL), where Peter held 65 per cent of the shares and Roger 35 per cent.

SHL was founded in September 1977, working from Peter's home in Claygate, Esher, Surrey and Roger's home in Putney, south west London. The aim was to revolutionise the way psychologists supported organisations. Holdsworth possessed the attention to detail and organisational skills that Peter often lacked. Peter, the imagination and sales flair. The first step was to create psychometric measures that were scientifically sound, that could be delivered quickly and looked good – backed up with excellent training. Peter was savvy enough to realise that image meant much to organisations. The standard tests of the time contained an uninteresting array of written content, were very old, overly complicated, lengthy and not designed for the occupational market. Publishers of the day could not understand the negative impact such draconian looking tests could potentially have on the applicant. Tests could take many weeks to arrive, often leading to illicit photocopying.

Peter went even further by suggesting that materials should be printed in colour. Roger disagreed, saying this would add to costs. However, Peter won the argument bringing his brother, John Saville, in to professionally graphically design SHL's first suite of tests. John was Director of Design at Her Majesty's Stationery Office and also designed SHL's first brochure. The SHL brochure was to cause much consternation amongst psychologists, as being 'too commercial'. It reminded Peter of the time the NFER took over the tests of the NIIP in 1974. The reply of the head of the NIIP, when Peter asked which of their tests sold most was, rather disparagingly, 'We are not in trade you know'. There were multiple copies of NIIP tests in their office on Wimpole Street, London, which had been stacked there collecting dust, for over 30 years.

The first tests published by SHL were the Personnel Test Battery, a collection of Verbal, Numerical and Error Checking tests, for sales, clerical and general staff. The Technical Test Battery, a group of eight Verbal, Numerical, Visual Estimation, Spatial and fault-finding tests for craft and technical apprentices. The Advanced Test Battery consisted of Verbal and Numerical Critical Reasoning and Abstract Reasoning Tests for management, graduate and professional groups. The Critical Reasoning Test Battery was for supervisory and more senior sales roles, the

Programmer Aptitude Series, for developers and analysts and the General Aptitude Series for counselling and careers guidance at work. Assessment centre materials were also created, consisting of in-tray exercises, group exercises and a management interest inventory. In 1984, after a four-year research programme, the Occupational Personality Questionnaires (OPQ) were published, which the BPS called 'ground-breaking for their time'. Included in the OPQ Suite were two 32-scale questionnaires called the Concept Model which were developed by deductive methods, 14-, 8- and 5-factor inventories, called retrospectively the Factor, Octagon and Pentagon Questionnaires. The Five-Factor Pentagon Model, published in 1984, was said by the British Psychological Society to be the first commercially available version of the Big Five, or what is sometimes referred to as the Five-Factor Model (FFM). The FFM is now used extensively by academics globally in researching personality. However, Peter while accepting the efficiency of the Five-Factor Model has preferred to work at the facet level of personality, to give more depth. For example, Peter has maintained that conscientiousness needs to be broken down into sub-factors such as reliability vs drive to provide further detail at the individual level for use in the workplace.

In 1997, SHL was represented in 40 countries and had been floated in the London Stock Exchange, reaching a value of £240 million. Everyone benefited. Occupational psychology in the United Kingdom was changed forever. It was now possible to demonstrate that psychologists had something significant to offer to industry and psychological testing was advanced because Peter had challenged assumptions, that had long been taken for granted about fairness and equality in testing. All SHL staff benefited, as they had been offered shares at 10 pence, which later had a value of £2.50.

By the late 1990s Peter was listed as one of Britain's top ten psychologists, the only occupational psychologist cited. He had worked tirelessly to demonstrate the absolute need for psychologists to make decisions on fair and objective data. Unusually for a psychologist, in 1998 Peter was listed amongst the UK's top 100 Entrepreneurs in an award sponsored by Lloyds Bank and KPMG. In 2001, Peter was presented with the British Psychological Society Centenary Award for Distinguished Contributions to Professional Psychology. His portrait hung in the National Portrait Gallery, London. The BPS citation read,

Peter established Britain as the centre of Psychometric excellence and cemented the notion of fair and objective assessment in Human Resource departments across the world. As a skilled Psychometrician and visionary leader, Peter Saville has made a significant impact on professional psychology in the UK and beyond. The widespread use of SHLs tests by major companies and public bodies is a testament to the influence of Pete Saville's remarkable ideas.

In 2003, Peter left the board of SHL in support of his co-founder Roger Holdsworth. Asked back, he refused and formed Saville Consulting (now Saville Assessment) developing the Wave Questionnaire with his team. Willis Towers Watson acquired Saville Consulting in 2015. During this time, Peter was made an Honorary Fellow, the highest award the British Psychological Society can bestow. The citation stated, 'Professor Saville's services to the field of psychology in terms of applying the science to the workplace and creating the global gold standard for psychometric tests are exemplary'.

Peter left Saville Assessment in 2016 to form 10x Psychology, to provide modern assessment tools, predictive analytics and innovative solutions, spanning the entire employee lifecycle from hiring and leadership to employee wellbeing. At 10x he was re-joined by the Managing Director of SHL and Saville Assessment staff. Peter Saville twice took legal action when SHL objected to his using his own name. Peter won on both occasions but jokes that he may now change his name to what his family used to call him, Tommy Trouble.

Peter Saville, the father of occupational psychology, is often credited with starting a whole new industry. Ever a passionate football fan, he has been chairman of three football clubs and he and his second wife Jemaine are benefactors of the Outward Bound Trust and the Willow Foundation. Jemaine lost her first daughter to a rare teenage cancer – the Willow Foundation provides special events for seriously ill young people. Jemaine and Peter have 9-year-old twins, Faye and Jack, and nine grandchildren. Peter's son Jack has been assessed as intellectually gifted but dyslexic, described at school as 'highly creative – but talks too much' (personal communication).

Major works

Holdsworth, R., Saville, P., Hawkey, D., Blinkhorn, S., & Iliffe, A. (1980). *The Advanced Test Battery (Higher Level Psychometric Tests of Numerical Critical Reasoning, Verbal Critical Reasoning, Spatial Reasoning and Logical Analysis)*. London: SHL.

Saville, P. (1972). *British Supplement to the Wechsler Intelligence Scale for Children (WISC)*. London: The Psychological Corporation.

Saville, P. (1972). *The National Adult Standardisation of 16 Personality Factor Questionnaire (16PF)*. London: NFER.

Saville, P. (1977). *A Critical Analysis of the 16PF, PhD Dissertation*. London: Brunel University.

Saville, P. (1983). *The Development of the Occupational Personality Questionnaire (OPQ)*. Harrogate: Presented at the National Conference of the Institute of Personnel Management.

Saville, P. (2015). *Peter Saville Unplugged: Entrepreneurship, Leadership & Chairing a PLC. Keynote Speech: Association of Business Psychologists Annual Conference 2015 'Business Psychology in Action'*. Reading, UK.

Saville, P., & Blinkhorn, S. (1976). *Undergraduate Personality by Factored Scales*. London: NFER.

Saville, P., & Blinkhorn, S. (1981). Reliability, homogeneity and the construct validity of Cattell's 16 Personality Factor Questionnaire (16PF). *Personality and Individual Differences*, 2, 325–333.

Saville, P., & Hawkey, D. (1979). *The Technical Test Battery (Psychometric Tests of Verbal, Numerical, Mechanical, Spatial and Logical Reasoning for Engineers)*. London: SHL.

Saville, P., & Holdsworth, R. (1979). *The Personnel Test Battery (Psychometric Tests of Verbal, Numerical and Checking Skills for For Sales, Clerical and General Staff)*. London: SHL.

Saville, P., Holdsworth, R., Nyfield, G., Cramp, L., & Mabey, W. (1984). *The Occupational Personality Questionnaire (OPQ)*. London: SHL.

Saville, P., & Hopton, T. (2015). A History of Leadership Theory. In *Business Psychology in Action*. Altrincham: Troubador.

Saville, P. with Hopton, T. (2016). *World Anthology of Psychologists Series: From Obscurity to Transparency in Psychometrics – Collected Writings of Peter Saville 1972–2015*. London: Routledge.

Saville, P. & MacIver, R. (2017). A very good question. In B. Cripps (Ed.), *Psychometric Testing: A Critical Perspective* (pp.29–42). London: Wiley.

Saville, P., MacIver, R., & Kurz, R. (2009). *Saville Consulting Wave® Professional Styles Handbook*. New Jersey: Saville Consulting Group.

Saville, P., & Nyfield G. (1975). *Psychometric Testing*. London: HTS Management Consultants.

Saville, P., Sik, G., Nyfield, G., Hackston, J., & MacIver, R. (1996). A demonstration of the validity of the Occupational Personality Questionnaire (OPQ) in the measurement of job competencies across time and in separate organisations. *Applied Psychology*, 45, 243–262.

Saville, P., & Wilson, E. (1991). The reliability and validity of normative and ipsative approaches in the measurement of personality. *Journal of Occupational Psychology*, 64, 219–238.

Bibliography

Richard Kwiatkowski interviews Peter Saville. (2007). Still in love with psychology. *The Psychologist Magazine*, 20, 306–307.

Chapter 24

Daniel Goleman
Emotionally intelligent

March 7th, 1946

Just as the great intelligence debate seemed to be running out of steam, Daniel Goleman's emotional intelligence kick-started an entirely new debate. Our capacity to read the emotions of others matters more than our IQ.

Daniel's parents, Irving and Fay were both born to immigrant parents. Both worked as professors at San Joaquin Delta Community College; Irving was teaching in the humanities and Fay, a social worker who taught in the sociology department. Irving, a baby-boomer, thinks he was probably conceived around Victory in Europe day, towards the end of World War I. The family were settled in Stockton, California.

Daniel performed well at school, becoming high school president and then attaining a leadership scholarship to attend Amherst College, Massachusetts to study anthropology. He went to Amherst because his friend had been so enthusiastic about it, but Daniel had never been to the College before his first day of term. Daniel found it difficult to settle, and his academic performance suffered. Eventually, he managed to transfer into Berkeley for the majority of his degree, only returning to Amherst to complete his honours project on the historical, anthropological and social perspectives of mental health.

David graduated magna cum laude (the equivalent of a 1st class degree in the United Kingdom system) which he considered to be a miracle given his poor early performance. A scholarship to Harvard from the Ford Foundation secured him a place on the clinical psychology programme. What was then the Department of Social Relations at Harvard, was a good fit for David. It was known for its dynamic interdisciplinary culture where anthropology, sociology and psychology created an environment for students to explore the human mind through multiple perspectives. Daniel's supervisor David McClelland was instrumental in supporting Daniel's interdisciplinary interests and with the award of a travel fellowship, Daniel was able to travel to India to study the religious practices of the Asiatic religions and the function of ancient systems of psychology in those cultures. These experiences shaped Daniel's PhD towards mediation as an intervention in stress arousal and eventually led to Daniel's first book, *The Meditative Mind*.

His first position came at the magazine *Psychology Today*. When the *New York Times* recruited him in 1984, his career as a scientific journalist was secured. He spent the next 12 years immersed in the science of journalism. The *New York Times* offered much in the way of media presence, but Daniel was increasingly finding that the requirements for newspaper writing conflicted with the exploration of ideas that Daniel wanted to pursue.

During 1990, he had stumbled across the framework contributed by John Mayer and Peter Salovey which addressed the role of accurate emotional appraisal in the self and others as the mechanism to a functioning life and good mental health. Mayer and Salovey offered a new way of thinking about what contributed to success. Mayer and Salovey were the architects of emotional intelligence, but it was Goleman who brought it to the public's attention, but he did some tweaking along the way.

Daniel had been writing about emotions and the brain and was convinced that the topic needed a book. He left the *New York Times* to dedicate his time to *Emotional Intelligence*, and to his surprise, it became a number one best seller in 1995.

Goleman's theory was that emotional intelligence mattered more than intelligence in the cognitive ability sense. Emotions are there to keep us regulated, whether it be loss or love, frustration or fear, our emotions help us to manage tasks that are too important to leave to intellect alone. When those emotions are not adequately managed, intelligence is of little use, which means that emotional intelligence is more critical to success than ability and, to secure the future success of our students, schools ought to teach emotional intelligence as part of the curriculum.

Before the book came to press, Daniel was already pursuing the idea of emotional learning in schools with a group of educators and researchers, forming CASEL, the Collaborative for Academic, Social, and Emotional Learning in 1993 with the venture philanthropist, Eileen Growald and activist Tim Shriver (who went on to become the chair of the Special Olympics). The group worked to expand the scope of life skill development in schools around the world. Research and evaluations suggested that these interventions were having a wide-ranging impact on children's lives. Incidents of violence, substance abuse and unwanted pregnancies reduced, and children were more engaged in their learning, improving their performance by as much as 15 per cent.

The uptake in the business community was no less impressive, and by 1998 Daniel had published *Working with Emotional Intelligence*. His research led him to explore the competencies of high performers across industry and government departments; the best leaders had the components of emotional intelligence in large quantities. Self-awareness, regulation, motivation, empathy, social 'skill-can', are traits that go beyond self-control and getting on with the job. These ingredients enable good leaders to understand themselves and others to move people together in the same direction for a common purpose.

Educators enthusiastically adopted the concept across the world. Thousands of schools began providing social, emotional learning programmes, and by 2007, the pull towards Daniel Goleman's EI brand brought together 75 global leaders in education, including George Lucas, to scrutinise the latest scientific findings behind EI. However, some of Goleman's claims were becoming problematic for the academic community. In particular that when the contribution of technical skills, ability and emotional intelligence to performance was calculated, emotional intelligence was twice as valuable as any other variable, for all jobs at all levels. Ninety per cent of the difference between star performers and more average members of a team, was attributed to emotional intelligence over cognitive ability.

This analysis overlooked the fact that top performers will all have above average cognitive ability scores, the range is restricted and at his 2008 speech to the American Psychological Association, Peter Salovey, now Dean at Yale, slammed Goleman's statements as outrageous. Salovey continued in an openly critical assault in the *American Psychologist*, arguing that Goleman's journalistic accounts of EI were raising unrealised ideas that were in no way supported by research. Goleman had in fact changed and extended the framework of EI which was driving inflated ideas about what EI could achieve. Mayer and Salovey were setting themselves apart from Goleman's work, publishing their own EI books aimed at non-academics, the EI instrument the Mayer-Salovey-Caruso-Emotional-Intelligence Test and making it clear that other models were available.

There are three major EI models Mayer and Salovey, Bar-On and Goleman, of which Goleman was the most recent, Bar-On was the first to discuss what he described as 'Emotional Quotient' his doctoral dissertation of 1985. These three approaches diverge in how EI is constructed and framed, but the three models have commonality in the aim of understanding how emotions impact on human effectiveness. Bar-On, Salovey and Mayer are undoubtedly the original pioneers of Emotional Intelligence, but it was Daniel Goleman's best-selling book and the initiatives that followed, that successfully piqued the interest of the public, academics and industry. This attention created a new wave of research which could examine legitimate EI questions. Not just questions about the nature of EI, but questions that examine how, if at all, EI can be developed. If indeed EI is a skill, then there are moral and ethical issues about its development which require more careful thought and study because the enthusiasm for the pro-social advantages of EI, has obscured its darker side.

Daniel Goleman is married to the psychotherapist and educator Tara Bennett-Goleman. He has two children from his first marriage to Anasuya Theresa Matthews, Govinddass and Hanuman.

Major works

Goleman, D. (1995). *Emotional Intelligence*. New York: Bantam Books.
Goleman, D. (1998). *Working with Emotional Intelligence*. New York: Bantam Books.

Bibliography

Ashton, S. G., & Goldberg, L. R. (1973). In response to Jackson's challenge: The comparative validity of personality scales constructed by the external (empirical) strategy and scales developed intuitively by experts, novices, and laymen. *Journal of Research in Personality*, 7, 1–20.
Bar-On, R. (2006). The Bar-On model of emotional-social intelligence (ESI). *Psicothema*, 18, 13–25.
Salovey, P., & Mayer, J. D.. (1990). Emotional intelligence. *Imagination, Cognition and Personality*, 9(3), 185–211.

Index